Alexander the Great is  because he had no mo... present-day adventurers i... parts of the world left un... justify what it takes to ma... are a remarkable exceptio... in London, he has bee... greatest walkers. He usually journeys alone ... describing what he sees with fresh understanding. He strode the length of Britain, through Europe from the North Sea to the Mediterranean and across parts of boreal Canada and tropical Africa. Mr Hillaby is, moreover, a distinguished natural historian who for years wrote for the *Guardian* and *New York Times*.

The author has written four highly popular books: *Journey to the Jade Sea*, *Journey through Britain*, *Journey through Europe* and *Journey through Love*.

£1.50

JOHN HILLABY

Journey Home

Granada Publishing

Paladin Books
Granada Publishing Ltd
8 Grafton Street, London W1X 3LA

Published by Paladin Books 1985

First published in Great Britain by
Constable and Company Limited 1983

Copyright © John Hillaby 1983

ISBN 0-586-08492-4

Reproduced, printed and bound in Great Britain by
Hazell Watson & Viney Limited,
Aylesbury, Bucks

Set in Ehrhardt

All rights reserved. No part of this publication may
be reproduced, stored in a retrieval system, or
transmitted, in any form, or by any means, electronic,
mechanical, photocopying, recording or otherwise,
without the prior permission of the publishers.

This book is sold subject to the conditions that it
shall not, by way of trade or otherwise, be lent,
re-sold, hired out or otherwise circulated
without the publisher's prior consent in any
form of binding or cover other than that in
which it is published and without a similar
condition including this condition being imposed
on the subsequent purchaser.

To Katie

Contents

Note

During our journey we met many old friends, such as
Leonard Harrison Matthews and his wife Dolly, who know
the extent of our obligations and gratitude. For different
reasons, three classes of creditors can lay just and legal claim
to acknowledgement. The first are the editors and publishers
of the *New York Times* and *New Scientist* where portions of
what I have written first appeared. The second are copyright
holders of works which proved extremely informative, especially in unfamiliar territory. Among them are Winifred
Pennington and Molly Lefebure of Cumbria, Christopher
Morris, the editor of *The Journeys of Celia Fiennes*, David Joy
of *The Dalesman* for his unrivalled knowledge of our early
railways, and Edward Storey and David Yaxley of East Anglia.
The third group are the clergy of England, those genial
dispensers of Christian knowledge and excisable liquors. We
encountered many between the Lake District and the outskirts of London and rarely left their company without
learning much about their neighbourhood. We also drew
heavily on the knowledge of Major Brett Collier, the representative of the Ramblers' Association in Lincolnshire, and
Alan Mattingly, the General Secretary of that invaluable
organization in London.

As usual I am deeply indebted to Mr Douglas Matthews
and his staff at the London Library who could not have been
more helpful. The lines beginning 'And so he conjures up the
boy . . .' are borrowed from one of the many exuberant poems
by Iain Hamilton, friend of long standing and former colleague on the *Guardian*.

Throughout the journey we managed to keep warm and dry
in Grenfell jackets supplied by Messrs Haythornthwaite of
Burnley and Goretex rainproofs from Berghaus of Newcastle;
and we know of no better tent than our portable igloo
manufactured by the Phoenix Mountaineering Company at
Amble in Northumberland. Good boots and shoes are diffi-

cult to come by these days but, not for the first time, Eric Sleath of Marrum Sports Ltd (Hochland Romika), Northampton, looked after my footwear. Most of the pictures are our own, but Corry Bevington provided us with several fine ones including the photograph on the jacket. The maps are from the studio of my companion on many a walk, Giovanni Caselli, a Florentine archaeologist, illustrator and the pioneer of the Etruscan Highway. For abundant information we should also like to thank Mr J. Neil Place, a managing director of Tilcon, a company which quarries gravel without hurt to the land. Lewis Penny, the distinguished geologist, Walter Poucher, that Grand Old Man of the mountains, Alfred Wainwright the pathfinder, Desre Behrman, Martin Burton, Michael Clegg and Peter Wenham of York, Frank and Crokie Allen, and not least my publisher, Ben Glazebrook and his staff at the Constabulary, deserve more than a word. But there is no space for more than *li ringraziamo tutti*.

J.H.
1983

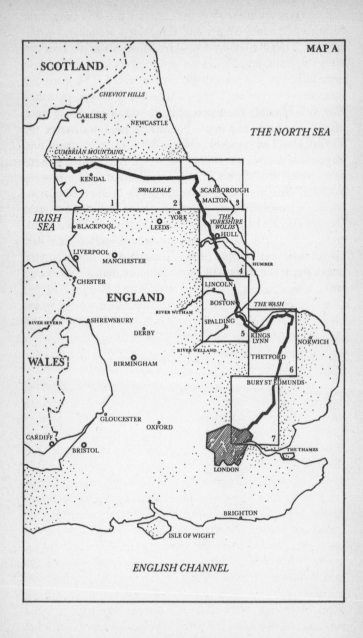

MAP A

Introduction: how it all began

With the possible exception of the equator everything must start somewhere, and this account of a brisk walk from the Lake District to London, a splendid walk as it turned out, began essentially in the city of my youth, Leeds, in what used to be called the West Riding of Yorkshire. Not a lovely city perhaps. Bernard Shaw considered the place fit only for Marxists and millionaires. But among much else these days Leeds houses a huge television company from which a brash fellow 'phoned to ask whether I would undertake a short walk on the coast of Norfolk, describing what I saw. Couldn't be done, I said. As a small recompense for good companionship when things hadn't been going at all well I had promised to take Girl Friday to Provence on the date they wanted me in Norfolk. They foresaw no problem. She could be put down on the production schedule as a Personal Assistant, a cosy contemporary expression for baggage superintendent, tea-maker, and brow-soother in general.

After the usual anxieties of production were over and done with, we had all the time in the world to look around, to wander along the margins of sand, shingle and saltings tenanted only by plaintive bird life. A good place, as we saw it, to be included in a more ambitious walk. But to what end, and from what starting point? Our cottage high up on the Yorkshire moors would provide us with the necessary contrast for a foray south and east into the milky shires of Saxon England, but we wanted something different, something we hadn't seen before. Slowly, gradually we extended our proposed line of march north and south. Eventually we settled for a rough diagonal from the fells of the north-west to the estuary of the Thames. By linking up the highest, the most ochreous, portions of those coloured prospects of liberty, the pages of an atlas, we worked out a route. We tried to avoid roads as ardently as we sought old tracks, the upper reaches of rivers, and the homes of friends of long standing, believing

11

there to be something prescriptive and reassuring in their presence.

On paper it promised well, offering much that had been missed on an earlier walk through Britain where, by clinging for the most part to the west, I had mainly seen rough pastoral country, the refuge of the Celts. But what of the Cumbrian hills, and the differences between the dales and the moors, to many of us the better half of Britain? Why not take in the Wolds, Danelaw, the Lincolnshire fens, and that vast tract of cultivation between the Norfolk dunes and the urbanized symmetry of the Home Counties? Here we hoped to find scope for exploration, for though I had sampled a bit here and there as any tourist might, the essentials, I knew from experience, could be seen in the round only by passing from one ward to another on foot.

It will soon become apparent that Girl Friday, a robust person by any standards, is also an exceptional walker. As the widow of a tea-planter in Ceylon she had become accustomed to hills but not to sheer drops or even very steep slopes. She suffers from vertigo and this posed problems, for Helvellyn and Kidsty Pike loomed ahead. We had less than a fortnight to assemble our gear, including a new line in tents. Even the light-weights come in all shapes and sizes, from transparent envelopes that weigh less than a pint pot to box- and ridge-shaped affairs in which you could seduce a hockey team.

Holding, as I do, that a tent is merely a form of insurance against unexpected bad weather, especially thick mist, I have become adept at sleeping in barns, outhouses, and in the lee of hedges, walls and rocks. This cuts out all that fiddling about with a fringe of guy ropes like bits of string which, when you want to put the thing up in a hurry, may be fairly compared to milking a mouse. Moreover, once inside, the lack of headroom reduces you to a brutish posture, especially if it happens to be raining when you're pulling your pants on. Clearly this wouldn't do for the Queen of the Night, nor me.

After crawling into a variety of contraptions on the floors of sports shops, I was offered by a manufacturer the loan of a Phoenix, a double-skinned igloo spacious enough to house four lusty mountaineers. It had, in fact, been used on the slopes of Everest. The thing was upheld by four lengthy but

12

feather-light tubes of aluminium which, when fully extended and pushed into seams on the outer skin, could be bent over into the shape of a ribbed hemisphere and pegged down securely from within and without. There were literally no strings to it. Notwithstanding a Homeric tussle when we tried it out for the first time, it looked as if we had found a portable home from home.

Homeric? No more, no less. There was that time when Telemachus, the son of Ulysses, strove, like a modern analyst, to find out why his father couldn't settle down quietly on the family estate at Ithaca. The All-seeing Hera told him he would have to pin down Proteus, the Old Man of the Sea, who knew what was the matter. But Proteus was not to be subjugated that easily, certainly not by a merè stripling. Moreover, like that hemispherical tent of ours on a windy morning at the top of Chimney Bank in Rosedale, he could assume a dozen shapes at will, turning from an immense bat into an octopus, a bucking horse, and then a wild boar. To get to grips with the thing for the first time we should, of course, have chosen a quieter day, but with careless abandon we spread it out until it resembled an enormous starfish. Katie, for such is her real name, shoved in the tubes whilst I stood by with the camera, whereupon, like the phoenix it was, it arose from the flaming gold of the bilberry. To my dismay, my helpmate promptly disappeared beneath the flapping folds of material which first turned themselves inside out and then all but gave her a lesson on hang-gliding. The Bank stands above the steepest hill in this country. We put the thing to rights eventually and set off for an amble round the Dale to get the feel of unaccustomed weight.

In my salad days I had trained for a transalpine excursion by carrying sixty pounds of weight lifters' weights sandwiched between the pages of the London telephone directories, but today I wouldn't wish that masochistic exercise on a dog. We compromised by splitting the load in Girl Friday's favour, but found that the spring-scales inched ominously down when into our rucksacks we squeezed a small butane cooker, pans, cutlery and unbreakable crockery, and a bag of dehydrated foodstuffs which, we discovered during the first week, all tasted much alike.

Books presented a problem. The eight on the short list included E. V. Rieu's pocket-sized translation of *The Odyssey*, Gilbert White's *The Natural History of Selborne, Three Men in a Boat,* and a field guide to the *British Mosses and Liverworts.* Madam said she wasn't too keen on liverworts, but we agreed on *A Coast to Coast Walk* by that marvellous man, Alfred Wainwright, whose guides to the Lake District are classics of the genre. And at the last moment we slipped in a small edition of *The Journeys of Celia Fiennes*, that much-travelled daughter of a Cromwellian Colonel, reckoning we should cross and re-cross her lines of route in several places.

After rites which have no place in the narrative at this stage, we arranged for maps to be sent on at intervals, locked up the apartment in London, and drove north to the foot of the fells.

Into Cumbria

Ravenglass, a mere pocket-handkerchief of a place on the Cumbrian coast, gives the impression that it fell asleep on its bed of shingle centuries ago and now stirs uneasily only when the little trains from Barrow and Carlisle chug in and chug out, venting shrieks that echo back three-fold from the fells around. But if asleep that port and fortress known to the Romans as Glenaventa has much to dream about. Here it was that the Emperor Hadrian, conqueror of the Parthians and builder of The Wall, considered plans for the invasion of Ireland under the Eagles of the Sixth and Twentieth. Earlier still, the Estuary of the Three Rivers (the Irt, the Esk and the Mite) afforded sheltered landfall for the sifters of gold from that Eldorado of the West, the Shannon – gold which was carted across the fells and dales for eventual shipment to Scandinavia and Gaul. That route we had a mind to follow. In brief, we took to the hills from a township at the end of its tether, a place that clings on only because time has forgotten to wipe it out.

The gentle swash and fetch of the waves were as the breathing of an exhausted man whilst far out across the saltings there appeared no distinction between the sea and the sky, only a flight of sea birds, flake-white specks against the grey like cigarette ash caught in a beam of sunlight.

That leaden sky worried us somewhat. Did it betoken rain? Were we in for a downpour before our venture had fairly begun? No matter. Our waterproofs were at the ready. However, as no account of an excursion through these islands of the grey winds can be reckoned complete without some reference to the weather, it must be said that within an hour we had the best of it. On Muncaster Fell that morning the lowlands were as bright as scarves, and later, when the great circle of mountains from Scafell round to Crinkle Crags and Harter Fell uprose behind Ellerhow Moss, that range which has been nicely called the volcanic roof of the North, we felt in every sense on top of the world.

15

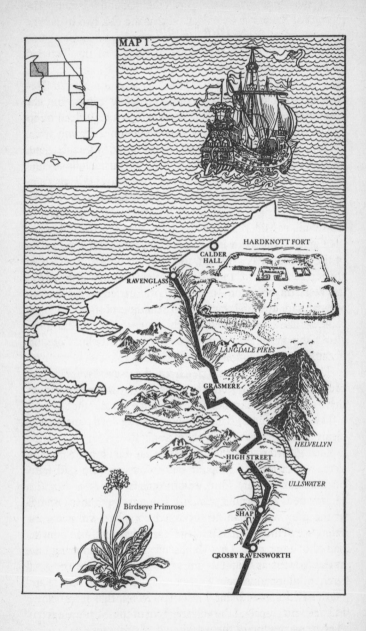

MAP I

HARDKNOTT FORT

CALDER HALL

RAVENGLASS

LANGDALE PIKES

GRASMERE

HELVELLYN

HIGH STREET

ULLSWATER

Birdseye Primrose

SHAP

CROSBY RAVENSWORTH

Of the three rivers that lose their identity among the saltings of Ravenglass we decided that the Esk had by far the most to offer. She rises far to the north-east under some crags with the improbable name of Knotts of the Tongue; she skitters around the Great Moss and Birker Fell and then, as if conscious of what lies in wait for her at Glenaventa, she starts to meander, modestly displaying her lower reaches from behind a screen of larch. Judged upon her merits in the round, a well brought-up, a mature river. By contrast, the Mite has no youth to speak of and the Irt a distinctly shady background, escaping as she does from the depths of Wastwater. So we went up the Esk or, more accurately, we looked down on her, respectfully, by keeping to the shoulders of the valley until we got closer together in the woods of Milkingstead.

At the beginning the going is not so much difficult as confused. Of the Roman fort behind the station at Ravenglass little remains except the cyclopean blocks of the bath-house; the rest has been knocked about by the engineers of the railway and obscured by a quite inexcusable profusion of rhododendrons and birch. Through that misplantation an ill-marked path winds furtively, as if ashamed of not living up to its well-mapped credentials. Close by Decoy Wood the labyrinth opens out into a deer park where, if the going had been less steep, we should have cut a merry dance in praise of a great down-pouring of sunlight.

The path over the fell is steep but purposive, and leaves ample time to take in what becomes clearer at each crest gained. The tarn near the summit is an exception. Seen from afar, these isolated pools normally wink at your approach: you can assess their actual size, and speculate how best they can be rounded. But on Chapel Hill the tarn is almost entirely screened by more rhododendrons, which in turn are girded by trees. We ventured among those curious tunnels of growth, peered at their reflections in the wind-pewtered water, and scrambled out among the infinitely more pleasing cover of heather, bilberry and whin.

When those of us gypsily inclined are setting out for a long walk in the spring of the year, there come mornings so vibrant, so deserving of that simple word *primavera*, that it

17

taxes language to say more than one would drink in every drop of it – and this was such a morning. The wind blew fresh and aromatic from a ridge of distant pines; high up, two buzzards, mewing softly like kittens, mounted an invisible spiral in the sky with no more effort than slight uplift of their rounded wings. Stone-chats chinked, grouse gabbled, and big bees bumbled irritably as, in their zeal to squat in deserted mouse-holes, they fell over in their efforts to get in. When to all this a mistle-thrush in the dingle below rolled out slow notes that could be heard the length of the fell, life seemed eager, brimful, at all levels.

There is a place here for what Winifred Pennington, a distant relative of the founders of Muncaster Castle, says of her native land about which, as a biologist, she knows a great deal. 'Why does the landscape look as it does?' she asks. 'Can we look at it not only as it now appears, but going back through time until we understand the reason for what we see?' Surely the time she refers to also includes the Proust-like remembrance of things which seemed unimportant in youth but which, through the years, have become bright corners in our store of memories.

This came home to me with uncommon force at the foot of Hooker Crag where, leaving Katie to adjust some chafing strap or other, I clambered up the pink granite the better to see what lay around. To the north-east, beyond Miterdale, the broad shoulders of Scafell stood out among a host of lesser peaks, dove-grey for the most part but patterned here and there by shafts of sunlight that brought out warm hues of amber and oyster-blue as you may see them in Hebridean cloth. To the north, the Commons of Nether Wasdale sloped down to forested valleys drained by the Irt and the Bleng, whilst more to the west the chimneys and high towers of the atomic power station at Calder Hall stuck out with curiously irritating incongruity.

When in the company of newspapermen I first visited those silent generators of power I could find nothing more striking to say than that close by, at Dring, archaeologists had unearthed the earliest known evidence in the Lake District of Man the Tool-maker. There, on the one hand, were bits of flint believed to be seven or eight thousand years old, whilst on the other we were allowed for the first time to gaze with becoming awe at the marvel of its day, the prototype of the nuclear oven. The nation's economy, we were told, was on the brink of transformation.

This, surely, is one of those points on which the gain of many years teaches us a different wisdom. Today I am solidly on the side of a reporter from a tabloid who on that occasion had the impertinence to ask one of the atomic knights on the platform if it wouldn't be cheaper, certainly safer, to squander the fortune they had spent on harnessing the tides instead. I forget how they brushed him off, but recalled the occasion that morning when, from the highest point of Muncaster Fell, I looked back on the huge arc of the Irish Sea.

The sea! The sea! Those triumphant words and what they meant to the ten thousand under Xenophon are just about all I can remember of one of the greatest marches in history. I remember them because, having failed to write on time a short essay about how those hungry, hard-pressed men reached the Black Sea from Babylon and their excitement at getting there, I was ordered by a homosexual classicist to write them out a hundred times.

I suppose I saw the sea for the first time on the sands of Margate where, stumbling about in nappies, I learned to toddle. Most memories of that period which, analysts assure us, is important, have faded, but I know that at the age of two or thereabouts my parents took me to a menagerie, where a monkey, irritated perhaps at close scrutiny, grabbed hold of my infantile hair so tenaciously that it pulled out a handful. Later, in the wild imagination of childhood, that monkey became a gorilla of such ferocity that it took the combined efforts of the whole zoo staff to save me from a broken neck. This went down particularly well with youthful companions who could match it only with elaborate tales of bites from neighbours' dogs. The story gained pictorial substance at Pontefract in the home of my paternal grandfather, Old John, a cultured if tyrannical reprobate to whom I attribute all my imperfections. Before he squandered a lot of money inherited from the manufacture of those liquorice confections called Pontefract Cakes which still bear our name, Old John had built up a fine collection of pictures and books, including many about exotic travel. Among them I recall a huge leather-bound volume about the exploits of one of the first white hunters, probably Frederick Selous or perhaps Trader Horn. It was illustrated by full-page etchings of a variety of animals, the most striking of which was an outsize in gorillas standing upright with jaws agape and fangs exposed. A golden opportunity. In a hushed voice I explained to young and impressionable cousins that the animal was *none other* than the one from which I had been providentially rescued. We were obliged to speak in whispers since the volume, perhaps because it depicted bare-breasted black women, was one of those kept in gran'pa's study.

When the old man was out and we were confined to the house during the unutterable boredom of Sunday afternoons we staged brief forays into that forbidden territory. Dare we look at the awful creature? Well, yes. Perhaps just a glance. Certainly no more. We crept in; we opened the book, pausing before we turned that well-thumbed page. The moment we saw the gorilla we shrieked. We banged the book shut and fled, our excitement for the day over.

In his youth Old John had cut a fair figure as a fell-walker and amateur wrestler, a fact attested to by a framed sepia photograph of him in white combinations, admiring his biceps in the guise of Mr Atlas. He had also sailed, and raced horses, unsuccessfully. His pictures were mostly Lakeland scenes, turbulent seascapes, and his expensive thorough-breds that never quite made the grade at Doncaster and Tanshelf, the local course.

As my father, a distinctly unathletic company director, was averse even to throwing a ball about in the garden at Leeds, I egged the old man on to tell more stories, especially that one about how, after arguments at the local hustings, he had put a hammerlock on the town clerk, 'a damned Whig with no beard', until that unfortunate had put to rights some real or imaginary irregularities in the distribution of voting papers. There was another story, supported by cuttings from the *Pontefract Advertiser*, about the sequel to Old John's venture into the orchid-growing business. Inspired, I suppose, by the huge greenhouses of the local gentry, he ordered one of his own and stocked it with more orchids than he could afford.

When he discovered that the temperature and humidity made it unsuitable for sitting there at night to drink and keep out of grandmother's way, his enthusiasm evaporated. However, a friend had presented him with one of the new HMV gramophones with a heavy winding handle and tin horn. I found the remains of it in the cellar. With his mind still on isolation, gran'pa decided that for a one-man auditorium with shelves ready-made for the discs, there could be nothing better, nothing more resonant, than the orchid house. He sat there, night after night; and bought so many records that the company presented him with one of their emblems, the plaster dog listening to His Master's Voice. But another problem arose. The high-pitched arias of Melba and Galli-Curci attracted less melodic cats, which quickened the music lover's sporting instincts to the point where he started taking pot-shots at them with a powerful air rifle. Wind of this reached the newspaper through indignant neighbours. In a small but incisive paragraph on the front page, the editor wrote: 'News has reached us that, in his declining years, Mr John Hillaby, the sweet manufacturer, has taken to shooting cats in the dark. We suggest that, for the safety of the local feline population, he loads his gun with liquorice allsorts.'

I loved those stories, punctuated as they were with oaths and aphorisms, but when grandmother, a grey-haired wraith, entered the room unexpectedly, chilling the atmosphere, he would promptly switch to some quite irrelevant local history – perhaps about the castle, or how *his* father, another John, had started the business experimentally by boiling liquorice in a fireman's helmet. But though he was as adroit at changing subjects as he was at concealing whisky glasses behind the coal-bucket, his spouse would catch a key word to some oft-told tale of derring-do, and from experience knew that anecdotes about cock-fighting and the like prompted the old man to unlock the liquor cupboard to which, I suspect, he kept a duplicate key. 'The boy would do well to learn more about matters of improvement,' she would say primly, an almost direct reference to the fact that I took little interest in the works of the Georgian ladies which she sent me year by year on my birthday. They bored me, a standpoint fortified by one of her husband's extravagant comments to the effect that

Charlotte Brontë was a dried-up old bitch who would have done better by herself and the world in general if she'd married one of his draymen. He preferred Surtees and Henry Fielding.

Notwithstanding his robust attitude to life, Old John had a keen eye for paintings, especially water-colours of the Lake District. With the exception of Gilchrist, I have long since forgotten the names of both the artists and their works but clues to the character of their owner came out in his attitude to them all. It wasn't so much the placidity of the scenes or their beauty that fired his enthusiasm. It was the contrariety of the picture as a whole. What force had reduced that slope to a wilderness of tumbled boulders? Remembering, perhaps, his fell-walking days, he asked what one might expect to find beyond that promontory or in the depths of some shadowy valley. With grandfather there was no room for neutrality of opinion. He grabbed your arm; he demanded an opinion. What was the artist trying to *say*? Could one afford to take liberties with, say, perspective if the effect was right? In short, did it or did it not come off? Otherwise, as he put it in a phrase often used by my father, one might as well throw the damn thing out of the window.

This passionate, subjective approach to art came out clear in his choice of seascapes. They were mostly of storms on the east coast, of lifeboats being launched, ships demasted within sight of wave-thrashed harbours. All fine swirling compositions.

Although Pontefract stands foursquare on some of the thickest coal seams in the country, even today the countryside is curiously attractive. When grandfather and I walked down leafy lanes to see the 'Ings', those sheets of water caused by mining subsidence, he taught me the names of scores of plants. The reward for remembering: perhaps a thin slab of Swiss chocolate. He didn't hold with those damned pious sweet-makers at York; they were Quakers, and liquorice was fit only for the lower orders. The penalty for forgetting: a sharp clout on the ear. No child should be struck in cold blood he said. The upshot was that I learned a great deal and hankered after larger vistas.

For some reason I never managed to reach the Lakes until

much later in life; in fact I believe I saw Mont Blanc before Bow Fell. But the sea! The sea! I yearned for the harbour steps, the fishing-tackle, the peppery smell of ragworm, the best bait for codling. Not for me the storms that stirred grandfather's imagination – they put an end to fishing, sometimes for days. For all that, I knew what effect the sea had on a youngster who had never seen it before. His name was Alfie, a mere titch, the youngest, the smallest treble in the choir of St Chad's, Headingley. I hated him. He turned up ten minutes late for the appointed start of our annual trip to Scarborough.

Where was Alfie? Nobody knew. The tenors and three bass voices had already swept off in one of Waddington's shiny charabancs accompanied by crates of bottled brown and the vicar's warden, an impious man. Why couldn't we go without the kid? We couldn't, said the organist. The little chap, an orphan who lived with an aged uncle, had been talking about the trip for weeks.

Almost in tears the laggard arrived, pulling at his uncle's arm. He wore a nearly new pair of grey flannel trousers, lent with some misgivings by the people next door. In his excitement to get to the church he had wet his own. 'Mind them pants,' were his uncle's parting words. He conferred briefly with the organist. A coin changed hands. A two-bob piece, quite a bit of money. It was offered to me if I would look after the brat. Conflicts arose: avarice versus youthful stirrings. Barred as we all were from my beloved harbour, I had hoped to ogle the girls on the sands in the company of our leading soloist, a lecherous lad who had taught me a thing or two. His voice was beginning to break. Avarice won. Off we swept to the coast, with Alfie on the seat next to me. He jumped up and down. He had never been beyond the city limits. I hated him more and more.

The old port of Scarborough lies under Castle Hill, a promontory that juts out between two extensive bays. With a cultivated sense of theatre, the driver cruised through the back of the town and pulled up his coach on the edge of the North Cliff, the better to present the view right across the bay. With their eyes on an ice-cream stall, nobody much cared. Nobody, that is, except Alfie. He could scarcely speak as he

23

scrambled down and ran to the railings, staring open-eyed, open-mouthed, at what by any reckoning is an almighty big bathful of water. I followed, holding his hand, worried about what he might do. He continued to stare. Eventually he gave a strangled cry and looked down at those nice flannel trousers. Alfie had done it again.

The sea! The sea! Seen from Hooker Crag, the water that washes the Cumbrian coast is not so much a bathful as a pale blue ribbon, broken at low tide by the shingle beds and the saltings.

> . . . plus vague et plus soluble dans l'air

Verlaine caught it nicely, and on Muncaster Fell it matched the mood of the mountains.

I returned to find Katie looking intently at something far down in the valley. A bird? I asked. She nodded and handed me the glasses. A bird indeed. A fell-runner, a marvellously built young woman in T-shirt and shorts who loped along so purposefully, so lightly, that even in the close-up of the Zeiss, she scarcely seemed to touch the ground. It could have been Atalanta herself. Had she seen me, I would have blown her a kiss, and yet at heart I had the rather snobbish feeling that, in the scale of enjoyable gymnastics, we had the edge on that girl as much as she had on, say, a jogger or one of those arm- and bottom-waggling competitive walkers.

A light walker imposes little more than his own weight on each foot. He doesn't jolt his framework. The runner may impose up to four times that weight, whilst the pounding of heavy joggers on hard surfaces is incalculable. To judge from their grunts, their agonized expressions, the ecstasy lies in the agony. You feel they wouldn't be doing it if they weren't contemplating the imminent demise of those who take next to no exercise at all. Hard words these, but sensory impressions are progressively diminished when we move more than about five miles an hour on foot; below that speed one can see trees as well as forests, and in towns people as well as crowds. Possibly the walker has found the peace that the runner still seeks. But that couldn't be said of Atalanta. She tripped along as delicately as a deer. For reasons of her own she disappeared, briefly, behind a boulder and then on she went, neither slower nor faster than before. One could say of her, as of Lady Macbeth, that no compunctious visitings of nature could shake her fell purpose.

A large slab of rock below Hooker Crag, called Ross's Camp on the map, is as fine a place as anywhere to enjoy the view. The name intrigued me. I drew blank among the comprehensive *Proceedings* of the Cumberland and Westmorland Antiquarian and Archaeological Society. In a letter, Walter Poucher, that veteran mountaineer and photographer, a man whose profile puts you in mind of the south face of Great Gable, said he could find nothing about the place in his extensive library of Lake District books. But I found a clue among the history of the age-old affrays on the Border.

During the struggle for the throne between Matilda and Stephen during the twelfth century, at least five hundred 'adulterine' keeps sprang up in the Debatable Land. The contemporary Anglo-Saxon Chronicle says, 'Every shire is full of castles and every castle filled with evil men.' Later, in the sixteenth century, Scottish raids were so incessant that it was proposed to build another wall with 'esconses' or forts at every mile. Treachery was so rife that the Wardens of the Western Marches were ordered to take immediate action against those who employed Scottish servants or had taken Scottish wives, the punishment for which was death. This, as I saw it on slender evidence, must be where Ross marched in. He was a close relative of the great Buccleugh of Lanark whose coat of arms is still supported by two virgins 'habited only from the waist downwards'. Their motto is *I love*, and they were not earls to be trifled with in love or in war.

A fair niece had become hopelessly enamoured of a local lordling, but had been 'thrice fyled', that is testified against, by one of the Warden's agents. She had been imprisoned. At this news Ross walked through the night with thirty tried men. Things went badly for the incursionists. Their escape route to the east was cut off by Mouncey, the self-appointed king of Patterdale. They narrowly escaped capture by clambering round Wastwater at night to a keep of the Grahams, who were as often as not in league with the Scots. But before he left Ross laid his hands on that stone below Hooker Crag and swore he would return.

As we sat there, two good folk, a retired baker and his wife from Todmorden, trudged up the slope from Eskdale Green. Quite a haul they said, but they'd enjoyed it. Their first visit to the Lakes, they confided, but they would certainly come back. At this I told them about Ross and suggested they, too, should put their hands palm downwards on that hewn slab. I make no excuse for this. It is a good thing if you can persuade people they are somehow partakers in a mystery. It makes them feel *bigger.*

In Eskdale for lunch an hour later we encountered a sad youth who had fallen out of a tree. We also made more enquiries about Ross, the outcome of which I'll come to when I've dealt with the youth. He was carrying a crash helmet and was clearly at odds with one of the leaders of the local Outward Bound School. He wasn't, one felt, cut out for commando stuff. As a reprimand for something ineptly done he had been ordered to fix up a rope-ladder for his fellow adventurers whooping it up in the woods below. But that, too, had gone badly. A knot or two had given way. He had hurt his shoulder and was in for another ticking off. But he wouldn't get it, he said. By God he wouldn't. He was going to eff off for the effing station, outward bound on his own.

As for Ross, neither the landlord nor any of the oldsters in the George the Fourth knew anything about him. But weeks later, hearing about my enquiries by a roundabout route, Mrs Hodges, wife of the former vicar of Eskdale, sent us a courteous postcard. The story of the camp, she said, had taken some running down, but it transpired that about a hundred years ago a certain John Ross had been in charge of the Muncaster estate. It was his custom to serve out food and drink for guests at his lordship's shooting-parties on that stone. Ah well, legends sprout as mysteriously as legs on a tadpole. The emissary of the Buccleughs could, of course, have been one of his ancestors. Maybe he *did* return.

I wish our way had lain more among trees, for they are among the most companionable of societies, but gone are the days when it was said a squirrel could leap from Skiddaw to Furness without touching the ground. For the most part the

26

trees have now been laid low or, worse, replaced by a corduroy of conifers. Nevertheless the woods of Forge and Milkingstead were fine to walk through, dappled as they were by sunlight. It's possible, I suppose, that a few of the old pines there were the descendants of those that once sheltered wolves, wild boar and Scots engaged on villainy, but the majority were civilized trees, especially the rose-stippled larch introduced to the Lake District in the late eighteenth century and (notwithstanding what Wordsworth said about them) none the worse for that. Originally they were natives of central Europe, a strain which doesn't do too well in the south of England; but these, I was told, came from vigorous Scottish stock.

Beech and oak have been planted there, and sycamore too, a tree I could well do without. The lovely birch, I assume, came in by itself, flanking the glades. A sure test of a healthy and aesthetically pleasing forest – which are more or less the same thing – is what grows *between* the trees, no matter whether they are conifers or hardwoods. I cannot abide crowds anywhere.

The Esk kept us company for most of the way, babbling in deep groins of granite and then reappearing unexpectedly in a different guise, close to the path, swirling round and round on a mosaic of coloured pebbles. This is a nobody-about sort of place, for the simple reason that it can be reached only on foot. The road lies on the other side of the river; the climbers are off in their hundreds to Helvellyn, the Langdale Pikes and that enormous lump of volcanic ash, Great Gable. I can't think why so few people appreciate Harter Fell which dominates Eskdale as you may see it from the floor of the valley.

We managed to keep off the road until the footbridge beyond the Old Drift, the place where the river wanders off for some business of her own under Birker Fell, and the cars grind up the Hardknott Pass. After inspecting three or four sites for that most English of occupations, an afternoon cup of tea, we settled on a bower which couldn't have been bettered for Marie Antoinette in the woods of Versailles: a concealed loop of the river, a hummocky bank like a sprung settee, and an orchestration of willow warblers. Here I had intended to say something about my relationship to Katie but that must

27

wait a quieter moment since, on the authentic note of anti-climax, I tripped over my pack.

As we lolled back and nibbled scones overlaid with quince jelly a small butterfly fluttered into view. I glanced at it without much interest, and then stared, fascinated. A Mountain Ringlet, a rarity, our only true Alpine, a relic of glacial times. I leaped in pursuit as one might after a wind-blown five-pound note. Unfortunately, at the point of take-off I knocked over the open rucksack at my feet, breaking four badly-packed eggs and damaging my exposure meter.

Undeterred, I pounded after the creature which, showing an uncommon turn of speed, fluttered round our tea-table at least twice before making off for the safety of the opposite bank. Egg-white is penetrative stuff. It took us ten minutes to scrape it out of the canvas pocket. In that time I consoled myself with the thought that it might not have been a Mountain Ringlet, but possibly a Large Heath; and, on a more pious note, with the reflection that if it was a rarity it should be left alone – which, of course, was to take credit for something I could not help.

When I came to set this to paper Katie said she didn't think I was altogether justified in discussing the peculiarities of something I wasn't at all sure about. This underlines a nice point of difference between us. She knows more than a fair amount about natural history, but doesn't often speculate. She prefers other people's points of view. They are more likely to be right, she thinks. On the other hand, as a rambling naturalist I regard myself as a self-liberated man, sustained by the childish belief that everything I think about, everything that happens to me, is of general interest. Only a person who is congenitally self-centred has the effrontery and the stamina to write the way I do.

There was nothing we liked about Hardknott Pass more than getting to the top of it. Had we hurried instead of ambling along the riverbank, the traffic would have been far worse. As it was we swung on to the road in the light of the lowering sun, and trudged and trudged, stepping aside only to enable an occasional car to pass, cars that seemed to relegate us to tourist class. On we went, cutting off the corners on some of the bends, often with chins down so low that the

28

crags on either side of that great *cirque* loomed up almost unnoticed until we were deep in their shadows. A few cars were parked on the brow, and I wondered if we should have difficulty in settling down for the night close to one of the most famous sites in Cumbria, the ruins of the Roman fort of Mediobogdum. And if the ruins were all I hoped for, what about water? I glanced down at the gill some three hundred feet below. That surely was not the source on which the garrison had relied? It could easily have been sieged by invaders. Question after question whirled round, like waltzing mice. Had I been pushing Katie a bit too hard? She had never carried a pack before. Should we call it a day and, if so, where?

I see no reason to disclose where, in fact, we settled down for the night. Enough to say that whoever built the best-preserved Roman fort in Cumbria south of the Wall ensured our privacy by siting his battlements high on a ledge hemmed in by mountains. It might fairly be compared with the British garrison of Landi Kotal at the top of the Khyber Pass or Chitral in the far frontier hills. At Mediobogdum (literally 'the fortress situated in the middle of the curve') Sir Mortimer Wheeler said he felt closer to the grandeur of Rome than he did in that untidy builder's yard, the Roman forum. It guarded the vital Roman road from Glenaventa, the port to Ireland, to High Street above Ambleside, the road to Scotland. How and when it fell nobody knows, except that the Brigantes probably closed in. From an inscription discovered in the *porta praetoria*, the south-east gate, it is known that in the days of the Emperor Hadrian, Hardknott was garrisoned by a cohort, that is five hundred auxiliaries from Dalmatia, now part of Yugoslavia. A war-mad people, says Strabo. 'Their home lands are poor . . . they live for the most part on spelt and millet . . . and they are tattooed.' Spelt, a crude form of wheat, must have been hard on the teeth.

Using a freshet of water which might have been there since Roman times, we did rather better with soup, dehydrated chicken *mexicaine*, followed by almond tart and coffee. The wine lasted until the most distant fells had been devoured by the dusk.

A feature of our northern skies is that from mid-April

onwards daylight lengthens so rapidly that within a month darkness, as we usually understand it, is of scant duration, and in the absence of much cloud becomes merely a lowering of the afterglow. So it was that night. With no sounds beyond the occasional bark of a raven and the needle-thin squeaks of fieldmice, sounds that served only to emphasize the silence, we talked and we talked of things of no great profundity. They had to do with the laundry lists of life, the rearrangement of our bits of property, our need to do something about her car. In setting this down as simply as I can, I take enormous pleasure in dwelling on that word, 'our', because Katie and I were married in London before we set off to walk back to that city. From time to time as I lit my pipe I caught a glimpse of her face, so warm, so full of compassion that I cannot better what R. L. Stevenson said of his night among the pines: '. . . even when I was exulting in my solitude I became aware of a strange lack. I wished a companion to lie near me in the starlight, silent and not moving, but ever within touch. For there is a fellowship more quiet even than solitude and which, rightly understood, is solitude made perfect. And to live out of doors with the woman a man loves is of all lives the most complete and free.'

In our sleeping habits Katie and I are by fortunate chance synchronous, which is a high-falutin' way of saying that we can both go to sleep and wake up at the same time, or at least with no more than a gentle shove on her part or mine. But on that morning under Hardknott I had a mind to be out and about uncommonly early. The reasons were in part those that had prompted the Atalanta of Eskdale to similar activity; I also wanted to look at the place seen only briefly the night before, and say good-morning all round; and Katie, I assumed wrongly, would be very tired after her first day's walk. Besides there might be some busybody about.

Outside, all appeared as through veils of muslin moving gently in the lightest of breezes. Only the topmost tip of Raven Crag pierced the opacity like the up-ended bows of a ship which has all but sunk, an illusion heightened by the curious wave-like pulsations of the water vapour. Gradually, that's to say within a few minutes, the visibility clarified.

Streamers of mist swirled away until most of the mountains came into view and objects in the foreground stood out in hazy silhouette.

Through the broken walls of the fort I saw what could have been an irregular column of rock, or perhaps a motionless figure. That chap from the Parks Department whose Land-rover we had seen the previous night? We were trespassing, I suspected, and in split seconds I rehearsed a confrontation in which, as I usually do in these imaginary encounters, I came out rather well. But it wasn't the bailiff, although, if you could have seen that shape as I saw it in my mind's eye, it might well have been Liccaeus of Liburnia on the last sentry-watch of the night on *Kalendiae Maiae Anno Urbis Conditae CXXXIV*.

Four Auxiliaries had patrolled the fellstone battlements from the last hour until dawn. Two were his fellow country-men. Not bad chaps. At least you knew what they were talking about. The other was that Greek bastard Tykas who owed him fifty sesterces. What was it Centurion Rufus said when he complained? *Graecas calendas solvere*. Greeks never paid. *Never* paid? Bet that sod Rufus got a back-hander for sticking up for him. Funny how he wouldn't let him see the Commander. Still, it didn't do to argue the toss with the Centurion. Never knew where you stood with him. Blew hot and cold, he did. One day he'd hint that if you went on cutting more stone than anyone else he'd put you in for a *principalis* so that, instead of sweating your guts out, you could stand around and do damn all. *And* be paid for it. Then, sod it, the next day he'd break his bloody *vitis* on your back. Liccaeus thought ruefully of that time a year back when his first job each morning had been to sweep out the Centurion's room. A doddle that was, a cosy little pad next to where the lads, eighty-five of 'em, polished their leather and slept like cooped-up fowls.

He'd learned a lot, he had. Before his transfer to *Victrix* at York, the Centurion Vesuvius Rufus from the Great City had fought under the Eagles of Hispana. He could show off the scars of eleven wounds, and none of 'em on his back. Five of 'em, collected where the fighting was hot, they'd brought him in a handful of gongs – three embossed discs, the *phalerae* and two *hastae purae*, the coveted silver spear-shafts for bravery in single combat.

31

Rufus had told him a bit about what they were up against at Hardknott. The cohorts were being pulled back from Scotland to the Wall. The bloody Brigantes were massing in the mountains. The attack would come from there. They were too smart to show themselves on the road. Why, said Rufus, if you haven't served north of the Wall, you don't know what bad weather is! Not to be outdone, Liccaeus had told him that back home in Liburnia, the Bora could blow the arse off a mule. No Roman could stand up against it: you had to be *born* on the Adriatic coast. That did it! Insubordination! Bang went the chance of a *principalis*. He remembered the clout he got and jankers on the parade ground for a week afterwards. What made Rufus so bloody touchy? What with his wounds, his gongs, and his length of service, he'd be out in a year or two. Lucky sod.

As he waited for his relief to turn up, Liccaeus yawned and looked up at the deserted pass. Although it had been a quiet night, thank God, he could do with some kip. If the weather held, maybe they'd get some leave. Leave! He thought of those tarts down at Glenaventa, especially that black-haired Celt with the huge tits. Cost a packet, she would. Liccaeus remembered the fifty sesterces he was owed, and sighed.

Katie didn't altogether believe what I told her about Liccaeus and, come to think of it, I wouldn't swear to his name myself, but years ago I had seen his homeland, which lies between Istra and coastal Herzegovina on the Adriatic coast.

Around the roof

On that second day we shouldered our portable home from Hardknott to the flanks of Helvellyn. By taking into account a number of side shifts which had almost nothing to do with where we proposed to settle down for the night, the going amounted in all to about twenty miles. A pretty fair stint by most standards, but then, in the manner of a medieval ox with its set acreage to cover, or, if you prefer it, like Thursday's child, we had far to go.

Within an hour of adjusting our straps against the sensation of being pulled backwards, we had topped one pass only to find ourselves confronted by another. This was Wrynose which, in its extremities, seemed to be making a determined effort to climb into the sky. It lies in the shadow of Ulpha Fell. What Wrynose means I'm hanged if I know, unless it has something to do with the reaction of travellers confronted by that switchback. But Ulpha surely is cognate with wolf? There is a hamlet and another fell of the same name not far away. If to these old lupine resorts you add Ulverston, Ullswater and Ullock (*ulfa-leikr*, the wolves' playground) the animals in Saxon times must have been more common than badgers. Well, maybe they were, but speculation on this point was considerably dampened when, after some enquiries, I learned more about the acquisitive habits of two local warlords called Ulf and Wulfere. The origin of place names is a muddy tarn in which presumptions are quickly drowned.

There were a few fluffy clouds on the horizon but they were making off towards Shap Fell. The common opinion is that rainfall hereabouts is consistently one of the heaviest in Britain. This is a half-truth. Gordon Manley, whose opinion would be hard to fault, has pointed out that the climate does not, in its essentials, differ much from other parts of northern England. However, because of the mountains, in wet seasons 'the extremes of rainfall and the persistence of cloud may be a little greater'. Lakeland devotees put it rather differently,

33

claiming that when it rains it does so *harder.* Quality rather than quantity, as it were.

What is apparent to anyone within sight of Scafell is that the peaks of that savage barrier of rock are highly productive cloud-factories. A mere breath of moisture-laden air from the Atlantic is enough to generate whole schools of whale-like cumulo-nimbus which sail overhead, ponderous and serene, in groups or at intervals. Molly Lefebure, a dedicated Cumbrian cloud-watcher, once likened the progress of a particularly large one to that of Moby Dick when Captain Ahab wasn't on his tail.

The top of Wrynose – called *Raynus* by the locals – is marked by the Three Shires Stone, the place where, until civil servants started to play about with the boundaries to their own advantage, the three old shires of Cumberland, Westmorland and Lancashire rubbed shoulders for nearly a thousand years. Today the oldsters of Appleby, Penrith and Furness are more than dismayed about losing their identity. They are very cross about it.

With our backs to that stone we looked far down the valley towards Ambleside where, nestling among the fells, the surface of Little Langdale Tarn winked like a watery eye in the constantly changing light. It blinked, it winked, it half-closed as if tired of glaring at the sky and then, suddenly, in a blaze of sunlight, it flashed so fiercely that you might imagine that the basin of the Brathay had been turned upside down for one moment, leaving behind an ingot of solid silver.

In the early part of the nineteenth century Little Langdale achieved a felonious reputation as the resort of moonshiners, who, backed by an efficient sales department (the local smugglers), brewed potent stuff in places known to almost everyone except the harassed excisemen. The business required no more than a hide-out with a supply of water and grain of almost any kind, sometimes mouldy stuff which horses wouldn't touch. Their skill lay in coaxing the temperature of 'the worm', the condenser, up to that point between steady distillation and a diabolical explosion.

From 1823 onwards the duty on liquor amounted to two and threepence per wine-gallon; whisky was looked down on by the gentry who tippled brandy; commoners drank themselves blind on gin at a penny a glass. What Two-Finger Jack, Lanty Slee and his fellow-moonshiners concocted was far from nobody's business. Hundreds were engaged in the trade. There were skirmishes on the pass between the law and the lawless. Boulders were rolled down on a coachload of excisemen. Mary Larg, a notorious wholesaler, went to the gallows, whilst Lanty Slee, who is reputed to have made some of the best stuff in the country, went to gaol several times before he died a rich man.

As with Hardknott, you sweep up to the top of Wrynose, pause for a moment as a roller-coaster does, and swing down to what on the map is called Fell Foot. Close by lies a terraced mound, Sphinx-like in its enigmatic origins. It could be a moraine sculptured by successive ice-sheets, a Celtic burial-ground or, from its resemblance to Tynwald Hill on the Isle of Man, a Viking Thing-mount, a place for peaceful argument. With a lingering predilection towards those wild fellows, I am all for the Norse explanation.

When the kids at school used to boast how their dads had collected a gong for ramming a U-boat or capturing God knows how many Uhlans single-handed at Ypres, it saddened me somewhat, for I knew darned well that father had been turned down by the Green Howards on account of his flat feet or varicose veins, I forget which; but with the exuberant imagination of adolescence I slowly achieved renown at a school for the sons of indigent Methodist missionaries by claiming descent from Ketill Flat-Nose, Siggytrig Silky Beard, and Olaf the Fart. That last one grabbed those who didn't know Fart meant the Journey-maker. And come to think of it, there could be a grain of truth in what I said, since my family came from the East and North Riding; we bear a Scandinavian name; and it was from Hedeby at the root of the Jutland peninsula that Black Gottfrid launched hundreds of those long ships with their terrible prows. Moreover, when I was in shorts in the days of the Peacemaker, we spent much of the summer at Scarborough, a town named after an old pirate who set fire to the place.

After the sacking of Lindisfarne, the Vikings, as distinct from the Danes, had a rough time of it on the Yorkshire coast and found it more profitable and less hazardous to sail north, around Scotland, and down into the Irish Sea, establishing colonies at Dublin and on the Isle of Man as useful bases for attacks against, and the eventual colonization of, parts of Cumbria. They probably felt at home among the fells; certainly *Cymry* and *Cambroges*, meaning fellow-countrymen, are Celtic words. The Norse were the forebears of the Cumbrian statesmen, that is flockmasters who owned and gained their livelihood from small farms with an acreage of garth and intake for their sheep, together with an apportioned share of the fellside, the *heaf* for summer grazing.

Apart from the characteristic Herdwick sheep, a few Viking crosses, and of course that Thing, if Thing it was, the most enduring and endearing local relics of the occupation are Scandinavian words that still crop up in the dialect of elder statesmen. There is, for example, *ootgang* for a right of way which if it happened to be *brant* (steep) and *slape* (slippery) would cause an 'oss to go *kyavellin aboot.* To *dunk* a doughnut is, literally, to render it like a moist field. To *addle* is to earn, to *laik* to play, whilst *lowsin'* time is not when sheep are dipped: it indicates that the job in hand has been done. Due, I suppose, to the radio and television, the dialect is getting loused up in the American sense of the phrase. Some *shippons* or byres have already become cow parlours, which is a step on the road towards milk bars.

The last we saw of the Thing through glasses was from the track across Blea Moss which wer' us brant and slape us an owd muck-midden. It leads up to the Langdale Pikes, but to achieve that noble prospect we were obliged to grapple with the rhododendrons around Blea Tarn. No doubt that shrub looks fine on Mount Pisgah or in the vales of the Meander, but escaping, as it has done, from hundreds of lordly estates, it has become a downright pest, a menace to horticulture, forestry and the view. It's a costly business to eradicate the alien or even keep it in check. It is resistant to most herbicides and it smothers everything within its shade. I would have it out, root and branch. Xenophon suffered from it: his soldiers in Asia Minor were poisoned by eating honey from the flowers of the plant that nowadays pollutes Blea Tarn. Mind you, apart from that we rather liked the place.

From a prominence reflected in the water you look across

at the most photographed, the most picture-postcarded, the most easily recognized, group of hills in England, the Langdale Pikes. Since that occasion long ago when Pavey Ark was first assaulted, climbers have been flocking around the Pike o' Stickle, Crinkle Crags, the Gimmer with its smooth and vertical faces, and many more. No small part of the attraction of these volcanic cathedrals lies surely in their fine brave names. What of Swirl How, which has about it the smack of winter gales? Or Glaramara, Blencathra, Seatallan, and Dollywaggon Pike? From the way they slip off the tip of my pen, you might think I'm on intimate terms with them. Certainly I have cruised round their flanks, but I could no more climb Walker's Gully than I could St Paul's. Through a combination of ignorance and misadventure, enough rough scrambling came my way in the Alps and Africa to make me extremely wary of anything precipitous. As I understand it, the difference between a walker and a scrambler is that the latter uses his hands now and again, whilst dedicated climbers regard both walking and scrambling largely as means to get to where they intend to risk their necks. For all that, I revel in the company of climbers; I extract vicarious excitement from hearing how, in the old days, the intrepid have been forked off high ledges by the antlers of red deer who resented intrusion. I recall how once in a pub in Borrowdale a young lad from Manchester described what happened to another lad whom they had just taken to hospital with fairly substantial injuries. It seems he had been in the lead. For some reason he had detached himself temporarily from the almost fully extended rope a moment or two before he slipped. 'Aye,' said the narrator, who had been patiently waiting on the rock-face below, 'he didn't half whizz past.'

As for Katie, there was in her conduct among those mountains something I'm diffident about setting to paper, lest it suffer from clumsy handling. Although she had lived and worked with her late husband on several tea-estates in Ceylon, one of them at a height of more than five thousand feet, she suffers, as I've said, from vertigo of a high order, certainly more acutely than ever I have. But she regards that swirling of the senses, that flabbiness of the knee-joints, as something to be endured, not as a deterrent.

She loved estate life with its rigours and hazards that included bringing up babies among ticks, scorpions and cobras, with hospitals thirty miles away and neighbours thin on the ground. There were storms, and home-comings by ship, and a background, always, of exotic life: the jungle with its screaming birds, the lianas and the orchids; the geckoes chirruping on the walls of the nursery; and, outside, the tall casuarinas and the terraced hills. It was often hard going but much, almost anything, she considers, can be endured if the blood is sufficiently purposeful; and she took to our tramping together with a zest I have never known before in a woman. And whereas my knowledge of natural history often seems bookish, she knows almost instinctively about how things grow, and what water and nutrients and slope mean to the clothing of the soil.

In addition to what rears up into the slowly-moving clouds, some three thousand feet of igneous rock lie below the ground close to the prominence where we stood that morning. A glance at the famous lakes from a small-scale map or from a high-flying plane shows that they all radiate outwards from the region north of Langdale. They are depressions which have been smoothed and deepened by glaciers of an age which, by comparison with the explosions around Borrowdale, was but as yesterday.

On our brief venture up into where the action was, that is between Pike How and Swine Crag, we encountered more rooks, crows and ravens than I recall seeing together anywhere else. Among the trees in front of the Dungeon Ghyll Hotel the rooks cawed, their voices much less harsh than those of their raucous cousins, the crows. With their characteristic swagger, their shaggy trousers and bone-white faces, they are, in my opinion, handsomer, more acrobatic and, under modern conditions, better able to look after themselves as well. They dominate the motorways, rising precariously close to approaching vehicles and promptly falling back on whatever they have been feeding on, which is far more likely to be a flattened crow than a flattened rook.

The crows that morning were quartering the fells in search of their usual spring fare, the placental remains of new-born lambs; and given a chance no doubt they would pick the eyes out of the helpless too. In this scavenging exercise they were much beset by parties of yelping jackdaws who, unable to share in the feasting of their fiercer relatives, indulged in mock attacks undertaken, it seemed, just for the hell of it. An impertinent, a mischievous-looking, a delightful bird. And above all soared the lords of the Corvidae, the high and mighty ravens with their massive bills and vulgar vocabulary which ranges from a sepulchral belch to a cork-popping noise.

The willows alongside the Langdale beck were beset by looper caterpillars of at least two members of that huge family of moths called Geometrids from the way their larvae seem to be measuring the leaves on which they feed. Like so many moths, their names are a pleasure to say aloud in both English and Latin, which is usually half Greek. The first we came across, the Pale Brindled Beauty, is *Phigalia pilosaria.* Now why the hairy creature *(pilosus)* should be attached to the name of a town in Arcadia I can't say, but the binomial slips easily off the tongue and the grubs look like animated twigs. Most of the others were the progeny of the July High Flyer *(Hydriomena furcata)* which nicely describes the watery appearance of the forewings of the adults marked, as they are, with two-pronged forks.

For many years I used to attend the famous Verrall Supper for entomologists where among the old timers you would hear talk of the habits and distribution of Pugs and Pygmies, the Ledean Piercer, Minnion's Carpet, the Green Brindled Crescent, Depressed Midget, Parenthesis Sober and Wakeley's Bentwing. The medieval writers took little interest in butterflies and moths and named only two or three, with the result that Linnaeus had to make up his own scientific binomials. The great eighteenth-century lepidopterists, the Aurelians as they called themselves, invented the vernacular names, and what names they are. They called a drab-coloured creature with no specific sexual life the Virgin Smoke, whilst the larvae of the Puss Moth with its twitchy antennae at the rear is *Cerua vinula,* the Horn-tailed Wine Dispenser.

Once upon a long time ago I revelled in the *Jurgen* of James Branch Cabell. I have never managed to get very far with *Lord of the Rings* and wonder how many of my generation can, but perhaps one day when I am really old and grey and full of sleep I shall recreate the fabulous Kingdom of Hexapoda and people it with hideous Pugs and Pygmies constantly at war with a goodly band of Heather Twists and Water Veneers. They will live under the shadowy power of the Purple Emperor and his fallen familiar, the Death's-Head Hawk. Lackeys and Flounced Rustics will hurl their almost invincible Gregson's Darts at the Enchanter's Cosmet and, should that fail, they will unleash the Ghost Swifts. What they will do on Minnion's Carpet to the Brindled Beauty of Rannoch, I scarce dare say. Enough to reveal that Vernon her lover will be only a Half Mourner when he discovers she has already been scuttled by a Lulworth Skipper.

With one of several routes to choose from we had a mind to strike up Stickle Beck and work down towards Grasmere by way of the ridge, but something about the appearance of our fellow-travellers festooned with rope recommended caution. 'Much of a climb?' we asked, nonchalantly. They nodded, grimly. That settled it. After all, we had been walking since first light. Better to save our energy for the flanks of Helvellyn. We therefore clung to the floor of Langdale until we reached Chapel Stile where there were no more than a couple of steep hills between ourselves and Grasmere. If asked about the Pikes, those great walls of volcanic rock, we say we have rarely seen a more theatrical backcloth.

In the most populous parts of the Lake District the locals will tell you they live double lives. There is the tourist season when everything is directed towards catering and salesmanship, and there is their own season from October to April when, if you happen to be there as an outcomer, you may catch the essence of Westmorland: the fox-hunting, the whist-drives, the coffee mornings, the local hops, and that most popular of regional institutions, the merry neets for the menfolk. Almost anything may take place at those excuses for a get-together, from singing, card-playing and drinking to wrestling and face-pulling contests, which often amount to the same thing.

Proud though I was to learn that Old John had been a wrestler, I have seen the Cumbrians at it only once and, probably through ignorance of the finer points of the rules, account their kind of wrestling a dull sport. Only the contestants seem to know what's going on. For much of the time it appears to be a grunting match between two tightly-locked and almost motionless men clad in white combinations and black knickers. Then quite suddenly the deadlock is broken when one massive fellow heaves his equally massive opponent off his feet, holds him up in the air for a moment, a miraculous moment, and then chucks him face downwards on the mat. The best of three falls wins the encounter.

Face-pulling contests are self-explanatory, except that some rugged local fellows seem to be unfairly endowed with in-born advantages. In fact, it's on record somewhere that, after a bout which went on for ten minutes at grave risk to the contestants' jaw muscles, the first prize was awarded to an old chap who, it was discovered afterwards, had just looked in to see what was going on.

When it became apparent that we couldn't reach the lake without resort to lengths of road rendered dangerous by cars full of tourists in a hurry to get to the truly palpitating heart of Wordsworthland, that stretch between Chapel Stile and Grasmere put us thoroughly out of sorts. There are good stands of trees on either side of switchback lengths of tarmac, and glimpses of Elterwater, Loughrigg Tarn and Rydal Water are to be seen in between them. The sun poured pure gold on the vale of Rothay. If the approaches could have been partly rid of that nose-to-tail traffic, the lakes, I'm sure, would have rarely looked more lovely – but, as we know, all power corrupts and horsepower corrupts absolutely. Some unfortunate fresh-air seeker had stalled the engine of his flying skunk across the road in trying to get into the car-park of the youth hostel, and the air thereabouts became blue as cars, unable to climb up or race down that hill, added to the local smog. 'But,' says Daniel Behrman in his study of car-poisoned mankind, 'don't let the exhaust fool you, it's only a smoke screen. Run an automobile on steam, electricity, sunshine or early morning dew, it'll still get you. Put on bumpers and eiderdown, bring back the man on horseback waving a red flag, and the automobile will *still* be lethal.'

For this and other reasons we didn't get on at all well with

41

Grasmere, a victim of its own popularity. We dropped in for supplies and advice about how to avoid the main road north to Keswick. You will think, rightly, that we should have relied on our own maps. Unfortunately we didn't discover until it was too late that, owing to lack of overlaps on the new, cheap, and ill-done sheets, Grasmere is tucked away in the north-west corner of the one map we didn't carry.

Although I'm pretty sure the two good souls at the Information Centre could have told us in their sleep about how to get to Dove Cottage, Rydal Mount, and the church-yard beautiful and green, they knew nothing whatever about local footpaths nor where we might park our rucksacks for a couple of hours. Strange, this, in walking country, but I give it as a fact. With splendid disdain for what was thundering up and down the A591, we rejoined the tumult.

As Dorothy Wordsworth has described almost every nook and cranny, every footpath and lane that leads out of the town, it is virtually impossible for anyone even slightly acquainted with that marvellous mish-mash of gossip, poetry and passion, her *Journals,* to leave Grasmere without being aware of the begetters of one of its principal industries. Lytton Strachey thought the history of the Victorian age would never be written because we know too much about it. 'Ignorance', he says, 'is the first requisite of the historian.' Much the same could be said about the Wordsworths, except that behind all the volumes of biography and criticism, including the theories of neurosis-hunters, are one or two still-unanswered questions which are much more important than William's relationship with his sister. They are whether or not the poet was consciously aware that he was quick to take advantage of almost any opportunity that turned up, believing, as he put it, that he was predestined to wear a wreath of laurel on his brow and that his art was, therefore, subject only to its own laws. Was he blind to what he was doing or was he so steeped in the conventional morality of the age that he could justify almost anything in carefully modulated verse? There are probably no straight answers to those questions, which brings us back to Strachey's paradox.

Wordsworth says he was 'fostered alike by beauty and by fear' which were 'much favoured' in his birthplace, the town of Cockermouth in north-west Cumberland. He was surrounded by superb country, but his mother died when he was eight and his father, an attorney and land agent, had almost no money at all when he followed her to the grave not long afterwards. The young Wordsworths were farmed out to relatives. Here were two critical factors in his life.

A more puzzling factor is what took him to Paris in the van of the Revolution of 1791. There are tales of him marching with the mob, waving the Union Jack, and being watched by Pitt's secret police, but the story of how he seduced a pretty young girl, Annette Vallon of Blois, and left her with a child, his daughter Caroline, was not known except to two or three people including his sister until forty years after the death of the revered Poet Laureate. *'Aye, think on that my heart and cease to stir . . .'* Could it be that something beyond orthodox morality was creeping in? How else can one explain his repeated use of such words as 'betray' and 'cowardly'?

More understandable is why he took up with Dorothy, first at Alfoxden in Somerset and then at Dove Cottage in Grasmere. She gave him warmth. Of that there is no doubt. She was wildly in love with him. Her beloved has only to leave her for a few days: she is prostrated. She weeps. She mopes. She wonders what to do, and then, 'Oh happy, happy morning!' She hears a footfall beyond the gate. 'It was William . . . after our first joy was over we got some tea. We did not go to bed until four o'clock in the morning.' Thereafter we find her petting him on the carpet, lying with him in a ditch, wondering what it would be like when they were dead and buried close to each other.

On a coach trip she buttons herself up in his overcoat, and 'never rode more snuggly'. A strange relationship. Were they engaged in a sort of erotic brinkmanship akin to the controlled paedophilia of Lewis Carroll and the Reverend Francis Kilvert of Clyro who, though unquestionably an honourable man, was forever kissing little girls in their nighties? It could be. And believing they were engaged for life, just the two of them, Dorothy took it more than hard when her beloved William told her he intended to marry that 'phantom of delight', his childhood sweetheart, Mary Hutchinson. That was his final step as a poet of the first order.

Dorothy had done far more than prepare his food, mend his breeches, grease his boots and smooth his brow. She provided him with pieces of verbal jewellery. She had the eye of a poet. Her *Journals* are filled with brilliant observations. The first paragraph, written at Alfoxden, begins: 'The green paths down the hillsides are channels for streams. The young wheat is streaked by silver lines of water running between the ridges, the sheep are gathered together on the slopes. After the wet days, the country seems more populous. It peoples itself in the sunbeams.' William used hundreds of her lines. He had become accustomed to her marvellously simple way of seeing things. She was far better at it than he was but, of course, he wouldn't admit it. Here, for example, she is describing a carter and his young friend. She says he was 'cheering his horses and talking to a little lass about ten years of age who seemed to make him her companion. She ran to the wall and took up a large stone to support the wheel of one of his carts and ran on before him with it in her arms to be ready for him. She was a beautiful creature and there was something uncommonly impressive in the lightness and the joyousness of her manner. Her business seemed to be all pleasure, pleasure in her own motions, and the man looked at her as if he too was pleased and spoke to her in the same tone in which he spoke to his horses.'

Poor Dorothy. She helped William to square things with his former mistress, Annette. It sounds a dreadful story. Brother and sister took the stage to Dover and the packet to France. What on earth did the great moralist say to the woman? We know that on that day trip he dashed off a sonnet which starts, 'It is a beauteous evening, calm and free'. Did he read it to her? At least it would go down rather better, one would think, than the poem he had written earlier about the woman abandoned with an illegitimate child.

> O guilty father – would that death
> Had saved him from that breach of faith.

Three days later we hear of the Wordsworths in Yorkshire for the wedding. Dorothy couldn't face the ceremony, but the night before she slept with his wedding ring on her forefinger and went through the routine of falling on his bosom the next morning before he went to church. That done she says, 'I could stand it no longer and threw myself on the bed where I lay in stillness, neither hearing nor seeing anything.' And that, substantially, is the end of the story. William's Phantom of Delight, a woman who rarely said more than 'God bless you', became:

> A creature not too bright or good
> For human nature's daily food.

After achieving the respectability of marriage, the author of those tremendous lines about Newton voyaging through strange seas of thought alone, wrote little else for which he is remembered. As for Dorothy, her *Journals* came to an end within two months of the wedding. Friends say she came close to the very doors of insanity. Decorate it as you will, the *ménage à trois* is a dismal house.

For special occasions the Wordsworths hired horses from the owner of a livery stable called George Mackareth who used to be the landlord of the Swan Inn a mile or two out of Grasmere. We noticed The Swan because a large card in the window said *Leave Your Rucksacks Outside.* We noticed, too, that not far beyond the tavern an inviting track curled off to the right and disappeared into the hills. A sign-post pointed *To Helvellyn* and thither, as Dorothy so often said, we went.

Out of sheer relief at leaving that dreadful road we took to the track with enormous affection. Mossy-banked and partly paved by well-worn stones, it kept company with a noisy torrent appropriately called Tongue Gill. In no time at all she met up with her more conversational sister, the Little Tongue. This offered us two ways of rounding a huge grassy knoll marked on the map as The Great Tongue, though in shape, like those clouds from Scafell, it was whale-like. A somnolent whale which had surfaced somewhat sleepily from the Sargasso. In the failing light it looked rather sinister. Keep right, advised Walter Poucher, and right we kept, though thinking him wrong when, in an effort to avoid some precarious stone walls, we came hard up against an intolerable slope, too slippery by far. So down we went and up again and around we went and on. A square dance, a rare dance on what we trod upon.

On the second, or maybe the third, circumambulation we squared up to one of the walls which, of course, is something you shouldn't do. They are antiques which should only be handled by wallers. If, however, you are hard-pressed they can be climbed over by ensuring you don't push anything sideways. They are slightly tapered towards the top, and laid down to stand straight up.

Tiring of the upping and downing, we followed the gill for a few hundred yards, a rough scramble that enabled us to sample the water. Owing, I suspect, to the presence of iron in that volcanic rock, it tasted as beer sometimes does from a pewter pot, that is of boiled railway engines. However, a nipperkin of malt improved it considerably, and we pressed on.

The going much steeper now. Weird clumps of rock appeared jet black against a sky that would have made a fair showing for the last act of *Götterdämmerung*. Ochreous for the most part but shot through with blood-red streaks towards the west. Over our shoulders reared the silhouette of Seat Sandal, with Fairfield Brow and Black Crag immediately above. With an audible stream for guidance nobody could have mistaken the way, but in the almost dark it was difficult to distinguish between successive platforms of rock. Each one appeared to be the rim that separated us from our hoped-for rest beside the shores of Grisedale Tarn. When, after much scrambling, we found ourselves in a massive but rather moist amphitheatre, we decided to stop there.

The problems as usual were to find a dry and reasonably level patch to put the tent down, and to locate a supply of fresh water not too close for the trickling noise to create intolerable discomfort through the night. Try sleeping near a dribbling tap. For our couch and kitchen we compromised with a gentle if irregular slope by putting sheaves of rushes around the knobbly bits. By shifting a double sleeping-bag backwards and forwards and lying on it as you might try out a new mattress in a bedding department, it's surprising what can be done with the humps and hollows of a peaty knoll. We used some lumpy bits for our pillows and others to loll up against for back support. This done we simply cast the tent over our bed, swivelling it round judiciously to avoid crawling out into a particularly moist patch near the front entrance which served as a cookhouse.

Leaving Katie to the business of sorting out the kitchen gear, I went off in search of water. In the afterglow it had to be done by sound which, under the echoing walls of Gavel Crag, was often deceptive. I tried out that echo with a great shout. It came back from two sides and disturbed the ravens. What I took to be the faint sound of a rivulet turned out to be a waterfall high up on Sandal. By bending down and listening as you might to the movements of a fieldmouse among dry leaves, I heard a trickle almost at my feet. By torchlight I located the spring and managed to scoop up half a bucketful by laborious cupping. In the process I captured a fine specimen of what used to be called the common frog, but it croaked so dismally between my lightly closed fingers that I let it go. A prodigious leap and it disappeared. Though I could see Katie in the glow of the gas stove, I tootled on my whistle to show she had married a man who was not only a water diviner but one able to hunt by torchlight.

I suppose we should have eaten regional delicacies that night – say, tatie-pot, fat-crowdie or maybe Dove Cottage Pie – but we were travelling light. Within twenty minutes we set about soup and reconstituted beef which, it said on the packet, had been specially made for astronauts. The dehydrated potatoes were splendid. They had acquired a sort of piquancy from that water.

Dawn broke out at half-past four by which time we were heartily tired of lumps of volcanic rock which appeared to have come up during the night. A struggle with the outer zip of the fly released such a shower of ice-cold droplets on my naked back that washing entailed no more than a brisk towelling down. Warned by my yelp, Katie did rather better by inching sideways, and there we stood, almost starkers, yawning, stretching, looking round sleepily, feeling as if we'd stepped out into some obscure corner of the Stone Age. Didn't she feel that way? Ice Age, she said, and slipped back into the tent for some wind-proof underwear.

In the dusk we had ventured into a corrie. An old track for

47

packhorses stood high above our pitch. The remains could be made out with difficulty amid a confusion of boulders, a landslip that formed a natural ramp, and we scrambled up it towards the untroubled surface of Grisedale Tarn.

The impression is of a lake which has almost filled the crater of a volcano. The walls of that natural dam were shored up by glaciers. If they were to give way, one could imagine the almighty *whoosh* as billions of gallons of water plunged down a thousand feet into Patterdale. A few ducks paddled about on the surface. They looked somewhat disembodied in that early morning light, but they were undoubtedly duck, common duck, mallard, breakfasting on snails and waterweed, and I don't think Wordsworth quite hit it off when he apostrophized them as

> . . . feather'd tenants of the flood,
> With grace of motion that might scarcely seem
> Inferior to angelical, prolong
> Their curious pastime . . .

The lines are from the poet's *Guide to the Lakes* which by 1830 had become so popular that, according to Matthew Arnold, a naïve clergyman once asked the poet if he had written anything else.

On the far side of the tarn a zigzag zigs up the summit of Dollywaggon Pike, a name to be toyed with if ever there was one. What could *that* mean? A fish found only in Thirlmere? The great ram on the battle cars of the Brigantes? Perhaps the maypole at Grasmere sports, or maybe an old expression for waggonettes filled with children wearing huge straw hats, coloured pinafores and expressions of deceptive innocence? The proper meaning of a name, says that erudite Cumbrian, Robin Collingwood, 'is never something upon which the bird sits perched like a gull on a stone; it is something over which the word hovers like a gull over a ship's stern. Trying to fix the proper meaning in our minds is like coaxing the gull to settle in the rigging.' The most probable origin of the name, he thinks, is from *dolgr* meaning fiend or giant in Old Norse and *veginn* meaning lifted or something carried. It seems to be a local variant of the Devil's Armful. 'Quite the troll's work,' says Professor Collingwood cautiously.

With a day's stage that promised much in the way of ups and downs, we scuttled round the outfall of the tarn. We paused, briefly, as every newcomer does, to read the plaque which commemorates the place where Wordsworth said farewell to his brother, John the sailor, not knowing that within weeks he would go down with his ship; and then, determined on making the most of the long slope in our favour, we slipped easily into a stride that was a notch or two above normal cruising speed. With a light breeze against us, the sun on our backs, and a small fortune in kinetic energy to squander, we could have been walking through the first morning of the world.

Until an ant-like column of climbers came into view beyond Grisedale Brow, we had only the unobtrusive companionship of thermal-riding buzzards which floated up towards us, circling in slow motion until, losing their steady uplift, they broke formation and glided down to where they could mount another aerial staircase. As they appeared wholly indifferent to each other I assumed they were males out to enjoy themselves on a communal flight confined to neighbours. They are robust hawks, among the biggest of their family and ferocious-looking at close quarters. A bird I once surprised on the ground where it was feeding on a rabbit looked for a moment as if it were about to attack. It lowered its head, arched its wings, and chittered angrily.

Pliny called the bird *Buteo* from the Greek meaning 'to hoot', something it next to never does. The males present their potential mates with green sprays as a love token; they certainly hiss excitedly during copulation and, if lucky, they will bring up a pair of youngsters – lucky because their eggshells are often softened by pesticides in their food and broken in the nest. After fearful persecution, they are not doing too badly nowadays. There are probably about ten thousand pairs in Britain, which is not really a lot since tough old birds have been known to live for a quarter of a century.

The exhilaration of the morning was somewhat dampened in Patterdale where, after dropping down into pastoral beauty at the foot of Ullswater, we thrashed about a lot, looking for that great ridge on which the Romans built their highway in the clouds. The Mounceys of the region called themselves

49

kings, but there seems to have been trouble at the palace even in Dorothy's day. Her friend Peggy told her that the Queen 'had been brought to drinking by her husband's unkindness and avarice. She was formerly a very nice tidy woman. She had taken to drinking but that was better than if she had taken to something worse (by this I suppose she meant killing herself). She said that her husband used to be out all night with other women and she used to *hear* him come in in the morning for they never slept together – "Many a poor Body a wife like me, has had a working heart for her, as much stuff as she has had,"' confided Peggy as they 'sate snuggly round the fire'.

Dorothy also records how, upon what appears to have been a pittance, a local clergyman brought up ten children, sent two sons to college and left £1,000 when he died. The man's wife was very generous and had a passion for feeding animals. She killed a pig through feeding it overmuch. When it was dead she said, 'To be sure it's a great loss, but I thank God it did not die clemmed,' a northern dialect word for starved.

After a meal in that hamlet we were well on our way again within an hour. This entailed back-tracking towards the Kirkstone Pass and striking the contour behind the youth hostel. Up we went, confident that we should have an early night, but then one of those boggarts, banshees or sprites that beguile tired travellers to their undoing offered us an easier path, which had everything in its favour except that it came to a dead-end overlooked by Her Majesty's Ordnance Surveyors. And there we were, faced by the dismal prospect of trudging back or going over the top, which is just what we had tried to avoid. It was not a cliff face, mark you, but the need to climb came at us hard and didn't improve until we struck the path leading to a recognizable landmark. On the way the track had crumbled which meant going up a gully and rock-hopping until we coasted down to Angle Tarn. And by God, we had one really nasty moment!

Although there are as many evocative place-names in Cumbria as you could hope to find in the Italian Alps, inspiration seems to have run out, temporarily, after the first-comers had coined some beauties like Glaramara, originally called *Houedgleurmerhe* and try running *that* across the back of your throat. It has something to do with a shieling on the edge of a chasm. But what is both puzzling and makes for confusion is the number of Lakeland names, such as Ulpha Fell, Staveley, and Seat Sandal, which are used more than once when they are quite close to each other. There are I don't know how many Blea Tarns and Tongues, two Borrow-dales and two Angle Tarns. The one that appeared below us is matched by another under Bow Fell, but I doubt whether it could have looked more serene in the evening light. The water tasted good. No trout dimpled its surface, which meant that there were no flies to pester us. With gear spread out in front of the dome-shaped tent, we must have resembled a family of nomadic Lapps.

After supper all the light had gone from the land, and amid the softest of breezes the stars crept out cautiously and were reflected in the water as chips of silver that wriggled like tadpoles. It is at times such as these, says Hilaire Belloc, that great works are conceived but rarely put to paper. I'm not so sure about that; the greatness may be lacking, but under proper stimulus I find that I am constantly giving birth, like a hamster.

If haste is the resort of the faithless, then both Katie and I stand reproved for trying to get across the roof of England in four days. We headed for High Street at dawn, and were well on the way to Shap Fell before the thought occurred that we were overdoing it a bit. There are good reasons for hustling between the Tarn and the Knott, for the ground is boulder-strewn and soggy and the view ahead is unrewarding. Better to pause and peer down into Hayeswater Gill, or stop and turn right round to where Helvellyn, like an ageing prima-donna, is making her last and somewhat faded appearance. In outline the Knott is more of a protuberance than a fell, but it's possible that the weird boulders thereabouts caught Wordsworth's eye – or did Dorothy draw his attention to them first?

> As a huge stone is sometimes seen to lie
> Couched on the bald tip of some eminence;
> Wonder to all who do the same espy;
> By what means it could thither come, and whence;
> So that it seems a thing endued with sense:

51

> Like a sea-beast crawled forth, that on a shelf
> Of rock or sand reposeth, there to sun itself . . .

The mere sight of High Street, that die-straight highway through the upper air, is ample compensation for almost anything. There we sat down for a pint of tea, and during the making of it I read out some fine passages from the *Journeys* of Celia Fiennes (her name rhymes with lines) in a parsonical voice.

Celia is no woman to be sketched in easily with a few broad brush-strokes. An ardent Non-conformist, a pre-eminently Whiggish lady whose life (1662–1742) spanned the aftermath of the Civil War and the reign of William III, she is by turns brash and bigoted, compassionate in the face of the needful, prim and censorious, but above all she is brave and adventurous to a superlative degree. On horseback she rode thousands and thousands of miles, criss-crossing the whole country from the Scottish border to the Kentish ports and outermost Cornwall. Within that network of atrocious roads and tracks, there must have been innumerable people, high born and simple, who saw Celia Fiennes and the servants who accompanied her clip-clopping by. And notwithstanding her saddle-bags and dusty clothing, they saw a very aristocratic lady.

Christopher Morris, the scholarly editor of what little we know of her travels, says, 'Celia had lived through a social as well as a political revolution for it was the age in which the business man became at last able to buy himself into "good society" outright. He had crept in deviously for a century or more but by the end of the seventeenth century the last barriers were down and hence-forward he could enter quickly and openly, hardly troubling to ring the bell. A sub-aristocracy with a frankly plutocratic basis was growing up. To this the family connections of Celia Fiennes bear excellent witness.' Her grandfather, Viscount Saye and Sele, had married a Temple, his half-sister a Villiers, and his eldest son James a Cecil. His other children had married scarcely less well, 'for Celia's aunts between them had married one peer, two baronets, a baronet's son and the son of a mere knight'. The intriguing question is, what induced Celia to ride so far for so many years?

An eye to investment, perhaps? She was always quick to enquire about mineral deposits, drainage schemes and new manufacturing processes. She was obviously beset by that little-recognized virtue, abounding curiosity in almost everything. Who else would inspect villains strung up by their necks in an advanced state of decomposition, providers of fodder for starving deer, lace-making, newts in her firewood, and a hill called the Devil's Arse in Derbyshire? In that rude place she ventured into a cave 'so low you stoop even upon your breasts' and thought it a wonder. Daniel Defoe thought the only wonder lay in the coarseness of our ancestors in thinking of 'so low a sirname ... but it seems they talked broader in those days than they do now'.

It may be too that, among other reasons, Celia rode far to find out who, if necessary, might be counted upon to support the Republican cause. She had been steeped in it since birth. Her father, Colonel Nathaniel Fiennes, had been condemned to death for surrendering Bristol to Prince Rupert. The sentence, however, was remitted and after a few years abroad he returned to take part in political life. Celia's three uncles and five uncles by marriage had all been Roundheads.

There is no evidence that she ventured up on to High Street on her way to visit Lowther Castle 'and several genteele seates' thereabouts. (Her spelling, to put it charitably, is often phonetic.) But she rode around 'Lake Wiandermer ... where there is good marble among those rocks'. 'Thence', she says, 'I rode almost all the waye in sight of this great water; some tymes I lost it by reason of the great hills interposing and so a continu'd up hill and down hill and that pretty steep even when I was in that they call bottoms which are very rich good grounds ...'

High Street is massive. For fifteen miles it rolls on towards Carlisle at a height of more than two thousand feet, but it must have been higher, much higher, before that incredibly ancient bastion of volcanic debris was clawed at, carved, sculptured and finally polished by ice. What renegade Celt, I wonder, was bribed or tortured to point out the mountain gangway to the advance guard of the Sixth Legion? He cannot have foreseen that engineers would soon build a major road, used thereafter by thousands and thousands of men, the majority on foot, their captains in chariots or slave-borne litters. The Romans were concentrating on their north-west frontier. The reputations of Hadrian and his successor, Antoninus Pius, were at stake. They were operating in enemy country, from forested valleys scooped into the flanks of that highway. Heltondale, Riggindale, Cawdale, and Measand Beck, as we know them today, could hide hundreds of painted slingers and spearmen. But in close order on the top, the men behind the Eagles were nearly invincible. Nevertheless there were desertions, mostly among the Auxiliaries, but sometimes the Romans themselves were given to ignobility. Writing earlier, Pliny deplores how he managed to obtain a centurion-ate for his fellow-townsman, Metilius Crispus, who set out with an advance of 40,000 sesterces to buy some kit for foreign parts, perhaps for Britain, and was never heard of again.

Before Magnus Maximus led the last of the legions back across the Alps, High Street began to crack up in what Victorian archaeologists described as its discriminatory pro-portions. This I take to mean that thereafter it would be downright dangerous to drive a chariot between Rampsgill Head and Kidsty Pike. But, this, of course, didn't deter borderers and brigands in general from venturing south and picking up transportable loot wherever they found it, espe-cially if it could be driven home on four legs.

Three features became immediately apparent as we coasted round that coxcomb of a crest between The Knott and Twopenny Crag which, since it sits atop an almighty drop, is a pre-decimalized understatement if ever there was one. They were first, that when you actually set foot on High Street it gives the impression of being an elongated plateau; it's curiously flat on top. The second is that notwithstanding the illusion that it goes on for ever and ever, Amen, the sense of breadth is deceptive. A short stroll to the left or the right of the roadway, and you are looking down on a swirl of cliffs and chasms. The third feature is that wherever there is grass to be grazed men have built walls without mortar, walls which run up and down the fellsides like live things. This is far from being a Cumbrian peculiarity. We have splendid constructions in Yorkshire but not, I'm obliged to admit, in such variety. They are of silver-grey limestone in Furness, mottled pink granite in Eskdale, sea-green slate around Tilberthwaite, and of rusty-red sandstone in the Eden Valley. Those that plunged down around us that afternoon appeared to defy gravity. Irrespective of slopes so steep in places that neither gold nor a rare butterfly could have tempted me to climb up alongside them, all the stones are laid horizontally. They are locked tight by the intricate distribution of the load. In the eighteenth and nineteenth centuries, travelling bands of wallers camped out on the fellsides for weeks on end, utilizing whatever loose stones lay to hand or hauling them up from quarries on wooden sledges. By comparison, you might think it was a far easier, if more protracted, job to build the Great Wall of China. Contemporary inspectors noted that when a true craftsman had picked up a stone he would not put it down until he saw precisely where it would become an endurant part of the whole.

Apart from one lone walker who scurried ahead until he was able to stand for a few minutes, Cortés-wise, on the topmost pinnacle, we had the visible length of High Street to ourselves. Few people venture into those high corries now that Hawes Water is a reservoir and Mardale almost a dead valley, drowned, like the wooded banks of Thirlmere, by Manchester City Corporation. Yet local folk can tell you how they organized horse-races up there for a shepherd's neet at the back-end, that is when the year's routine, from lambing-time to the big sheep sales, is over and done with. They wrestled too; they laid bets on fighting cocks; they guzzled hugely and drank themselves stiff on home-brew laced with hard stuff. Since the official business was the collection and return to their rightful owners of branded strays, merry neets were and, to a limited extent, still are a great feature of Lakeland life. But the shepherd, as opposed to the motorized flock-master, may soon be a figure from the past, like the charcoal-burner.

I am by nature somewhat superstitious, especially at moments of indecision. After much debate about whether to outflank Hawes Water by clinging to High Street or throw away our hard-gained height on the downslopes of the Kidsty

Pass, we heard the faint notes of what could have been the first bars of the Siegfried Idyll. A portent, I said, but, with no marked conviction about what it portended we tried to resolve the matter without resort to metaphysics. The sound came from far away to the east. Could it not have been the siren of the London-Carlisle express on Shap Fell? Good! So we were beckoned in that direction, and down the pass we went.

Alas! Sirens are notorious deceivers. Instead of continuing to inhale the heady air of High Street we were beguiled down to the dreary man-made shore of Hawes Water, which after the inundation should have been renamed Mortlake.

Later that afternoon a spry young chap told us he had done the coast to coast walk twice and considered there was nothing more dispiriting than the slog up Hawes Water's west shore to Burnbanks. Better by far, in his opinion, to cut down into the Measand Beck from Weather Hill on the Street. Be that as it may, we missed the opportunity.

Parts of the journey which failed to stir our imagination have but small place in this narrative. Enough, then, to say briefly that the face of Hawes Water is that of a beautiful woman who in her maturity has been forced to undergo cosmetic surgery more fit for the whore-house than the admiration of her old friends. It is the face of a courtesan, *sans nuance et sans charme.*

The great plateau

The Shapites, the folk who live on the northern slopes of Shap Fell, are reckoned to be as hard as the granite they quarry thereabouts. 'Just a bloody-minded bunch of stone-bumpers,' said an out-of-sorts fellow who, I learned later, had been ringed at a local sheep sale. He glanced up at the ridge where already, an hour before dusk, little wisps of mist were beginning to creep about on cats' feet, a sign that usually betokens a dirty night. 'Can't think why anybody wants to go there,' he said.

I thought of the great coaching days, of horses sweating up to the summit of the highest main road in the country. Through mist, the plaintive pipe of horns. Hooves clattering on the cobbled yard of the Shap Inn. Travellers went in fear of mist and snow and storms. Even in summer they were sometimes fog-bound for hours, and always, at any season, were easy prey for masked ruffians with a brace of flintlocks at the ready. Shap was the place where that incomparable labour organizer, Thomas Brassey, mobilized ten thousand navvies to blast and hack their way through the biggest obstacle in the path of the first railroad through to Scotland. On that ridge the Bonny Prince engaged in the last skirmish fought on English soil, and out on the moors, far beyond the village, there were the graves and stone circles of the Dawn People. But to humour that fellow, why I said, we were just passing through.

At heart I felt a bit bleak and hoped Madam didn't feel the same. We had been on the go since dawn. When we began to throw away hard-gained altitude on the featureless prospects of Hawes Water I knew what we were in for, a gradual diminution of spirit. On a long walk, says Hilaire Belloc, there is within us a small lamp which now and again burns low. Nobody seemed to want us.

Celia Fiennes must have known this soon after she turned up at Lowther Hall, now the seat of the Lonsdales. She goes on and on about the Noble Architecture, the flatte roofe, the exquisitely painted interiors by Antonio Verrio, the gold hangings in the bedrooms. But what of Lady Lonsdale? All we learn is that she 'sent and treated me with a breakfast, cold things and sweetmeats all served in plaite, but it was so early in the morning that she being indisposed was not up'. You can imagine her ladyship asking: 'Wilkins, has that talkative woman *gone?*' Celia, too proud to comment, merely says we 'returned back to Peroth' which is Penrith.

Our spirits brightened up a bit when, among the conifers at the head of the reservoir, we found a small but well-marked track which promised to lead us across the Lowther and up to Shap by way of the Abbey. Notwithstanding the reassurance of the reservoir engineer, a kindly man who took us in and gave us a cup of tea, it was, unfortunately, a promise unfulfilled. Or maybe we strayed on to a quite different track. It led us into bogs, across high-walled fields, over gates festooned with barbed wire and into muddy lanes that went nowhere. The upshot was that after half an hour of hard going we began to appreciate the profundity of Wainwright's Second Law, which is that route-finding in cultivated valleys is more prone to error and exasperation than among desolate mountains almost anywhere.

The only positive advice we managed to extract from the Job's Comforter of Shap was that we'd gain a mile if we stuck to the road above the bridge. We didn't. We decided to make for the ruins of the Abbey. At first we couldn't find it. Where there should have been a stile, some bloody-minded stone-bumper had walled up the public right of way. A light breeze blew the mist away, but by that time it had become too dark to see more than the mere silhouette of the Abbey, and in that fitful atmosphere, I slipped, I cursed, I said:

* * * * * * * *

Occasional asterisks, I think, lend starlight to a page. They brighten it up. Before Henry Miller and James Joyce risked gaol by printing what had hitherto been unprintable, the asterisk in literature was what the fig-leaf was to Victorian sculpture: it indicated an impropriety but concealed it. At one time, I thought, many novels would consist almost wholly of asterisks. Today they have a different meaning and those deployed above mark a transition both in time and mood.

It took some doing. Shap, the town with length but no breadth to speak of, looked shabby. We found a good pub and spent the night there, but the next morning we began to think that nobody knew or cared a hoot about the place. In fact if, after diligent enquiries at the vicarage, we hadn't managed to meet the man who in his youth had dreamed of finding treasure there, we should have passed through at one with Trollope who thanked God he hadn't been born on the fell. Apparently his carriage broke down and he moped about the village for days.

John 'Shap' Fairer – he's quite proud of his nickname – is a newsagent from necessity but an antiquarian at heart. He's not sure, he says, how it all began, but from the boxes of documents, the curios, the bits of stone that make it difficult to move about inside his house near the old Market Hall, a stranger might hazard a guess. The collection includes relics of the railway, the quarries, the Abbey, the neolithic circles, and walls of books and documents of what the Shapites have been up to for some hundreds of years.

Shap, as he puts it, 'has always been a convenient dormitory, a day's march from anywhere'. The railways and the quarries attracted labour from Aberdeen to Cornwall. Many of the in-comers married locally and settled down. The town which has now been relegated to the status of a village under the new county system has always had a reputation for diffusion. Old families are relatively rare. The Fairers are among them. William Fairer of Shap Grange, a squire and a philanthropist, died in 1637. He was suspected of Jacobinism and his lands were forfeited to the government. But the records are obscure.

For many years John Fairer, the collector and antiquarian, has been trying to unravel the identity both of himself and his birthplace. How had he become interested in local history even from his earliest days at school? He thought for a moment. 'Romantic stuff,' he said. 'As a kid I was always looking for secret passages and buried treasure, and I suppose the drive became stronger and better directed as I got older.'

His ambition today is to start a local museum. Far from being outflanked by the new motorway, the village has become a more comfortable place to live in, but he doesn't expect much support from his neighbours. 'You can't get 'em to pull together,' he said. 'They're independent and every man has his price.' Leaving me to unravel that cryptic remark for myself, he fumbled around for a document about the Abbey we had seen in the dark.

It was one of the many monastic houses that were established in England during the twelfth century. It belonged to the Order of Premonstratensians, a word that honours the foundation of their first house by Saint Norbert at Prémontré in Northern France. 'Shap,' said John Fairer, 'came from *Hepp* meaning a heap, a pile or a collection.' It referred, he thought, to the prehistoric stones found close to where the Abbey was founded. Within a century or two the name had changed from *Hepp* to *Hiap* and then to *Shap*, the form in use today.

From their characteristic clothes, the Premonstratensians were often called the White Canons. Their idea was to lead lives of personal poverty and austerity like monks, but they differed from monks in that they were allowed to undertake parish work in the neighbourhood of the Abbey. Very little is known about them as all the records have been lost, but they flourished, and towards the end of the fifteenth century one of their most famous abbots, John Redman, was appointed bishop of St Asaph. Nearly seventy years later his successor surrendered the Abbey's possessions to spoilers under the orders of Henry VIII.

With men like Thomas More and John Fisher in mind, martyrs who suffered death rather than submit to the repudiation of papal authority, I asked if the White Canons had put up much in the way of resistance. 'Stop them?' said John Fairer. 'They were bribed. It looks as if they wanted to be liquidated.'

The story, which sounds like a bit of decorated history, is that on 14 January 1540, the White Canons were told that Henry's henchmen were riding towards them on High Street. They may have been led by Thomas Cromwell himself. The brethren dedicated to poverty waited expectantly. Who knew what they might gain from the new deal? To their marked disappointment the spoilers rode on, and might well have passed from sight had not the canons rung their bells with such vigour that the leader turned and formally dispossessed them. Who could resist such a welcome?

That may well be legend, but documents attest that the last abbot was compensated with a comfortable pension of forty pounds a year. His canons received smaller sums but sufficient for their subsistence. They were also at liberty to supplement their dole by seeking clerical or other employment, and no doubt did so.

We set off across the great plateau of *Westmoringa* with a keen sense of anticipation, almost of a home-coming, knowing that beyond it lay our native Yorkshire. It's not surprising that even the mixed-up population of Shap are resentful at losing their identity in Greater Cumbria. Sense of place is a strange thing. We are mindful, perhaps, mostly about what we have lost. The weather, certainly, had no mind of its own. A shawl of mist hung over the fells to the west; the sky ahead looked bilious; but with the intention of ambling that day we could, if necessary, resort to our igloo.

The village stands above a six-lane motorway and the railroad that brought fame and an army of workmen to Shap in the middle of the last century. They were the pioneers of the track for the puffing billies. Today, without apparent effort, the electric-driven Inter-City expresses slide past at eighty miles an hour. Seen from the old coaching road, they look like toy trains. They are relatively quiet, clean and efficient. There appears to be no difference in the speed of those whirling up to and those whirling down from the summit, though a signal man said the drivers are obliged to brake slightly on the curved descent to the Lune Gorge. What does the daily run to and from Euston mean to the drivers? No more than an intricate exercise in signal-watching, relieved only by that spectacular switchback? Surely not heroic in the sense that the old-timers had both to thrash and curb their steel chargers.

Steam engines, even the famous ones, have never fascinated me, but as we stood on the bridge that morning I thought of the man, his name long since forgotten, who had coaxed one of the Royal Scots over Shap Fell for the better part of his life. A native of Dewsbury in Yorkshire, he was due for retirement. I was eighteen, a nervous 'prentice reporter on the local paper.

'Had to flog her a bit to get her over the top,' he said and his eyes glistened as he talked of short cut-offs and thrashing as they climbed up Greyrigg at first light. That long plume of smoke as the steam gauge began to drop, would he miss it? He nodded. Would he retire to Dewsbury? He rounded on me. 'Ah'd go *daft,*' he said. 'Ah mun go somewhere where ah can see the trains.'

Shap literally sprang to life in 1844 when, after innumerable delays, Parliament passed an Act enabling an optimistic company to raise public funds and build a railway track between Lancaster and Carlisle. By something more than a coincidence, it happened to be the year in which Turner painted 'Rain, Steam and Speed'. Railways were not only the most spectacular, but among investors the most talked about, invention of the early part of that century. Within two decades the mileage of track in Britain had grown from sixteen to well over two thousand. The country was on the verge of a railway boom.

The promoters of the west-coast route to Scotland were up against what to many seemed an insuperable obstacle, the Cumbrian Fells. After a careful survey of half a dozen projects, George Stephenson, the Father of Railways, came out with a route of his own which was both original and far-seeing, in that it was reconsidered and nearly accepted a century later by the engineers of the present motorway. He proposed to avoid the mountains altogether by striking across Morecambe Bay on a barrage from Lancaster to the low-lying coast of Cumbria. For obscure reasons of defence, the Lords of the Admiralty turned it down.

At this news, Joseph Locke, Stephenson's former assistant, a young and relatively unknown engineer, campaigned vigorously for the acceptance of his own plan to blast through the roof of Shap. Far too hazardous in winter, wrote Stephenson in another detailed report. The track might be covered in snow for weeks on end. Locke persisted, and gained the contract. Stephenson growled, and went on with something else. Wasn't the first time he'd had trouble with that cocky fellow. Locke, in fact, had considered a plan to tunnel through the fells but abandoned it in favour of an up-and-over route, arguing that any time lost in climbing would be regained during the descent. If he had any doubts about what would happen in the depths of winter to the little engines with their huge driving wheels, he kept them to himself.

A contemporary portrait shows a handsome dark-haired fellow with particularly large and luminous eyes, the face of a modest but supremely self-confident young man. Locke had confidence both in himself and in those who, after careful consideration, he chose as his associates. Unquestionably the most outstanding among them was Thomas Brassey, who has been called the greatest contractor the world has ever known. He built one mile of railroad out of every twenty constructed up to the point of his death. It has been estimated that the man who dreamed of building the first Channel tunnel controlled a labour force so large that had he gone bankrupt, the unemployment rate in Britain would have risen by one per cent.

Two less confident men might have thought they were doomed to failure from the start. Delays were caused by bickering among the backers who wanted the line to pass through places in which they had a marked interest; landowners were tardy in taking up offers; Parliament had been slow in giving its assent to the money-raising Act, and, worse by far, the contractors for the company behind the east-coast route to the border were ahead of them by seventy miles – the length, in fact, of the west-coast line. Moreover, in terms of longitude, Edinburgh lay to the west of Carlisle. For all that, Locke and Brassey believed they could put trains through to Scotland within two years. But where would their rivals be by then? Nobody could predict, but they took confidence in the fact that their rivals had yet to bridge the mouths of the Tees and the Tyne.

Within five months of the passing of the Act, Brassey's genius for organization became apparent. A labour force of nearly four thousand men and four hundred horses had managed to lay permanent track in deep cuttings on Shap Fell. The force was nearly doubled the following year when viaducts, marvels of agile architecture, were beginning to soar upwards, foot by foot, over the Eamont, the Lowther and the Lune. A start had been made on seventy other bridges over turnpikes and public roads. Such gigantic works, such a mustering of men, had not been seen in Britain since prehistoric times. The navvies used only picks, shovels, drag-lines, and gunpowder, but towards the end of the project in December, 1846 there were nearly ten thousand men on their payroll. And Brassey was by far the most active of them all.

He knew precisely what had to be done. He paid well. He offered piece work which brought him the best, the most dextrous of men, and when labourers of any kind were hard to find during the great railway boom of '46, his lookouts enticed casuals off all the main roads with offers of beer and money on the nail. After a hold-up such as a spell of bad weather the work went on through the night, in the light of paraffin lamps.

Despite careful labour management there were some outbreaks of disorder and rioting among the men, particularly between rival gangs of Scots and Irishmen, not helped by the fact, it was reported, that the English would fight anyone. The monthly pay-days were feared by native Westmorlanders who, after cases of assault, robbery and rape, petitioned for protection. A government Committee of Enquiry was told by a witness, a shocked clergyman, that in addition to the intemperance and fighting, he had found nineteen men and one woman in a hut built for two. But the line was laid almost on time, and at a cost below the estimated one and a half million pounds.

On we went, through an enormous limeworks drained by bile-green ponds on which the only signs of life were flocks of that cheerful red-billed bird, the oystercatcher, known to wild fowlers as the sea-pie. They trilled, they piped, they showed off their black and white plumage which, when they huddle together, puts you in mind of old fashioned mint humbugs. They hung around the path that winds through the quarries, and until we had wiped that slimy white slush off our boots, the birds and warning notices about blasting were all we had to look at.

By contrast with granitic Shap which seems anxious to hide its history in a fold of the fells, the landscape of the great plateau boldly displays the relics of its most ancient inhabitants, a landscape of stone circles and clustered settlements with tumuli or barrows on the skylines, barrows where the Dawn People chambered and venerated their dead. On the moor the granite lies deep underground. It is thickly overlaid with limestone, detectable in the springiness of the turf and a profusion of chalk- and limestone-loving flowers such as diminutive eyebrights and mountain pansies with petals purple or yellow, or both – a landscape for pastoralists.

For a curious naturalist an extensive tract of unploughed land is sprinkled with question marks, and Madam often managed to turn over more than I had answers for. But we rarely left them unanswered for long. Those little wild pansies, for example, the ones that country folk call heartsease, did they give rise direct to those common plants of the garden with their enormous petals, she wanted to know? I wasn't sure. Certainly they were all members of the violet family, the Violaceae. Everything can be placed in a natural family. But I couldn't tell the botanical difference between the delicate violet of the hedgerow and what must be one of the oldest flowers in cultivation.

A week elapsed before we discovered from a reference work in the cottage that the only differences were superficial ones of colour distribution, proportions and size. By skilful botanical selection, the petals of the pansy have been flattened out into a 'face', whereas those of the violet remain long and oval. It is matters such as these that fascinate us, not just occasionally but almost all the time we are out of doors together. Katie's questions are often so coincidental that she could have been eavesdropping at the doors of my thoughts. That same botanical work made it clear that a great variety of plants, the so-called calcicoles, inhabit limestones because they are dry, well aerated and warm, qualities that first attracted Man to the region.

The scenery of Britain can be read off the map, but not the map we know, for that is an artefact. When prehistoric man arrived in boats with leather sails, he found no protected harbours, nor roads, no fields to welcome him. The land was densely covered with forbidding forest and impassable swamps, and he was the first to make it fit for habitation. Fortunately the vegetation was not equally intractable. The low-lying clay lands supported oak woods with a tangle of thorny undergrowth, barriers to settlement and communication that only well-organized and well-equipped societies could tackle in the closing stages of prehistory.

However, when not overlaid with glacial clays, chalk lands and limestone hills could be more easily cleared of their scrubby vegetation. For this reason the Dawn People sought out the Downs of southern England and Yorkshire, and limestone plateaux similar to those on which we walked for two long days. Similar but with an important difference.

There is next to no evidence that prehistoric Westmorland has been populated for more than about four thousand years, a long time ago by most standards but much later than the colonization of the south and the west.

The shepherd-kings of the Bronze Age were warrior-pastoralists. They buried their dead singly in the foetal position surrounded by grave furniture of a curiously stereotyped kind: a flint knife, a rectangular 'bracer' for protecting the wrist against the recoil of the bowstring, a perforated button, and a beaker or drinking cup. What did they expect to find in the afterworld? Nobody knows. Nobody will ever know.

We came to the cairns and the circles armed with some knowledge, but were taken aback by how vast, how strange it all looked. Pagan godhead seemed inherent in a stone-laden landscape made the more mysterious by the cloud shadows that raced under a fitful sun. The sort of morning that turns in its sleep and murmurs of the spring. Some of the boulders, eight or nine feet in diameter and polished by the ice sheets, appeared as delicately poised as a golf ball on a tee, but they were wholly immovable. They are glacial erratics, shoved down from Shap Fell by tongues of ice. Others lie half-buried in the alkaline soil. The cracked limestone pavements gape alarmingly.

What did the first-comers make of them? Did they think they had strayed into one of the graveyards of the gods, abandoned, left open when their occupants took to the sky as a butterfly does from a fragile chrysalis? Limestone is soft. It weathers easily into a variety of shapes, petrified monsters which look as if they have crept out of the ground. On an open moor they engender a feeling of awe. It is significant, surely, that the most imposing monuments of neolithic man are found among the megaliths of nature. Their chiefs, one assumes, were buried in the barrows on the skyline where they could look down on circles used for seasonal rituals and sacrifice.

We walked round the biggest of the double circles and counted thirty-two stones within a diameter of twenty-two generous paces. Nothing, as I see it, can be made of these numbers, since many of the original uprights have been carried off by farmers in need of gate-posts or lintels for barns and crofts. Writing more than a hundred years ago, Canon Simpson, an archaeologically-minded cleric, says that at the centre of the circle we paced, now rather a jumble of stones, he found 'some burnt matter'.

The excavator was more fortunate in a nearby cairn where he unearthed 'the bones of a man of great stature, a portion of the antler of a deer much larger than those of our days, and bones of other animals'. Good as he was as a chronicler, in deploring the fact that the site on Iron Hill was 'conspicuous for that want of care which its prominence deserves' he may well, of course, have been justifying his own role as a barrow surgeon.

The sky began to darken; we looked up at the huge horizons; we felt the wind rising from the north, a wind which had about it the whispering rip of a scythe through the grass, and decided that of all places none looked more attractive at that moment than the adjacent hamlet of Oddendale which probably stands foursquare on a neolithic settlement.

A curious place behind a palisade of storm-thrashed sycamores. 'Do not disturb the sequestered privacy of this hamlet,' says Wainwright the path-finder. I cannot think why, unless, like a lapwing feigning injury, he is trying to divert attention away from Ewe Close, the best-known Romano-British village in the north of England. We found the Oddendalesmen, all three of them, not only friendly but anxious to do all they could for us. Ray Johnson, a bit stiff these days, he said, drove home the cows from the seat of his tractor, whilst young Tom, his son, went off to ask the neighbours in for a baptismal party the following night. Another little Oddendalesman had been born in the wilderness.

Ewe Close lies half a mile down the lane from the farm, but hidden from all except the most diligent history-seekers. It is the ruin of a walled village which was occupied nobody knows how long before the Romans came, and might well have survived raids by that old pirate Thored Gunnarson (A.D. 966) long after the legions had left. The walls are everywhere about six feet thick. The whole settlement, of about a dozen huts including a circular one with a fifty-foot diameter of floor space, thought to have been the home of their chiefs, covers nearly four acres of ground. The Collingwoods, father and son, who have done more for the antiquities of Westmorland than anyone else, think the Close was occupied by about sixty souls who grew grain and pastured their cattle on the plateau. Perhaps the most remarkable fact about the settlement is that the Roman road from Lancaster to Carlisle passed within twenty yards of the walls.

This is not a matter of some beleaguered Celts seeking the protection of their conquerors. For some very curious reason, it was the Romans who came to the settlement. To secure its loyalty when they could so easily have speared the inhabitants and razed it to the ground, a pioneer force of the Sixth diverted their main road westward from its straight course along the ridge, so as to pass by the dwelling of the Close's chief. To do so they were obliged to loop up and down the steep flanks of two lateral valleys. He must have been an important chief, perhaps the descendant of a long line of the shepherd kings of the Bronze Age.

What were the advantages to the Celts of having the Romans literally on the doorstep? They would get good pottery, certainly, weapons unlikely, but useful tools and new-fangled ways of grinding corn. Professor R. G. Collingwood is somewhat cynical. He says that chief must have been the northern counterpart of those southern British nobles whose Romanization Tacitus so deplores: less civilized, but glad to think that, according to the Augustan decree, they were Roman and a friend of the Romans. And as for his people – 'Perhaps they gave up the old habit of burying their chiefs on hill tops to be nearer heaven, but is unlikely that even by the end of the Roman period they had learned much about Christianity.'

Then what of those people out on the moors who refused to be Romanized? Some think they were Celtic bandits who at that time of unrest preyed on both farmers to the south and itinerant merchants carrying raw gold across North Britain from that Eldorado of the West. At first they were thinly distributed, but, owing perhaps to their attachment to their cemeteries and dancing floors, they began to settle down in communities which, until the legions arrived, changed extremely slowly. And then everything changed.

Although the region was a chaos of hills into which the Celts could slip away, Rome could not afford to leave them alone even if, as at Ewe Close, it meant building a road up to a settlement, perhaps of an important quisling. The Romans were for ever building roads and forts, but the Celtic pastoralists, an unsettled, an untidy, people, had no wish whatever to become urbanized. They moved about to and from the high tops spanned by the ridgeways. Their refuge and a rich source of food was the forest, which they gradually destroyed. In its natural state with the trees spaced out according to their requirements, good stands of timber cannot have been burned down all at once. But they could be progressively ringed and felled.

Grazing pressure around a settlement could be eased by sending their youngsters to outlying sites, the shielings, converting them into homesteads where tree seedlings would be kept down by grazing animals. That is how, through the ages, our forests became the artefacts to which we have become apathetically accustomed.

Today the youngsters of the high plateau are out and about, driving huge tractors as soon as they are considered fit to wear long pants. We stopped for a word with a likely looking lad who didn't seem to be more than about twelve, and was protected from the fearful-sounding noises of his machine by ear-muffs. At our approach he pushed them up and turned the engine off. In the silence that followed one could hear the murmur of wind through a handsome stand of beech, the *cheep* of nesting chaffinches, and behind it all, way out on the moor, the calling, calling of curlew.

It came out that it was his Dad's farm. One day, he said, he hoped he would be running it himself. He worked six days a week, mostly hauling and distributing muck, sometimes trenching or cutting hay, but almost always from the seat of that monster. I wondered how his grandfather would have felt about working in the spring unable to hear the marvellous clamour of birdsong. Could the lad hear *anything* above the noise of engines? Was he ever conscious of what he'd lost? It would have been an impertinence to ask. For that matter, what would be the answer of those miserable millions whose lives are spent commuting between the suburbs and an office downtown? The runners in the rodent derby? But I was curious to know what the youngster did on his day off.

With the pride of an owner of a thoroughbred, he said he took his bike out. It stood there in the barn, a lean-looking thing without mudguards or much in the way of an exhaust. On Sundays he went out on a mad helter-skelter with the neighbouring lads, scrambling he called it.

Little-known slivers of English history crop up in such unexpected places that I suppose we shouldn't have been surprised to find a monument to Charles in the middle of the wholly deserted moorscape miles from Shap. Yet there it was, erected, I suppose, by some pious Stuart, but not to the questionable glory of the Bonnie Prince whose ignominious retreat over Shap Fell has not, as far as I know, been memorialized in stone. The inscription read: *Here at Black Dub, the source of the Egremont, Charles II regaled his army on their march from Scotland, August 8th A.D., 1651.*

What I couldn't make out until I learnt more about it later was why King Charles, accompanied by nine thousand foot and four thousand horse, should have crossed a wilderness fit only for buzzards and moorcocks. It had never occurred to me that long before the track was hacked out of Shap Fell, the main thoroughfare from Scotland to England lay across these Ravensworth moors, though today scarcely a trace remains.

Charles was certainly a marked man. The royal womanizer

who had tried to save his father from the block knew well that Parliament had issued a proclamation 'that all who should recognize his son as his successor should be adjudged traitors and suffer accordingly'. In return for support in Scotland, he had on several occasions sworn to uphold what he most detested in religious practice, stark Protestantism; but even Cromwell had to admit that the Covenanters 'were so given to the most impudent lying and frequent swearing that it is incredible to be believed'. Yet they were religious fanatics.

At solemn communion which sometimes lasted for three days, a dozen or more preached to people 'in a state of trance . . . a solemnity unknown to the rest of the world'. They were particularly hot against Malignants (devoted Royalists), Sectaries (English Puritans) and witches 'which were never known to be so numerous in Scotland as at that time'. Women could be burned if seen talking to a cat. Hundreds died at the stake. The Presbytery of Lanark 'sent for George Cuthie the pricker who hath skill to find out their mark' by sticking long pins into suspects. Others much favoured vaginal examinations, 'knowing by certain protuberances or a sustained issue that suspects had had commerce with Auld Hornie'.

Charles, sometimes called Old Rowley after the name of his favourite stallion, knew what he was up against among the Covenanters, but from his bold conduct he cannot have suspected for one moment that his large army would be literally chopped to pieces at Worcester a month after his refreshment at the source of the Egremont.

The King is reported to have fought gallantly, urging on his men, first outside the walls and then, when his horse was shot under him, by making his way back into the city on foot. It soon became apparent that the day had been disastrous for the Royalists. Thousands were killed, thousands more were rounded up and whipped towards London where, three days after the battle, Lady Fanshawe wrote in her *Memoirs* that, 'about eleven of the clock at night, we saw hundreds of poor soldiers, both English and Scotch, marched all naked on foot . . .', thereafter to be sold like cattle in Tothill Fields to merchants who sent them off as slaves to Barbados.

Charles escaped and in various guises managed to elude capture until his friends smuggled him across to France.

Eight years elapsed before the King, his gallantry undiminished, 're-entered his Metropolis amidst the roaring of a thousand cannon, the pealing of innumerable bells and the deafening acclamation of the multitude'. It is not long before we hear about his irrepressible merriment. 'Old Rowley himself at your service, madam,' said the King, entering her apartment with his usual air of easy composure.

The Bonnie Prince, his grand-nephew, was less fortunate. Before he came to a sticky end through drink and clap, he too had a bad time of it at the hands of the English. From that same spring which feeds the Egremont, now called the Lyvennet, we looked back on the flanks of Shap Fell, where the lad who thought he was born to be king scuttled back to Scotland, defeated.

The infamous affair of the '45 began early in August when the Prince landed in Scotland and raised his standard at Glenfinnan. He did pretty well at the start. He first out-manoeuvred and then beat the leather pants off fifteen hundred men led by General Sir John Cope. After a quite unaccountable delay of six weeks, which enabled the English Government to call out the militia, raise new regiments, and bring in troops from the Continent, the Prince marched south at the head of a considerable army. Perth and Edinburgh fell like sandcastles and, mounted on a white horse and preceded by a hundred pipers, the be-wigged young man was proclaimed King of Carlisle, amid much hand-kissing and promise of royal favours.

On he went, through Penrith, Shap, Kendal, Preston, Manchester to Derby – where, for equally unaccountable reasons, he turned tail and retreated back to the Border with the Duke of Cumberland and eight thousand men close on his heels. It was only through sheer luck that he managed to evade General Wade and his crack troops who were waiting to swoop down on him from Newcastle.

They had a particularly bad time of it in Westmorland. They were stormed by a mob at Kendal, and by the time they reached Shap in bad weather on 14 December the retreat had some of the qualities of slapstick farce. At close quarters in the dusk the rival forces got mixed up, and men on the same side chased each other. The Prince disappeared, but someone claimed to have seen him dressed as a lady of quality rattling past in a coach. His hussars bolted, scared by rustics with hayforks whom they took to be Wade's pikemen; but his commander, Lord George Murray who came out of the affair better than anybody, refused to run for the Border but went back to Shap twice, to look for his troops which, after some brisk skirmishing, had managed to capture the Duke of Cumberland's footman and a few of his kitchen staff.

Asked what happened during one affray when the gallant, if over-confident, Colonel Honeywood received a Jacobite ball in his thigh, a Highland prisoner said: 'We fared nae so good 'til the lang man in the muckle boots came o'er the dyke, but his foot slipped on a turd an' we gat him doon.'

The last engagement fought on English soil ended ingloriously at Clifton, north of Shap, where both commanders claimed a victory. The firing lasted half an hour. Prudently, after it ceased Lord George drew back to Carlisle whilst, instead of pursuing him, the Duke thought his troops needed a rest and ordered them to spend the night there.

We decided we needed a bed more comfortable than a groundsheet on the windswept moorland, and struck north towards the isolated village of Crosby Ravensworth. We followed the Lyvennet, a mere trickle thereabouts but a streamlet which, through ample refreshment, augments the Eden on her way down to the Solway Firth. A mile below the squat monument to Charles, the refreshment was drawn from those swamps deceptively hidden by spikes of rush that gave the name of moss-troopers to men who lived by rustling Border cattle.

Under heavy clouds we sploshed and squished our way through those swamps until, almost miraculously, the sun came out as if to see what we were up to and then, apparently satisfied, left us on the firm banks of a beck hidden in places by the enormous, the tropical-looking, leaves of the butterbur which used to be wrapped round newly-made butter for storage in winter.

The leaf, to quote Old Gerard the herbalist, 'is of such widenesse that of itself is bigge inough to keep a man's head from raine and the heate of the sunne'. When powdered and

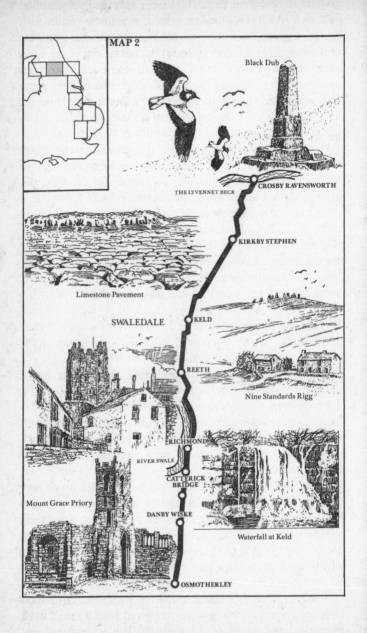

MAP 2

Black Dub

THE LYVENNET BECK — CROSBY RAVENSWORTH

Limestone Pavement

KIRKBY STEPHEN

SWALEDALE — KELD

REETH

Nine Standards Rigg

RICHMOND

RIVER SWALE

CATTERICK BRIDGE

Mount Grace Priory

DANBY WISKE

Waterfall at Keld

OSMOTHERLEY

mixed with wine, the dried roots were reckoned proof against the ague as provokers of perspiration, a herbe 'fit to drive from the hart all venom'. Altogether a most useful plant, but less beautiful by far than that jewel of our limestone flora, the pink or, as country folk call it, the Birdseye primrose. The petal stars so delicately poised on a rosette of pale green leaves remind you of those Japanese confections that open out in a glass of water. Are those marvels of our childhood no longer made, I wonder?

From a bedroom overlooking the graves of the Dawn People we lay awake, listening to that most haunting of the voices of the moors, the cries of curlew calling, calling, as, high up in the dark, guided perhaps by a fitful moon, they winged over the plateau from their wintering grounds on the estuaries of the Irish Sea. From their cries, at first half-heard and then becoming louder and louder as they sailed overhead, they were clearly late-comers on the move, looking for nesting sites in numbers greater than I have ever heard before. The curlew has a Latin name no less evocative than its voice. It is *numenius*, the moon-sliver, which nicely portrays its long crescent-shaped bill.

Over a more than tolerable breakfast of grilled ham and mushrooms there was a decision to be made: where to head for that day. When there were oracles on earth or, as Belloc put it, before Pan died, we might have seen portents in that lamb's blood on the iron bars of Lingalow. Perhaps we should have retreated to one of the sacred places on the moor, maybe the Thunderstones below Aslaby Scar, and considered what it meant, but although I know a sign or two, including one recommended by no less than Palinurus, the pilot in the *Aeneid*, I can't pretend it has ever done me much good. As it fell out, we tramped on into the very eye of the storm, but as we saw a number of curious things on the way I shall try and put them into some sort of perspective. This is not easy. It's like trying to make a précis out of a video-tape which insists on spooling backwards at speed.

Imagine then two ant-like figures toiling up the great slope beyond the curlew-haunted village of Crosby towards Bank Top where, an ancient assured us, we should be able to see for fifty miles. They are talking those two, talking earnestly,

75

for on that vista much depends: no less whether to part there, temporarily, or walk on together. They stop, occasionally, and through glasses scan the sky where wisps of curlew are still calling and still flying east purposively. Satisfied by that excuse for a rest, they resume their climb, walking in step, hoping that each crest will be the last for an hour or two – which, on the waves of springy turf that surround the plateau, it rarely is.

They talk of this and that, but especially of what to do with that jalopy parked in a stationmaster's yard beside the Irish Sea. Somebody, meaning Madam, has to drive it back to where it can be picked up again: unlike Belloc on his *Path to Rome*, her companion, the narrator, is too proud to make use of any wheeled thing on a declared route. In short, we decided to see how the day turned out.

The blood on the cattle-grid came as a surprise. Still wet, still warm. Had it not been for a faint whimper from below, we might have walked on. A newborn lamb had dropped into the pit below the iron rails. As I began to haul it out, it first sucked my finger and then kicked with such vigour that I had difficulty in hauling it out by the scruff of its neck. But where was Ma? The lamb knew. Almost hidden in the bracken nearby a ewe, lying on her side, heaved convulsively, her head up, her mouth agape as she strove to give birth to another wet ball of wool in an envelope. In its wobbly efforts to rejoin her, the first-born fell into the pit again. We left it there. Only a farmer could carry off the whole family.

A breathless half-hour brought us to the summit of Bank Top where as far as the eye could see the horizons were ringed with fluffy white clouds, like an immense tonsure. The outlook neither particularly good nor bad. So that's what the gods of the grey winds had to say: make up your own minds. The Pythian oracles at Delphi spoke in a similar fashion. Cynical Greeks described their answers as *aenigmata*.

Before I could spin a coin or indulge in any other form of vulgar divination, a man appeared on the fell-side. We waved and made towards him. On hearing about the lamb he nodded appreciatively. There were several 'yows in t'brecken', he said, but added that, 'Bess'll find 'em, smart.' At this he turned; he shoved four fingers in the corner of his mouth and vented a blast that made us wince.

Bess, at first invisible, appeared from behind a ridge at least half a mile away and ran towards him, pausing only to gather two more sheep unseen by the flockmaster. I have watched this happen scores of times but never cease to marvel at the uncanny rapport between man and dog. We left them to it.

Within a quarter of an hour the rings of clouds had partly dissolved, leaving only one patch above which, as if suspended in the sky, appeared a high and bright-lit range of hills isolated from all around and below them. Bunyan's vision of the Celestial City could not have been more inspiring since, by some trick of the light, in part a mirage effect, we were looking at Arkengarthdale far away across the Yorkshire border. That settled it. We were bidden to press on, but not with the unswerving resolution of Bess who, at another whistled command, had located three more strays and was trotting along behind a flock of five as her master, without so much as a look behind, strode up towards the lamb under the cattle-grid.

More barrows. Six within two miles, some not even marked on the map. The crowns of others had been sliced in half, the wounds of some bygone despoiler. Prehistoric treasure-hunts became fashionable again in the eighteenth century when barrow-surgeons like Lord Conyngham boasted of how many they had ravished in one day. Seven or eight was not uncommon. The operation was ritualized. A dozen or more labourers removed the earth from the top of the mound, whereupon the excavator, 'suitably attired in an exploring costume', had the seigneurial privilege of breaking into the chamber.

Those we skirted that morning might have gone unnoticed but for weathered signs on poles which read: *This ancient burial mound is protected as a Monument of National Importance under the Ancient Monuments Act of 1930 and 1933 – Ministry of Public Buildings and Works.* The petty official who ordered those boards to be put up probably knew no more about them than we did.

Our speed increased to about a hundred and twenty paces to the minute as bruised-looking clouds began to wipe out the horizon as effectively as a blackboard duster. Brisk going but far from arduous, especially downhill, where, with

77

momentum gained, we roller-coasted up the next ascent, around farms, across lanes at right angles to our route. On short-cropped grass in easy country this sort of striking out is beyond the comprehension of dawdlers. But we knew it couldn't last. In both senses of the word we foresaw the tumult ahead, and the curious silence in which even birdsong ceased made it the more ominous.

The storm hit us far beyond that point where Madam could have walked down to the nearby township of Appleby in time for lunch. We were obliged to keep going, and for what seemed an endless afternoon we tacked against head-on squalls of wind and rain like two close-hauled boats.

Towards evening we slouched into Kirkby Stephen, wet through. The rain had ceased but a damp sunset smudged the haze with uncertain dyes.

The swirling dale

According to Old John, my paternal gran'pa, everything everywhere and at all times is linked up directly or indirectly with something else, and by some weird logic of his own he once sought to convince me that when a buffalo breaks wind in Alberta or a pub is burnt down in Pontefract there is an infinitesimal ripple on the sands of the Sahara. I don't know whether the old man had ever read Hegel, but his philosophy was expressed quite simply by E. M. Forster in those two much-quoted words, 'Only connect . . .'

They have come to mind on a number of occasions but never so forcibly as they did at half-past eight in the morning in the market place of Kirkby Stephen, that handsome town on the river Eden. Madam had been given a lift to Appleby, there to take trains to the car on the coast, leaving me for at least two or three days to strike across a substantial part of Yorkshire alone. Alone to what end? I had been alone for too long. I had become dependent on her enthusiasm, her chatter, her dogged determination to tackle everything we encountered, and I thought of the day's stint of maybe fifteen or twenty miles with no great enthusiasm.

And then a curious thing happened. In one of those labyrinthine flashbacks of memory that occur in a matter of seconds, I heard the tinkle of a bell and saw as if reflected in the glass of a large rosewood bookcase the face of a bonny lass. The girl was real enough. At that particular moment she was setting up a stall in front of the pub where we had spent the night. Perhaps I smiled for she certainly did, but it faded as if she read my thoughts and, knowing what lay behind them, looked away. If there is a corner of the afterworld reserved for boilers of liquorice juice, gran'pa is smiling right now.

The bookcases were his. Among the leather-bound volumes of travel and exploration were most of the works of Richard Burton, including an unexpurgated version of *The*

Thousand and One Nights. In my mind's eye I can still see that volume, for although we were forbidden even to open it at Pontefract I managed to acquire that rich collection of stories when the house and its exotic contents were sold shortly after gran'pa died. On his eightieth birthday he was knocked down by a motorbike on his way home from a long walk. The book disappeared under rubble when fire-bombs fell like confetti on the West End of London. But what, you may well ask, brought that faint tinkle to mind in the market place of Kirkby Stephen? Only connect . . .

When the sultan Schahriah discovered the infidelity of his sultana, he decided to acquire a fresh wife every night and have her strangled at daybreak. Scheherazade, the daughter of the Grand Vizier of the Indies, managed to break that uncharitable decree by telling him stories so skilfully broken off at a crucial point that the sultan begged her to continue them the next night.

One such story ended, temporarily, on the decision of a merchant of Baghdad, or it could be Alexandria? I forget the details, except that he was reasonably well off in respect of worldly goods but singularly unfortunate in affairs of the heart. At long last he decided that whenever he felt himself to be in love he would tie a small bell to his foot so that perceptive women might know he was dangerous.

Whether that stallholder heard the tinkle is a matter for speculation, but it came to me loud and clear as I thought of Hazel and Monica, Megan and Mary, Pépé, the Cucaracha, and Flo, on my way out of town, across the Eden and up to the huge quarries on Hartley Fell. The tinkle, perhaps, of jesters' bells. Further reflections about how a whole pattern of life changed when Madam decided that we might well walk together in the vicinity of Thorgill were interrupted dramatically when quarrymen, invisible to me, blew out a substantial piece of the backbone of England.

The moorland road skirts the rim of that white gash in the ground. I had seen the flags, heard the whistles, but had walked on wholly absorbed in memories. The thumps as the cordite ripped open the rock were as distant gunshots, but the House of Usher came to mind when a vertical cliff of carboniferous limestone shuddered, gaped, and toppled over as if in slow motion, breaking apart even as it fell. Millions of years of prehistory had been reduced to the rubble of roads in a few seconds.

Much trudging up a distinctly wet track brought me to a pause as figures appeared on the skyline. They could have been crouching men, waiting for whatever might be imagined. Through glasses they were clearly piles of stone marked on the map as the Nine Standards. A compass bearing to within a degree or two of south-east confirmed their identity.

Wainwright the pathfinder is such a conscientious guide that I cannot for one moment believe that, like Palinurus who abandoned Aeneas to his fate, he would deliberately mislead the votaries of the Nine into a morass of remarkable extent. In fact he warns us against it. 'Resist the beeline offered by Faraday Gill,' he says. I resisted it with no hesitation. It looked foul. 'Keep to the bridleway,' he says. 'It is excellently graded and affords an easy and clearly defined route up to 2,000 feet in tough surroundings.' I kept to it. No Ariadne could have offered a more reassuring thread.

I climbed, steadily, on elastic turf that glimmered with blue-eyed flowers. Again the map confirmed the bearing. I thought more kindly of Palinurus who confessed to his Trojan lord – rather too late, one feels, since by then they were both among the Shades – that when he let slip the helm his 'weary'd eyes seized with fatal sleep'.

No such excuse could have been put forward by the dozen or more of us who lost our various ways that ill-begun morning, for it came out later that at least half of the party had started off on that bridleway. Perhaps the one recommended by Wainwright has long since sunk.

If I were the first to get be-mired it was of some comfort to discover that nobody saw me coursing about like a retriever which at a critical point has lost the scent. The others who were plunging about through something close to the Slough of Despond far below imagined that I alone knew the way. I didn't. Not caring how wet I got, I battled my way up to the summit and when I waved to those below me it was with no confidence, for when the elusive Nine came into view they were as sorry a pile of stones as ever I saw. At least that's how I felt as I sat down to scrape the mud off my pants. Bunyan says, 'As the sinner is awakened about his lost condition there arise in his soul many fears and doubts and discouraging apprehensions which all of them get together and settle in his place.'

Nobody knows how those nine beacons came to be built on the high plateau between Bastifell and Rollinson Haggs. They lie within half a mile of the Yorkshire border, and occupy a commanding position on one of the principal watersheds between the Irish Channel and the North Sea. Stories about how they were hastily erected to give marauding Scots the impression that an English army was lying in wait for them are as unlikely as their supposed associations with Druidry. They are not particularly old. They have probably grown, as cairns will, from stones inched into place by generations of disappointed walkers. That would at least explain their symmetry, but not why they seem to exude an air of gloom. Though the sun shone bright the air seemed damp and cold.

The stragglers clambered up in pairs. An elderly botanist, the one person in the party with whom I hoped to have something in common, was possibly the most reticent and churlish. Perhaps he had found something rare and wanted to keep it to himself. Perhaps that battered old collecting-tin contained only his sandwiches. He never opened it. The others had little to say.

Before we disappeared, the tweedy couple towards the pub at Tan Hill and the rest down the slope to the road, we were joined reluctantly by a nice young lad who got a smart cuff for not hurrying up. He had been having a whale of a time on his own and had found a huge hairy caterpillar. We had a few words about it, privately. I noticed, too, that his boots were much cleaner than ours. The air seemed fresher the further I walked away from my fellow travellers. Why on earth were they so unfriendly? I hadn't done them a favour.

Though there is much injustice in this world, being spanked by a parent has never struck me as an invasion of the soul's privacy. If you were raised in a poverty-stricken district you were lucky to have a father around often enough to do it. I contend, too, that if you knew at heart you deserved an occasional cuff at home or at school, it doesn't mean, as some think, that in later life you are ready to bring back the rope and the lash and join the National Front. Among much else, my own interest in trees was quickened in sweet innocent youth by being tanned by a little bald-headed dominie affectionately known by scores of us at a big school in Leeds as Bug Willie.

As his name suggests, one of Digby Firth's extra-curricular passions in life was the pursuit and classification of insects, but realizing that not all of us were equally fascinated by the larval activities of tiger beetles or plant bugs, he finished an informal chat one afternoon in the early spring by saying that instead of ordinary homework, we should turn up the next morning with the twigs of at least six species of trees and write down how the trunks differed one from another.

For some reason I either forgot or thought they could be picked up on the way to school. Gran'pa had taught me the names of quite a few trees. Unfortunately, without meaning to be even mildly funny, when questioned I said I was waiting for the leaves to grow. If I hadn't smirked when the class laughed, I might have got away with it. Instead, I was told to bend over and got six from his cane, which, he explained patiently, wasn't a twig but a tall woody long-living member of the grass family. As further punishment he ordered me to collect and sew on to a card not six but twelve different twigs that night. But for the chance discovery that the milkman knew more than a thing or two about trees, I don't know how I should have done it on my own. But it took even that knowledgeable fellow to find a round dozen. I never forgot them, and by rattling off the names in a pious voice the next morning, I discovered one-upmanship without knowing what it was. The card hung up on the classroom wall until the end of term.

I cared little for cricket, an attitude which came close to blasphemy in Headingley, but I knew that bats were made from the fastest growing species of willow in the country. It paid to know more about trees and towards that end, as in many others, I was aided and abetted by a girl-friend.

If analysts can convince you that a maid's first man is psychologically indelible, the reverse is not uncommonly true. I can no more forget the name of that precocious little moppet, Hazel (the *Corylus* of Virgil), than our walks together hand-in-hand through the great avenues of Temple

83

Newsome. I loved her with all the uncluttered passion of a thirteen-year-old, not least because she knew quite a bit about natural history. Moreover, to earn a little pocket money she conducted infirm but well-heeled ladies around the huge and hilly gardens of Weetwood. Affluence and poverty were commonplace in Leeds.

Hazel and I grew up together. We shared our sixpences on bars of chocolate and tram rides. We learned some of the vital facts of life from her father's preoccupation with beekeeping. With the decent timidity of youngsters we put them to the test at Catterick-on-Swale, but as the village lies along my route that story must wait awhile.

Of all the gills, becks and streamlets that tumble off Nine Standards Rigg, none are more wild nor more lonely than those that feed the Swale, 'the swirling rushing river', a cataract that scours through the whole history of the North Riding. The name is related to that swiftest of birds, the swallow. Bede knew her as the Swalwan stream. Of her most distant daughters, Ney Gill was the one I took to first, and then the Whitsundale beck that froths into the river below Ravenseal. From that squat farmstead an hour of downstream striding brought me to Keld.

An exciting hour. Confined as she is to a deep gorge, the infuriated river thrashes about like a wounded snake, falling down staircases of limestone, swirling round and round in foaming pools, lashing out blindly against the soft rock in her efforts to regain the open sky. Beyond Wath Force she holds to the banks sullenly, flowing deep, pausing as a boxer does in a clinch between bouts; and it is there you may hear the staccato song-phrases of the mountain blackbird, wild and loud – loud so they can be heard above the roar of water.

Although the word 'Keld' has a metallic ring about it, the sound you might think of sword against sword, in Old Norse it meant a spring or freshet and, even after an hour of cloud-shed, fountains burst out of Wham Bottom, Woofergill, Polly Gutter, and a hundred more. The springs are the source of water for the dalesman's black-and-white Friesians which have replaced his Shorthorn cattle. On all sides, even on the steep edges of the Common, are field barns, detached from the homesteads, but so individual, so beset with personal detail, that no two appear exactly alike. They are the most remarkable architectural feature of the swirling dale. The oldest are clenched tight with hewn beams, the younger ones bear marks of the new-fangled saw. They were built for the storage of hay and the wintering of a few cattle which return what they eat (an acre and a half of grass for each beast stalled from November until May) in the amorphous shape of fertile muck. From this grow the carefully tended intakes that wrest fodder from the acid soils of heather, rush, and wet-arse, the invasive sphagnum moss. Until the derelict barns began to be replaced by tin sheds and old railway waggons, and the horse by the tractor, the pattern of life in the dale had been much the same for hundreds of years, possibly since the time of the Norse invasion. The same small land-hungry holdings. Cattle were 'dried off' in the autumn, when the milk was preserved as butter or cheese. 'Aye, we did us milking in the fields them days,' said a little man in a black cap who was trying to drag a rusted cylindrical hayrake back to life. He looked at his fingers and added, 'There's nowt like armstrong machines.' I looked puzzled and he began to milk an invisible cow. He revved the tractor up again. 'Giddup yer bitch,' he growled, and slowly the steel tines began to revolve until, spinning round like demented coat-hangers, they threw up a shower of sparks from the cobbled yard.

To the north-west of Keld the gaunt shoulders of the moors have been slashed open and poisoned by mining operations, leaving only mounds of spoil and the ruins of abandoned buildings. The scene is one of desolation, the outcome of the lust for lead, most of it in the sixteenth and seventeenth centuries although the sombre-grey ore has been mined there since Roman times, and probably earlier. Gunnerside was the Klondike of Swaledale.

Fortunes were made by the few and lost by many, and always there loomed the spectre of bellan, the local name for lead poisoning. The symptoms were elusive: muscular weakness about the feet and the wrists, which could be the fatigue of a man who had worked underground from dawn to dusk. At least, they hoped it was that; but gradually they found they were unable to lift their pots of beer without pain. From the knees downwards they were afflicted with curiously persistent pins and needles. At night, in the light of a tallow candle, they saw the reflection of that ominous blue line around their gums. They knew that acute gut-ache, that condition known as painters' colic. They were in the grip of bellan. In some areas, hens could not be kept because the grit they picked up contained fragments of lead, and the streams that poured out of the deep workings were covered over with slabs of limestone to prevent stock from drinking poisoned water.

As I discovered at the cost of much sleep that night, the deserted buildings are widely tenanted by that ghostly bird with a voice so hysterical that it's almost impossible to reduce it to phonetics, the barn owl. At first the sound came from different quarters and so far away that one had to strain to hear it. Presumably they were out hunting among pastures more productive than the sterile spoil of miners. They were successful, it seems, for at least one pair returned after about an hour and kept up their long-drawn-out screams until past midnight.

This could have been a quarrel between two testy old cocks or a simple affirmation of love between a well-fed couple. It's difficult to interpret the niceties of barn owl talk. It all sounds much alike, especially in an area where courtship and territories amount to much the same thing. As I tossed and turned in my sleeping-bag, I reflected that if somewhere there were a home for neurotic birds there would be a lot of little grebes, blackbirds, stone curlew and barn owls among the inmates. Had they been within range I would have chucked a brick at my unwelcome neighbours. The last I heard of them was a sort of self-satisfied *tek tek tek* which I hoped meant, 'Well, Well. We'll resume this matter later.'

At first light I scrambled up into that desolation by crossing the river above the sad ruins of Crackpot Hall, and paused there to look around, not only at the delicate lacework of the waterfalls which are among the best in a stream renowned for its cataracts. I paused because, in the vivid cinematography of the imagination, I saw another walker hurrying up, stopping to look at his map, the twelfth he had used in his journey up from Cornwall. He was heading for the Border. He was hurrying because he was already a day behind his self-appointed schedule. Since there are maelstroms of thoughts that cannot easily be put into words, it is enough to say that I saw myself as I was nearly twenty years ago. It was the first time our paths had crossed.

This Crackpot Hall is everything you may imagine for yourself: a once-handsome farmhouse perched on a cliff so eroded, so heavily undermined by workings, that it cannot stand there much longer. Gingerly, as one might touch a pagoda built from a pack of cards, I pushed open a door swinging from one rusty hinge. The roofless beams sagged ominously; the floorboards had been gnawed by rats. A huge pile of twigs in front of the fireplace had fallen down the chimney from generations of jackdaws' nests. Among them were owl pellets which glistened as if recently varnished. Some of my noisy neighbours of the night had dined there. I clapped my hands and out of the skeleton of an ash tree flew, not an owl, but two jackdaws yelping. They had seen me coming. It took me an hour of hard going to get up on to the miners' trods above Swinner Gill, and it was largely wasted time.

The men who had to blast their way into the fault lines before they began to hack out the precious ore were known as gruvers, or t'owd men, a reference perhaps to their dark complexions or prematurely old faces. When first the tin and then the copper mining industry of Cornwall went bust, twelve thousand gruvers roamed the country, looking for something to eat. Many came to Swaledale to find that London Lead and the Old Gang Company were already dismissing men, and many of them were Spaniards. A visitor to Swaledale at the beginning of this century said that many villagers reminded him of Goya's paintings of miners from Asturias. They were in fact their descendants. The more fortunate ones had migrated to Canada and Bolivia. Once a miner, always a miner.

They worked by the light of candles, boring their way slowly into the hillside, in places for a distance of half a mile. No wages were offered to those who risked their lives in the levels of Bunting, Sir Francis and Old Lile. Pay was reckoned at so much a fathom of metalliferous ore recovered, the details being entered into what was prophetically known as The Dead Bargain Book.

On I went, scrambling around the barren fan-shaped screes

of spoil, peering into the gothic arch of a level which now supports a profusion of lime-green ferns and avoiding – where I could – the steep sides of a hush. This is a local term for an ingeniously contrived ravine. To find new seams without weeks, perhaps months, of laborious digging, the gruvers selected a stream on a steep slope. They dammed it near the top and suddenly released the accumulated water. It gushed down, exposing whatever lay beneath the soil.

On the edge of Gunnerside Gill where a few trees relieve the awful sense of desolation, an incautious scramble started a trickle of stones which developed into a small avalanche. Among them were spar and barytes which tinkled as they fell. It was here, perhaps, that old Neddy Dick of Keld collected the hard core of what, to venture a small joke, must have been the first rock band. With a good ear for music, he noticed that many stones produced a clear ringing tone when struck. By careful splitting and trimming, he assembled first an octave and then a variety of half-tones. It was his ambition to tour the country with his instrument on a donkey cart, but he died in the late Twenties still thinking about the idea. When an antiquarian tried to find the stones years later, Neddy's neighbours told him they had been stored in an old outhouse and thrown away when the building collapsed.

Keeping to a trod on which the rank grass had been kept short by sheep and spring lambs as playful as infants in a school yard, I managed to outflank the hamlet of Healaugh, wondering what the word meant and how it was pronounced but with insufficient curiosity to make yet another detour to find out. I wanted to get off the barren moor by the most direct route short of venturing among the coaches on the busy road below.

Boswell asked Samuel Johnson whether he thought the Giant's Causeway was worth seeing. 'Yes,' said the master of verbal precision, 'but not worth going to see.' It was a little sad to discover that, after an absence of years, I felt much the same about Reeth which, like the two villages upstream, has become a victim of its own popularity as a tourist centre. The same busy car-parks, tea-rooms, bric-à-brac shops, and pubs which serve the same instant food from deep-freezers.

Reeth used to be called the capital of Upper Swaledale, but

I doubt whether many of the thousands who nowadays drive in and, after a short stay, drive out have time to notice the enormous views from where the Arkle beck tumbles down to the Swale. You have to walk up to that platform. There is a fine hall, too, the Draycott, and a former hotel, the Burgoyne, with curious tripartite windows.

Feeling a bit like Canute I retired, sulkily, to the least popular pub in the village where Fred, a cow man, told me that Healaugh was pronounced 'Hee-law' and meant an upland clearing. Everyone knew that, he said. He was drinking, slowly, in the company of Tony who looked like a Spaniard but wasn't and the amiable Albert, an endearing giant of a man who could have lifted up the three of us and maybe the table as well. A blacksmith, perhaps. It came out, gradually, that Tony had been captured at Anzio and stayed on, undeterred by a year behind barbed wire in Scotland where today he runs an ice-cream business. 'An ex-Wop,' he said, apologetically. They were holding a fellow-prisoners' reunion that night.

Albert had driven in with a truck-load of young lads from Bradford who, after lemonade and sandwiches on the green, were intent on a ten-mile trot up to the source of the Arkle. He glanced out of the window to make sure they weren't 'pulling the bloody place to pieces'. I took to Albert on the spot since, among other jobs for a big man able to look after himself and others, he had, as he put it, 'done a bit in the grunt industry'. He had been an all-in wrestler. At this I nearly changed plans and went along with his lads for, back in the late Thirties, I had become the self-appointed authority on that sport for a local paper.

Until the lads started to shake their fists at him with mock indignation, we swopped tales about the Manchester Mauler, the Wild Man of Warsaw, and other grunters of a generation ago. 'There's big money in it today,' he said. 'I should have stayed on.'

'How old are you?' I asked.

'Six foot two,' he said, looking me straight in the eye.

The last I saw of him was amid a whirl of arms and legs. As a limbering-up exercise he had challenged them all to hold him down. Like a bloodhound rearranging its litter of pups, he picked them off the grass one by one, explaining patiently how to get out of a hammerlock or a simple crucifix. I waved, he waved, and off I went, feeling there was quite a lot to be said for some of the visitors to Reeth.

Looking back on that long day from Keld to Richmond, I feel I have done less than justice to the spectacular variety of Upper Swaledale. The lunar landscapes of the mines are harsh, but more peaceful by far than the unrelieved tourism of the villages. What is wanted is more and more footpaths. One of the finest in Richmondshire may be encountered a mile to the east of the Arkle beck where, past the priory of Marrick and on to Marske, an up-hill and down-dale track takes you within sight of the great plain of York, a distance of a little more than a dozen miles.

Two young fellows walked out of the gates of the priory, talking together with such gravity that at first I took them to be seminarists although they were dressed in the common uniform of the city: waist-coated suits, shirts with matching ties, neat but not gaudy, and shoes that looked as if they pinched somewhat. Certainly not footwear for an upland track. What were they about? They were lecturing there, they said. The local diocese had built an Adventure Club along-side the ruins of the priory. To youngsters who knew little if anything about the country, one of them, a trade union official, had been disclosing, I hope, the secrets of his trade, whilst the other specialized, he said, in business management. Two pompous people, I thought.

Against the enormous clamour of birds in Marrick Wood, the splendour of limestone cliffs, and, far below, the Swale swirling about to avoid outcrops of millstone grit, there seemed nothing more to be said about adventure or anything likely to interest the two lecturers. I walked on, wishing only that Albert and his lads could have turned up and asked them a few questions.

Between the foot of the wood and the little hamlet of Marrick four hundred feet above the priory, there winds a tree-lined path so steep that steps have been cut into it. At the top a man chasing a ferret told me there used to be four hundred, which gives some idea of the angle of slope. At first I started to count them, an exercise which ranks among the iron rations of the intellect, but tiring of that pastime I fell back on a thought-stream which began with Hazel in a hilly public park in Headingley and ended in an all-in wrestling ring. I made a note of the transitions when I sat down to rest at the summit, and have since backed them up with some yellowed cuttings from the paper which once employed me for about thirty shillings a week.

At that time my relationship with Hazel had developed from one where, with enormous timidity, I put my arm round her waist, to another where, as if by accident, I touched her bosom. Mistaking what was probably a look of disappointment for one of disapproval, I shuffled home to God alone knows what feelings of remorse. It was months before I plucked up courage to ask her out again.

By then I had a pair of aces up my sleeve; more precisely, they could be flashed nonchalantly in their celluloid envelopes. They were press passes, one for the Leeds City Varieties, a famous music hall which had been on the go since gran'pa's youth. I recall Monday nights revelling in the company of Tessie O'Shea, George Formby, Norman Evans, Sid Fields and Teddie Brown, the fattest xylophonist in the business. All the top-line stars of their day. But the other press pass was for the local all-in wrestling ring, where I felt more at home since I knew three or four of the regular maulers.

Forgive us our press passes. When I discovered that the sight of two enormous men grunting as they tied each other in knots turned Hazel on quicker than gin and lime, they nearly proved her undoing on her sixteenth birthday. But virtue invariably triumphed, not only in the ring but afterwards when, with a piece to write, I talked to the combatants until it was too late to do anything except take Hazel home by tram.

In this there are psychological truths unsuspected perhaps by folk, especially elderly ladies, who write to the Independent Television Authority in their hundreds saying they can't sleep really peacefully at night without first seeing bouts of mayhem on the box.

The ring was situated in North Street, the slum-ridden Jewish quarter of Leeds, where the leading ore extractors, apart from ready-made clothing manufacturers, were the

Brothers Green, the lessees of the stadium. The manufacturers exploited a host of penurious Polak and Irish immigrants. I wrote a passionate story about it all but, perhaps wisely, the paper never printed it.

My personal involvement in national politics faded when, during a rally on Woodhouse Moor, a notorious fairground between the slums of Meanwood and posh Headingley, some of Mosley's hoodlums started chucking large potatoes lightly garnished with so-called safety razor-blades at the supporters of the Red Flag. Safer by far, I thought, to watch them fight it out symbolically at Greene's place, where the followers of Wozzeck, the Wild Man of Warsaw, screamed with anger or enthusiasm when he tried to gouge out the eyeballs of Pat O'Dooley, the Gentleman from Cork. As I recall, Pat weighed about three hundred pounds in his fighting knickers.

A slow developer in some respects I might have been, but, with an eye for scientific detail, it occurred to me that Wozzeck couldn't really put Pat into the overhead aeroplane spin without the co-operation of his partner. He couldn't do it even had he been fighting my dear old friend Wee Georgie Wood, whom we had seen at the City Varieties the previous week.

Before he crashed on the mat in a blur of arms and legs, the slow curvature of Pat's spine convinced me that both battlers knew a thing or two about angular momentum which, as all physicists and balletomanes know, is what happens when you stand up and spin round with your arms extended. If you lower them to your sides during the *prestissimo* you all but chuck yourself off your feet. This is what the lads were doing. Thereafter the combat assumed the predictable routines of Gathering Peascods, or Sellinger's Round.

Pat kicked Wozzeck in the face, and Wozzeck, no doubt recalling the Anti-trinitarian King Sisimond II and his long struggle with the Roman bishops, pulled Pat's hair and threw him into a triple cartwheel followed by what acrobats call *tinsikas* and a back flip. At this the heir to the realms of Cormac McCarthy tried to saw his opponent's head off between the lower ropes. This clearly annoyed Wozzeck who, after turning through various shades from lettuce to beetroot, un-roped himself and spread-eagled our Irish hero, who could do nothing except assume the starfish posture and play pat-a-cake on Wozzeck's bum with his bare feet. I became even more sceptical about the depths of the engagement when, after seeing Wozzeck carried off groaning on a stretcher after the Irish lad's last resounding boomps-a-daisy to the navel, I rediscovered him shortly afterwards, playing darts for pints of Newcastle Brown in the tavern opposite the stadium.

'Want a photograph?' he asked. When he told me it was his turn to win the following week, I began to wish I had spent more time with Hazel.

I don't know what happened to British all-in wrestling until it was revived by the television companies. In America, according to Joe Liebling, that prince of sports reporters, it went into a profound state of depression owing to the laudable efforts of a number of wrestlers to defeat each other. With respect for what they get up to in Cumbria, wrestling honestly conducted is a dull sport to watch.

The promoters tried everything including nationalism, importing dreadful-looking Foreign Menaces, massive men of all colours, who eventually succumbed to local heroes, until we got back where we are today and where we were when Hazel, in a new and rather daring frock, nearly jumped out of her free seat. The public is interested in villainy as villainy and virtue as virtue. It's all very ethical. That's why those Christian souls can't sleep until they've seen Mick McManus and Steve Logan get their late-night come-uppance. There is still some justice, some decency left in this world. That's why I took Hazel home by tram, and not too late.

On the brow of the hill the ferret-chaser appeared in no mood for idle gossip. He had been smartly bitten when he tried to pick up the ferocious-looking thing, and had only just managed to net it when it scuttled towards another rabbit-hole. It was difficult to make out the story of the steps from a man who spoke broad Yorkshire with his thumb in his mouth, but from his nod and the way he waved his spade I gathered I had struck the right way.

Right it may have been but easy to walk on it most certainly wasn't, especially in the vicinity of gates where cattle had churned up the mud. Farmers need gates, but when they lie across a common footpath some farmers, I suspect, derive quiet satisfaction from the plight of walkers who, they will tell you, are a damn nuisance. They leave gates open. I don't accept this as a generalization, even if a few do so; but the going would be easier by far if farmers maintained the stiles over their walls. That, they say, costs money.

Beyond the fields of the ferret-chaser there appeared the ghost village of Marrick which can boast of some antiquity since it is set down in the Domesday Book as *Marige*, meaning the boundary on the hill. A nobody-about sort of place, with a sundial the size of a cartwheel above the lintel of the only cottage that appeared to be inhabited. Carefully avoiding a flock of aggressive-looking bantams, I wove through snickets (squeeze-through stiles in a cross-gartering of walls) and contoured up to about a thousand feet where, on the ridge top, presumably the boundary on the hill, I looked down on a superb track which seemed to wind on for ever. Within five minutes I had slipped into ambulatory over-drive.

This is a curiously disembodied, an almost mystical, form of motion which, I suspect, only long-distance solitaries can enjoy to the full. It is here that the walker who knows what he's about can put to good use some of the poise, the dramatic arrogance, of the trained actor who, though perhaps tired out after an exacting performance, sweeps forward to the curtain for his final bow, his arms partly raised, his feet seeming scarcely to touch the ground.

The trick or, if you prefer it, the practice, is to acquire such control over the rhythms of your leg movements that, like regularized breathing, they can be ignored. It is then that the central bureau of nerves, which in some moods we call *ourselves* can go about its business without disturbance, in the manner of a government office during a public holiday.

I once tried to put this over to a small audience of mountaineers, with some diffidence, suspecting that most of them knew far more about the co-ordination of arm and leg movements than I did. When we settled down for an informal chat and a drink, I was taken aside by a tough-looking chap who, I discovered afterwards, had climbed Everest at

94

least twice. He seemed uncommonly interested in the motion of rhythms and detachment. 'Yes,' he said. 'I can see what you're getting at. Y'know, I've been making love like that for years.'

Madam has a stride which almost exactly matches my own, but Rabelais, who had no love for what he called the unfair sex, said it's in the nature of our respective thigh bones for a man to walk like a horse and a woman like a cow. As to the comparative merits of walking alone or in the company of one other person – more than one becomes restrictive – it swings entirely on the nature of the relationship. Stephen Graham tells us he likes tramping by himself, but hedges his preference with a touch of condescension by adding that a companion is well worth finding.

There are qualities about the north as you may see it from Reeth to Richmond unlike any others known to me. The Cumbrian fells are wholly spectacular, the moors of Shap, Ravensworth and Gunnerside are weird and desolate, but around Marrick and Marske are vistas made the better by good husbandry which, like a rare spice, keeps them fresh and haughty, not preserved in aspic for tourist consumption.

You have to search for Marske. It lies hidden away among trees, and the villagers, I began to think, are equally furtive, for the only living thing within view – if you discount the talkative beck – was a melancholic with a face that much resembled Buster Keaton's or Watteau's painting of *Le Grand Gilles*. The face of a comedian is often more than a little menacing and dangerous. You can't determine what he is up to. This man shuffled off as soon as he saw me, walking over the old bridge held together, apparently, by moss. I called to him. He looked over his shoulder, in a shifty sort of way and then entered his cottage and slammed the door.

I could have handled a pint of tea with relish but felt that aristocratic Marske wasn't the place to ask for one. Until they turned the eighteenth-century Hall into a block of flats, it had been lived in for centuries by the Hutton family who built the great obelisk on the hill – and with some justification, since two of them were appointed Primates of York.

There is no way of giving an impression of that heart-touching walk up to High Applegate and Whitcliffe Scar beyond saying simply it contours gracefully, and everything to me seemed full of the evening. In large part my contentment arose from the well sign-posted route that steers you off the road about half a mile beyond the village to the foot of an immense cliff topped by a thin fringe of trees, like ivy on a ruin. The river, that same swirling stream from Keld, looped about far below, but there was no temptation to get on more intimate terms with her since the path, marked by the acorn sign of the National Parks, was both unswerving and high-minded. Without its assurance, nobody would think of making for that tunnel through the woods of Whitcliffe. From a distance they appear impenetrable. The path knows better. It dips, slightly; it climbs, gently. It led me out on to a plateau where, far below, the town of Richmond appeared, gilded on the edge of a far-reaching plain.

Celia Fiennes described it as a town 'one cannot see till just upon it'. But that of course depends on how it's approached. Celia rode down from Durham, and you have the feeling she was nettled at losing her night-clothes in Darlington. It seems the guide she had hired had left the things in a little bundle lying about somewhere. Celia was interested in the contents of almost everything, from the Queen's dowry to the contents of a ditch bottom, but she couldn't abide carelessness.

As so much in Richmond is unexpected – the Norman castle with its keep on top of the gatehouse, an eighteenth-century theatre, a school which owes much to Le Corbusier, St Joseph's church with a tower described by Nikolaus Pevsner as 'naughty' – I suppose I shouldn't have been surprised to find the girls making love to the boys and the market place loud with unlovable music. A festival of some kind. The youngsters were carrying their 'trannies', transistorized radios tuned to different stations. My thoughts were solely on a meal and a bed in a reasonably quiet pub.

A bath, a pint, and a couple of lamb chops worked wonders. Within an hour I was wandering about among the youngsters, recalling cobbled streets, the slender lacy towers of the Greyfriars, the bridge with its rounded cut-waters unseen for half a century. Richmond *wears* well, possibly because it has never been in any serious affrays except at the hands of town planners whose prints are plain from the lower storeys of buildings in the sloped market place. There, in narrow doorways, young girls pressed themselves against boys in a reversal of the usual roles.

Towards closing time that night a nicely-matched young couple settled in the bar of our pub with its mercifully silent juke-box. He looked like a farm lad, tall, bright-eyed, but plainly nervous. In her azure-blue jeans, she could have taken her place among the fair-haired trumpet-blowing angels of Fra Angelico. A beautiful girl. The clock ticked. They talked a little. Suddenly the lass said loudly: 'Gorn! Put yer arm round me.' At this the lad put his arm round her shoulders stiffly. She rounded on him. 'Do it *proper*,' she said, and grabbed his other hand and slapped it on her ample bosom.

The landlord beckoned me. As a concession, he said, he could fix up breakfast for eight. Normally it was nine but his barman had agreed to come in early. We talked of this and that, and minutes elapsed as I paid the bill before going back to my seat to write up some notes.

After that interval the couple appeared to be eating each other, unconscious of anyone else, but when Lothario's fingers strayed under her front buttons, she said fiercely, 'Give ovver! When I wanna tak' me effin clothes off, I'll tak' 'em off missen.'

As he gave me a receipt and said goodnight, the landlord confided that if youngsters went too far he had to chuck them out sometimes, but, as he put it, 'things are different these days'.

Holy Trinity had struck nine next morning before I walked out through the town gate and down to the bridge over the swirling river. Two fishermen hunched over their floats told me they had been out since dawn and caught nothing. I felt that, like the apostles in the Garden, they needed a miracle to cheer them up.

As for myself, I ached to be out and away. Though the route entailed some twenty miles or more of the Vale of Mowbray which is dull going from any viewpoint, consisting mostly of lanes through farmland, Madam, I hoped, would rejoin me before nightfall. We were resolved to meet at the Carthusian Priory of Mount Grace. As I saw it, something of a pilgrimage, both sacred and profane, since it was on that self-same stretch of river I had caught my first trout and lost my first girl-friend.

> There be three things which are too wonderful
> for me, yea four which I know not;
> The way of an eagle in the air; the way of a
> serpent upon the rock; the way of a ship in the
> midst of the sea; and the way of a man with a maid.

With rod and with book, with patience, skill, and learning, a sad-faced priest convinced me there is something equally wonderful and that is the way of a trout with a fly.

Within our limited resources for travel, Hazel, I believe, would have accompanied me anywhere: to the City Varieties, to the wrestling ring, out into the country. She had liked fishing too, she said, especially since, on the banks of the Leeds and Liverpool Canal, we sat close together for hours. As thoughtful women will she took it philosophically when, in later years, I went off for the day, always on Sundays, with a busload of fishermen from the Leeds and District Society of Anglers. Women weren't encouraged to go on excursions that invariably ended with lengthy sessions in pubs. But Hazel and I were much together until I got down to the ways of a trout, essentially a solitary occupation.

In time I had begun to dislike the small pink worms, the wasp grubs, and the smelly maggots of the float fishers, but, until I met the priest with the roguish Tups Indispensable stuck in his deerstalker, nobody I knew could instruct me.

He knelt by the side of a tree in the rain, but not in prayer: Padre Rueful Countenance had lustful eyes on a butter-bellied trout under the far bank, a fish lapping up Pale Wateries for breakfast. Without resort to a float or maggots, he caught that trout by whisking his lure backwards in the air and dropping it with such parsonical grace that the placid stream scarcely marked his cast.

Could I stand by and see more? He looked pleased. I could forage in his fly box if I wished. His basket was at my disposal. Would I like to try his rod? Should we not go upstream together? For an ardent tyro my Romish man was a practical Christian and may his flock be damned in sempiternal fires if they found him less accommodating in his priesting.

He taught me the mysteries of The Pause which lead to The Presentation and The True Entry; I learned the significance of the Loose Wrist and Tight Elbow. Within half an hour I was an up-and-coming acolyte in the joys of the Downward Stroke, the Wind Cut and the False Cast. In return I hung his leader up in trees; I scraped his delicate rod rings of agate against branches; I tied his line in knots; and cracked off flies with all the abandon of a drunken carter. He was very patient, and I learnt to cast, and in casting joined the glorious fellowship of the flymen.

Within a month I had bought a rod and caught a trout in that gravelly length of the Swale near the Farmer's Arms at Catterick Bridge. On that first occasion Hazel came along too, but not, I regret, to her satisfaction. By that time she had graduated to become a dispenser in a local chemist's shop. Her father, a well-to-do fellow, said quite plainly that if I managed to scrape together some qualifications and we continued to get on well together, who knew? We might be able to open a shop of our own.

Holy Trinity had struck again before I left the river for a disused railway track, which, as so often happens on these short cuts through dull country, started off splendidly on a raised embankment and came to a dismal end on the banks of a drainage canal far too deep to be waded. The company had pulled the bridge down.

After coursing about through soggy farmland for nearly an hour, I took to a small road that crossed the railway within a quarter of a mile of where I had left it. This provoked more indignation than I care to set to paper. A local man assured me that since they had widened the motorway there were no short cuts to Catterick or anywhere else, at which I trudged on.

Even Alfred Wainwright, essentially a tolerant man, found that featureless country not at all to his liking. He says those who believe the earth to be flat will find much to support their belief between Richmond and Osmotherley, where, 'Although in the midst of thriving husbandry, few people are seen; in fact one feels lonelier than in the mountains. There is nothing of interest to anyone but farmers. Walking as a pastime is unheard of and incomprehensible. There are no welcoming "Bed and Breakfast" notices; no signs that say TEAS or even TEA2. You feel out of place.'

The river which had plucked my youthful heart-strings reappeared at Bolton, but not, as might be expected, the river I remembered. The swirling stream had grown sullen. She had lost most of her timber, and when she swung south around Catterick Bridge, the scene of my embarrassing assignation, I could not even approach the banks. The river ran between enormous mounds of gravel. In one year, a foreman told me, they had carted off over a million tons. But that was some time ago. Production is now slowing down. The quarry owners are looking for unworked deposits up-stream, whilst they set about the laudable task of restoring what the bulldozers and grabs have despoiled.

Even in my imagination there were no fine-drawn garlands of a valentine around the sign of the Farmer's Arms, the pub where Hazel and I spent a night of long ago. I had difficulty in imagining how it looked that weekend, when the BBC had announced that the Führer's tanks were thundering down to Vienna.

As far as I can recall we drove up in a flashy sports car, the property of a former colleague who had gone on to better things on a national newspaper. He had brought along a girlfriend who took his mind off what we had come there for, the fishing. I talked about almost nothing else. It was safer. I was as nervous as a kitten. But even as I prattled on about the state of the river, the advantage of using this fly as opposed to that, I sensed that within an hour or two I should be required to slip upstairs and into bed, where God alone knew what might happen.

Rilke says somewhere that the lover is in physical danger because he must depend on the co-ordination of his senses, for they must meet in that unique and risky centre in which, renouncing all extensions, they come together and have no permanence. In other words, he's on his own.

Hazel went upstairs for some reason or other. With a glance at the wench sitting at his feet in front of the fire, my friend said it was about time we joined her. I don't know what

I said, but I remained downstairs and had another drink or two until after midnight. And when Hazel tiptoed down, looking worried, wondering what it was all about, I delivered such a moral, such a preposterous, speech that she ran back to her room, crying. And locked the door. I didn't see her again for months, and by then I had turned to Monica.

Of the twenty miles between that pub of long ago and meeting Katie that night at Mount Grace, I recall only endless lanes, a talk with a journalist, a woman I have no wish to meet again, and that restless river. A tame affair compared with the cataract that thundered down from Gunnerside when the country was populated by small bands of mesolithic hunters. Because of the opening-out of the landscape from deep-cut gorges to a bed of millstone grit, the prehistoric river must have been about two miles wide at that point, a fact attested by the extent of the gravel deposits. And in that sub-boreal landscape, the people who chipped small flints followed the red deer up into the forested hills.

Rigorous though it was, they lived a rich and varied life since, if they are to survive, people solely engaged in hunting and gathering food not only live close to their environment, they must both understand and identify themselves with it. There were the All-powerful Sun, the Great Stag, the Ever-watching Wolf, and the Owner of the Salmon, constantly to be remembered and propitiated at the appropriate seasons of the year. They knew that the Owner of the Salmon lived in a huge hut somewhere under the sea from which he released his charges only for those who deserved them. The bones of the fish they ate were dropped back into the river reverently, since the failure of the salmon run could mean slow death by starvation in the winter.

For a month before a communal seal hunt, the medicine men walked about pouring out buckets of water so that their prey out there on the sandbanks could have a refreshing drink before they died. This is not disordered reasoning. Even in the days of the Neanderthalers, men leaned heavily on art and mysticism in order to withstand the harsh realities of life. To judge from what we know of the very few remaining hunting and food-gathering societies in the high latitudes, the Pygmy

Flint People must have gone in for some fantastic rituals. These lay at the very heart of their existence. We have no such festivities, no such incentives today. We are forgetting how to live. Perhaps we have begun to warm up the wax that will seal our own fate.

Blackamoor

Some two or three hundred feet above the ruins of Mount Grace lies the bustling township of Osmotherley, the place where, on no authority, some will have it that Oswald with his mother lay. It is known that this son of Aethelfrith who eventually became King of Northumbria had been obliged to flee to the holy island of Iona for some offence I can't fathom. There is evidence, too, that his mother, Acha, sister of Great Edwin, was an extremely beautiful woman, but that there should have been anything in the way of an incestuous relationship between them carries about as much historic weight as the story of Little Red Riding Hood. The hard facts are more prosaic and relate, moreover, to an entirely different fellow.

In 1087, the year that the Conqueror died and St Paul's was burnt down for the first time, a local *leah* or grove was tilled by the kinsmen of Osmund, hence *Osmunderle*. That would seem to bottom the matter, but they prefer the more indecorous story at the local pub.

Osmotherley is justifiably proud of St Peter's which, aloof from secular matters, stands with its back to the triangular green, a handsome building with a Norman doorway and foundations which are older by far than Aethelfrith's beer cellar. Since Catholicism has a long tradition on this edge of the moors, Romish folk attend their priests in a generously bayed house on one of the two main streets; others go to the Lady's Chapel nearly a mile out of town where the view is for God's contemplatives, and seemingly for ever.

For twenty years or more the townsfolk have become accustomed to the arrival, especially on Saturdays, of scores, occasionally hundreds, of heavily booted youngsters intent on getting to grips with what for many is an extremely painful exercise, a traverse of the whole length of the blackamoors, from Osmotherley to the coastal promontory of Ravenscar, within twenty-four hours, a distance of well over forty miles. This is the famous Lyke Wake Walk.

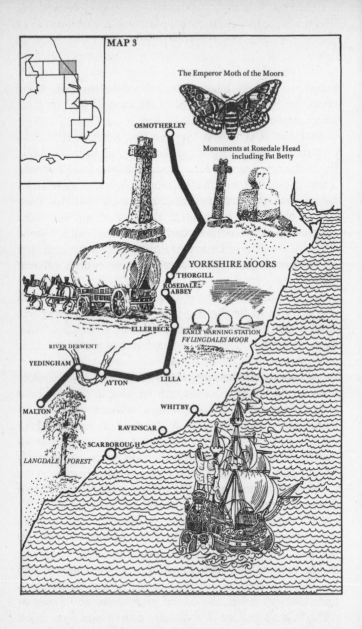

MAP 3

The Emperor Moth of the Moors

Monuments at Rosedale Head
including Fat Betty

OSMOTHERLEY

YORKSHIRE MOORS

THORGILL
ROSEDALE
ABBEY

ELLERBECK
EARLY WARNING STATION
FYLINGDALES MOOR

RIVER DERWENT

YEDINGHAM
AYTON   LILLA

MALTON

WHITBY

RAVENSCAR

SCARBOROUGH

LANGDALE FOREST

Holding as I do to the unswerving belief that walks of any kind should be in their essentials pleasurable, I am not at all in favour of the masochistic time-limits imposed by the founding fathers or, as they call themselves, not inappropriately, the Chief Dirgers. And as our cottage below Rosedale Head lies within a couple of miles of the halfway mark, Katie and I struck out for the high tops with far more to encourage us than a certificate for enduring blisters.

The Lyke Wakers have no time for detours; they walk in each other's footprints or at most abreast, their minds mostly on getting the infamous Whinny Moor over and done with before dusk. This means that across the longest diameter of this immensity of heather and wet peat, the trudgers have worn down a track so deep, and in places so sploshy, that I hesitate to describe the worst bits lest it deter those who don't know what they are in for. No matter. You can get used to anything which, in my opinion, is a shrewd argument against the existence of hell.

As for ourselves, we are essentially free-rangers, prepared if necessary to cut a corner off anywhere if it makes for dry and easy going. Though I tend at times to take a longer stride, in speed and gait the pair of us are complementary. From the waist upwards Madam puts you in mind of the figurehead of an eighteenth-century barque breasting the wind. When, as often happens, I'm tempted to stop and look at something that grows or flies or crawls, Katie keeps going. This may put her ahead by several hundred yards. If by chance she is moving resolutely downhill, I scamper after her and then, like Hazlitt with the green turf under his feet on the best of mornings, 'I laugh, I run, I leap, I sing for joy'.

For the most part these stops and starts are in the nature of a warming-up exercise, when belts and straps can be re-adjusted, and an opportunity to get the feel of the ground. Two occurred within half an hour of our turning our backs on the town.

The presence of several flattened toads on that rural road was not, I felt, a subject fit for discussion close on breakfast, and so when Madam noticed the pathetic cadavers I sugges-ted she should walk on. Curiouser and curiouser. There were forty or fifty in as many places, often in lines, one behind the other, like those damned souls in Dante who pressed on though their companions fell and were destroyed in their sight. Apparently some muck cart had passed that way the previous day, to and from a gate. A trail of the creatures had been in search of their breeding-ground, and a hard time they had had of it on the way.

I don't think toads are given the respect they deserve, and if Katie and I lived a more settled life I'd consider adopting a pair in addition to, say, a cocker spaniel bitch and a small flock of bantams. Toads are by all accounts docile and responsive to care; they will live on any living thing from ants to small fieldmice; they have pronounced homing instincts; and they live to a great age.

An old female toad, a friend of Thomas Pennant, the famous Flintshire naturalist, took up quarters under the steps of his house for over thirty years. It became a family pet and was visited every evening, emerging from its retreat when they approached whistling, waiting to be picked up and placed on a table where they gave it a meal. It died after being attacked by a raven.

Only prey that is moving is taken, but the amount of food a toad can consume is astonishing; some appear to have no sense of repletion. A large specimen kept by the great Boulenger of the Natural History Museum in London would swallow so many earthworms in succession that after a time they were voided alive.

A curious feature of toads' behaviour is attachment to the place where they live. It may be a hole in a wall, a cavity under a stone, or in some cases a low-lying bird's nest. If taken away and set down again, they are likely to return even though the journey back – since they are slow plodders and feeble hoppers – may take several days.

For reasons which have never been explained, all the sexually mature individuals of a local colony emerge from their hibernation quarters within a few days of one another, usually between mid-March and late April, according to latitude. At such times the males chirrup. The females, will feminists please note, have no voice whatever. And then off the colony goes to the same breeding-ground, year after year. Among toads the mass migration towards their Venusberg is

106

usually led by the males who, being noticeably smaller than their potential mates, seem anxious to be first into where the action is.

On the way their normal instinct for self-preservation is thrown aside. They will travel in daylight; obstacles such as walls that lie in their path are laboriously climbed. They are preyed on by a variety of raptors and, as I saw for myself that morning, they are crushed by wheeled traffic.

If a male can find a female before his rivals spot her, there is no courtship, no preliminary to mating. He promptly jumps on her back, grasping her firmly behind her forelegs and remains there until the eggs are squeezed out in gelatinous strings which are fertilized in the water. If there is much in the way of competition, orgiastic scenes are likely to occur. Unattached males strive to separate copulating couples and, if successful, they are frequently followed by others, until clusters of toads result. Up to twelve have been recorded with, at the centre, a female who was not only dead but had been dead for several days.

On such occasions the frustrated parties will grasp anything moving from the handles of fishing-nets to fish or frogs who just happen to be passing, minding their own business. Their surprise, their indignation, may be imagined since it's very difficult to dislodge a toad in *amplexus*, the amatory embrace.

I wondered where the toads of Osmotherley were heading for, but by this time Madam was pretty far ahead and I hurried after her. On the way, walking as fast as I could, noticing more and more flattened corpses, I came across a series of pools fed by a beck which emerged from a small reservoir. Somewhere thereabouts lay the breeding-ground which that year, I felt, would be sadly depleted.

Sweet are the beguilements of a naturalist in the presence of reed-lined water. The temptation to stop yet again came with uncommon force when the road swung close to the pools, and I all but ran into what a fisherman would call a massive hatch, a profusion of flies which were attracting most of the birds in the district, especially the warblers. Though the fragile insects fluttered about like wisps of smoke, they flew relatively high and were extremely difficult to catch.

107

After much leaping about, a difficult exercise with a rucksack on your back, I managed to nobble one or two which, from the transparent appearance of their larvae, are called phantom midges.

Before I could hurry on I noticed with considerable embarrassment that my capers had been watched from behind a gate by a local chap. His expression lay somewhere between curiosity and apprehension. Suppressing a ridiculous urge to say I was practising the Highland fling, I mentioned my interest in insects and showed him my captives. 'Yes,' he said, but he said it with no marked conviction.

Torn now between self-justification and the need to get a move on, I asked if he'd noticed the squashed toads. He said something about the paddocks were crawling which struck me as a singularly improbable place to find amphibia, and off I went.

Madam, who had been trying to photograph two coal-black lambs who seemed distinctly unpopular with the rest of their racially minded playmates, heard me out patiently. She even took kindly to the suggestion that, if the opportunity arose, we might try our hand at adopting a toad. Much can be done by devotion.

A crippled lady who helped to look after the reptiles at the London Zoo developed such an attachment to a Komodo dragon, a ferocious-looking creature about five feet in length, that it followed her around the Fellows Garden and, at her bidding, was restrained from snapping up the nasturtiums which were much to its taste.

The word 'paddock', I discovered later, comes from an Icelandic root and in some dialects of the north of England is used for both frogs and toads. My informant referred me to *A Child's Grace*, a poem of touching simplicity by Robert Herrick.

> Here a little child I stand,
> Heaving up my either hand.
> Cold as paddocks though they be
> Here I lift them up to Thee,
> For a benison to fall
> On our meat and on us all.
>   Amen.

From the reservoir the road inched up to close on a thousand feet in a series of ample curves. A little upon one side, and you catch glimpses of a seeming infinity of moors bounded by rough grazing, whilst below the other the landscape falls away sharply, down, far down, to the Vale of Mowbray with farms tucked away in the folds of the *Kliflond*, now the Cleveland Hills.

This is the watershed of two systems of rivers: to the north is the grossly polluted Tees, and to the south and south-east an aereation of troutful streamlets intermingle in the Rye on whose banks the Cistercians built their masterpiece, Rievaulx.

I cannot for the life of me understand why the Chief Dirgers settled on the muddiness of Scarth Nick for the start of the Lyke Wake Walk when there is good board and bed in Osmotherley, but there are, I suppose, strong elements of the Yorkshire tendency towards black humour in almost anything associated with death, and some parts of this roller-coaster-like route were used as corpse roads especially between the mid-eighteenth and nineteenth centuries.

When Britain underwent a prodigious cooling period known to climatologists as the Little Ice Age, the Arctic literally crept south. During the great frost of 1684 oak trees split in half with a noise likened to gunshots; numbers of forests were devastated. Much of the country's livestock perished. In temperatures that froze the Thames to a depth of several feet, people dropped dead in their tracks. In the north the winters were not only fearfully cold but extremely protracted.

When, in such conditions, moorlanders died in lonely homesteads, their bodies were stored frozen in outhouses perhaps for a month or more. Coffins were made ready for such events and when at last the ground thawed the corpses were carried by hand to the nearest cemetery. Dirgers accompanied them along these corpse roads, tracks set apart for the conveyance of the dead, and as they walked they sang. The words of at least one dirge are known. It is the Lyke Wake, the watch and ward over the frame of an unearthed and unsanctified soul.

> This yere neet an' ivery neet
> An' ivery neet an' all,

> Tak' fire an' salt and candle leet
> An' Christ redeem thy saul.

To the accompaniment of spine-tingling percussion and the braying of brass that rises, verse by verse, to an enormous, an almost frightening crescendo, Benjamin Britten put the dirge to music. Shortly before he died, I wrote to that enormously gifted man and asked him where he had found the words. He replied saying that he couldn't remember, precisely, but thought they came from an old anthology.

Credit for opening up the track is due mostly to a modest fellow called Bill Cowley who puts you in mind of Andy Capp. He comes from an old Cleveland family and when, after several years in northern India, he returned to his own grange under Black Hambleton, he thought often of those days in the Himalayas and set about a minor Everest of his own making, the opening up of a track across the highest parts of the moors. He said at the time he had no intention of doing the walk himself. He was too busy building up what today is a fine herd of cattle on several hundred acres of land. But as nobody took up his challenge to complete the route he envisaged in twenty-four hours, he set off with several of his old mountaineering companions and, with a few naps on the way, got through in a little more than half that time. Thereafter the lonely venture was doomed to success.

Thousands accomplish it every year. Some have done it more than a hundred times, and double crossings in the time are not uncommon. All successful entrants are admitted to a lively club of deadly serious dirgers who twice a year hold wakes or post-mortems. They are assembled in orders of tribulation according to what they have done or left undone. In addition to Chief Dirgers, the company includes the Melancholy Mace Bearer, the Misguided Foundation Members, the Cheerless Chaplain, and Past Masters in order of Passing.

The pity is that those who scramble and splosh their way from Osmotherley to the coast seem, like Belloc on his *Path to Rome,* to be wholly oblivious of what can be seen on the way. They complain about the weather, the miles still to be endured, the state of their feet, and the condition of the path which, God ha' mercy, is largely of their own doing.

110

The cairns on the skyline; the Emperor moths and Green Hairstreak butterflies; nesting golden plover; the sight, occasionally, of harriers slowly winging their way back to the forests of Hartoft – all this and more might not be there at all for the young collectors of badges and certificates. I find this wholly incomprehensible to many of the older folk I have talked to, veterans who have done the walk a dozen or more times. We may forgive it among the young for, let's face it, the lad who has not got slightly pickled, wooed a wench, been to Covent Garden, seen a blue movie, and walked or run at least forty miles, is as little to be trusted as an unvaccinated infant.

On the slopes below the high tops the eye is caught by declensions of grassy knolls or hummocks that become progressively more rounded as they fall lower and come to rest. They are known locally as slacks. When I first trod the blackamoors, the uplands of that dark soil, I assumed these slacks were bygone industrial workings for jet, iron ore, or pieces of crude brown coal which, from their tendency to explode on a domestic hearth, are called Danby crackers. The knolls, in fact, are beds of rock which have slid over layers of greasy shale.

On such a knoll stood a cheerful lad with tousled hair, the son of a local flockmaster. He was training a sheepdog as young as himself by chucking a ball down the slope and, by a series of whistles, ordering the animal to retrieve the thing or stand guard over it. They were doing fine. Between the young of all breeds there is an endearing rapport, for they can make a game out of anything. This surely is one of the fundamental differences between the young and the not-so-young. Substitutes are not acceptable to the mature mind, which desires the thing itself.

From the way the lad lifted his arms occasionally, gestures which, as far as I could see, had nothing to do with the job in hand, I realized that in his mind's eye he was bringing a dozen ewes round the last hurdle at a county sheepdog trial, and was intent on winning the cup, too. But when he saw us, or rather when his dog stopped and pointed, the lad hung his head somewhat and threw the ball less far and whistled less bravely.

Not an eloquent youngster, but then who would give away heart-felt secrets to any stranger who asked? How old was the pup? Eight months, he said. How had he come by it? He'd picked it out of a litter of five. What had he looked for? In a nice phrase he said his dad had told him to have a 'good look at the first 'un that spoke to me'. And that's how Tom of Cringle Farm had come by Gyp of Castleton. It had a good eye, not too fierce. His dad had told him to look for that as well, he said.

Zoologists are notably cautious about saying anything specific about the ancestry of the common dog. They will tell you it depends on what sort of dog you are talking about, and point to lightly hidden characteristics of the jackal, the dingo, and the wolf in various breeds.

> As hounds and greyhounds, mongrel, spaniels, curs,
> Shoughs, water-rugs and demi-wolves are clept
> All by the name of dogs; the valued file
> Distinguishes, the slow, the subtle,
> The housekeeper, the hunter, every one
> According to the gifts which bounteous nature
> Hath in him closed: whereby he does receive
> Particular addition from the bill
> That writes them all alike . . .

As Mark Twain put it in different context, the researches of antiquarians have already thrown so much darkness on the subject that, if they go on talking about the Laconian hounds of Sparta, the Molossus, the Tagetian tykes, not to mention Artemis and Actaeon, the chances are we shall soon know nothing at all. But, for all that, to me it seems indisputable that there is much of the wolf in the behaviour of the sheepdog, a fact I observed for myself whilst flying over the Canadian Arctic.

On three occasions herds of caribou were accompanied by, but not pursued by, packs of up to a dozen wolves which ran alongside them like cossacks on the flanks of Napoleon's retreating army. Game-wardens told me they had frequently seen wolves, acting presumably under a pack leader, first cut off and then strike down caribou, usually those with a calf to look after. How much of this has been brought out in the sheepdog, that wolf in dog's clothing? Local flockmasters were not particularly informative on the subject.

Like the young lad with the rubber ball, they emphasize the

importance of the eye which glares with a curious light when 'fixing' or restraining sheep from running away; they talk about their commands, either whistled or shouted. One of them made the thoughtful point that a good sheep-gatherer, the local name for a shepherd, should be able to 'read' his dog – that is, from its movements he should know what it is up to, especially when it acts on its own initiative, maybe to investigate something the gatherer hasn't seen; perhaps a ewe behind a wall in the first stages of giving birth.

The interpretation of what it's now fashionable to call cognitative behaviour among animals is, possibly, in part instinctive among shepherds, who are usually the sons and grandsons of shepherds. It could be, too, that some hermetic quality of their craft is such that they are unwilling to discuss the whole vocabulary of their signals with others.

They will tell you, most of them, about their basic commands: the sustained whistle which, from the Quantocks to the Kyles, means 'stop'. It's as imperative as a single note on the bell of a bus. There are local variants on whistles in sharp succession which to the dog mean, 'for God's sake get a move on' or 'turn left' or 'turn right' or 'bring the bloody creatures nearer' or, more difficult, 'move 'em away. We want 'em out on the common'. On a few points the more eloquent are prepared to talk at length. But until I came across the work of Gail Vines, a thoughtful student of animal behaviour, I could never make out what induced a well-trained dog to use its own initiative if it thought that circumstances justified something beyond the mere herding of sheep under supervision.

Dr Vines puts it down to a complex and, until recently, an unrecognized interaction between genetics and learning. The genetics of a working dog include behavioural traits or tendencies inherited from its forebears, those social carnivores the wolves. The investigation of those traits has been helped considerably by the fact that, for over a hundred years, the border collie, the commonest sheepdog, has been selectively bred to fulfil its role on the farm. The breed is now renowned throughout the world for its prowess which, like its ancestors', includes initiative.

Most caribou can run faster than wolves, so the wolves are often obliged to head off their selected victims and drive them

113

towards a point where one of the pack is lying in ambush, waiting for events it can envisage. It may be the pack leader or it may be an especially fast wolf conscious of its role within the pack.

The shepherd makes good use of this social response in dogs, and fosters it by acting as pack leader. A dog continually looks to see where he is, and, if temporarily uncommanded whilst, for example, the shepherd may be talking to a neighbour, the dog will circle the sheep and hold them contained until told what to do next. Some flockmasters consider it unwise to let a young untrained dog run with older dogs because the youngster may come to regard a mature dog as pack leader and begin herding sheep towards that dog.

Stories abound of the sheepdog's comprehension of what he is required to do. Dr Vines has recounted how, at line up to the shearing pen, one dog would always chase and bring back sheep escaping from the pen if they had not been sheared, but would leave the sheared sheep alone, though it had not been trained to do this. Another could tell, presumably by smell, which ewes were near lambing and bring them home unbidden. A dog can learn to pace sheep, automatically adjusting their speed and distance to the ups and downs of their territory.

Dogs often experience difficulties when faced by an aggressive ram or a ewe reluctant to leave her lambs. One such ewe had wandered away from the main flock and refused to be moved. It faced the dog square on, stamping its hooves. Stalemate? Not a bit of it. The dog returned to the main flock, cut off several sheep and drove them towards its stubborn charge. The ewe promptly rejoined her companions and the dog, with a sense of orderliness, drove them off together.

Since there is something curiously sheep-like in the sight of walkers trudging along a foul track only because thousands have tramped that way before, I tried to pick a route that avoided the worst places. Inevitably we strayed into heather, which makes for difficult going, or, worse, we encountered bracken which can be wholly enveloping; but until I tried to take a short cut to the top of the scarp and then, much later, a wholly wrong turning, things went pretty well.

In this business of striding out in the open air there is no

114

grand crescendo from hour to hour, or even from day to day. The wonder of it lies in moments enjoyed and unexpected sights seen, not in distance done. The going is made a lot easier when things such as backache – which makes the not-so-young feel they are even older than they thought they were – are tackled before they get out of hand. Lumbar pains envelop you with the stealth, the inevitability, of dusk. We experienced them, both of us, on that funicular beyond the sad-looking hamlet of Husthwaite pronounced 'Huss'ert' but not otherwise remarkable. A surprise, a disappointment in its way.

The fine timber of Scugdale had been admired, the stream forded, and the hamlet forgotten as we crunched through the pine needles of a fire-break in the forest. By a series of gentle contours we might have climbed up on to the misnamed heights of Live Moor without anything in the way of back-ache, but Old Nick who develops our consciences led us to the foot of an enormous incline, a cut through the trees. As the notice in bold print said, *Private – Keep Out*, we took to that staircase with added relish.

Up we went, up and up, avoiding fallen trees and mucky ground, at times literally clinging to the ascent. When at long last we thought we saw the open sky beyond the ridge ahead, it turned out to be that great dispiriter, a false crest, and we both felt that nagging sensation not unlike toothache among the lower vertebrae.

The prescription is to treat it at once. Without breaking or even lessening your accustomed stride, the trick is to bend or bow down from the waist as courtiers did and the pious still do. The relief is tremendous, and is bettered by doing it at intervals of about a dozen paces.

For those intent on sleeping *à la belle étoile*, the pack containing all the comforts of the night can be endured far more comfortably during the day simply by shifting the load from the shoulders to the hips, or vice versa. This can be done with a low-slung belt like the girth of a gunfighter in a Western. But a word of warning: the padded affair is attached to the frame by such a criss-crocheting of elastic strings and buckles and straps that it's best to work out how it hangs together before something which has worked loose has to be done up at an awkward moment. This provides as good an excuse for a short rest as the sight of an unusual bird.

Live Moor is high and windy, but ecologically dead. It could be that, in an effort to keep the bracken down, it has been over-zealously sprayed from the air. A wasteland. Not a beetle, not even the larva of a midge or daddy-long-legs. A gloomy half-hour elapsed before we saw a bird, a golden plover that skimmed over the exposed ridge of peat like a petrel across a petrified sea. With the exception of a detour around the equally barren runways of a gliding club, the inescapable route clings to the very rim of this blackamoor. It was sad to think that for thousands of years here were the forests of Cleveland which attracted the first colonists after the Great Melt.

They were the Bog People, the Maglemosians from Denmark and southern Sweden, who slowly poled and paddled their way across the swamps of what is now the North Sea. Who the first-comers were will never be known, but news of what they found in Yorkshire must have reached their less hospitable homeland, since a long series of Scandinavian settlements culminated in the great Viking colonization of the ninth and tenth centuries, events which took place nine thousand years after the Maglemosians arrived. The modern method of carbon dating is absolute. It is precise to within forty or fifty years.

Up to that time, probably for a million years or more, most of Britain had been honed smooth by successive waves of glaciers, but the dating of the Pleistocene, based largely on the scratch marks and the debris the glaciers left behind, is no more reliable than contemporary weather forecasts. The long-term clocks of geologists have yet to be equipped with minute hands.

The glaciers crawled south, but the Yorkshire moors escaped the main impact for by the time the Scandinavian ice-sheets reached the Cliffland, they had used up what, initially, must have been a fortune in kinetic energy. They had grown tired from much travel, but they effectively blocked the estuaries of the Tyne, the Tees, the Esk, and the Humber, and behind those dams of ice a thousand feet in height the swollen waters of half a hundred rivers began to rise and form

116

lakes which today are the fertile floors of the Vales of Pickering and York.

A cold unclear picture, a waste of ice as indecipherable as the Arctic, but, after the Great Melt, the setting for the flowering of Britain on an unprecedented scale. Among enormous beds of golden-yellow saxifrage, *dryas*, and the purple of gentians, there appeared the pioneer of our high latitudes, the birch, the slender tree that heals the contusions of the earth's face more quickly than any other. When Goering's airmen poured fire on the City of London, birch sprang up on the rubble of the bomb-sites within a couple of years.

As the moors began to lose their heavy burden of water, the pollen sequence in beds of peat shows that birch became intermingled with hazel, aspen, and willow and, eventually, stands of pine which, in isolated localities, have about them the quality of a bugle blast. Pine forests brought in wolves and red deer, the favoured prey of the Bog People who had established winter quarters in the Vale of Pickering.

Bows and arrows were their principal weapons – arrows tipped with slivers of flint known to archaeologists as microliths. With these all-purpose tools, mostly trianguloid in shape and no more than about two or three centimetres in length, they struck fire; they made knives for skinning and fish spears; they drew primitive pictures. And they left the little flints lying about in such profusion that one may assume that in summer the blackamoors were thickly populated by hunters. But the Bog People vanished as mysteriously as they came. What did they do with their dead? Their bones have never been found.

By contrast with the unutterable feeling of loneliness on Live Moor, the merry-go-round of bird life above Carlton Bank brightened us up no end. A host of rooks and gulls were making the most of a vortex of air that swept up from the plain below. Among them tumbled yelping jackdaws whilst high up, so high it was difficult to make them out, a dozen or more raptors including a fine pair of harriers slowly soared in circles.

On the ground, nesting among pools of sour water, we

117

came across a community of black-headed gulls. A bird on guard duty flew at us, cackling harshly. Without meaning to intrude, we disturbed a pair of snipe which zigzagged off, bleeping. Skylarks and pippits trilled, grouse gabbled, and anxious lapwings peeweeted their folk-name. On a patch of hummocky ground scarcely larger than a football pitch, at least eight species of birds were raising their families on the principle of the more we are together, the safer we shall be. The chances of a fox or a stoat sneaking in unnoticed were pretty small.

Hasty Bank hove up, and with our stint more than half done I discovered, too late, that I had turned off too soon, thereby adding at least five miles to what otherwise would have been a comfortable home-coming. My excuse? To my annoyance I had no excuse beyond that of over-confidence. I tried to bluff it out by saying we could get a better view of Farndale from the west, which is rather like claiming that St Paul's can be seen best from the top of Hampstead Heath. Although Madam put on a rather far-away expression, she took it well, I thought.

Up to the eighteenth century, the old name of blackamoor was widely used to distinguish between the extremely acid and badly drained land to the north and east of the plateau and the richer calcareous soils to the south. Blackamoors conceal at least three distinctive layers of forest in which the Maglemosians hunted red deer with their flint-tipped arrows. In his *Forty Years in a Moorland Parish,* Canon J. C. Atkinson, that Gilbert White of Cleveland, relates how one of his labourers engaged in drainage suddenly 'sank down bodily to a depth of at least three feet below that at which he had been working a moment before. As he sank a quantity of thick, black, puddly liquid gushed up all around him with the effect of giving him a most uninviting-looking bath far above his hips ... from his feet to half way up his thighs he was confined in a narrow cylinder'.

It appeared to be the ruins of a single tree, probably a Scots pine, which thousands of years ago had been destroyed by rising water during a climatic change. Or it may have been ringed and the upper part of the trunk burned by the land-hungry incomers. Like Irish bogwood, the roots are literally

118

pickled in the acid soil and, as a local put it, 'thoas auld tree troonks *will* work oop'.

Farndale, so unlike the blackamoors that hem it in, is renowned for a handsomely wooded rivulet, the Dove, and for a profusion of wild daffodils which each year attract coach-loads of admirers. Most of the visitors are carefully got up for the day's outing in fur-lined anoraks, knee-breeches, and socks turned over the tops of their daffodil-watching boots. It has become standard wear.

Only a few were in flower that mid-April afternoon when, more tired than we cared to admit, we looked up at the heavy clouds and the Blakey ridge which stood between us and our place at Thorgill.

The daffodils are the wild form of the cultivated plants seen most commonly in municipal parks, in my opinion a rather stiff and inelegant product of commercial nurseries. By contrast the wildling, *Narcissus pseudo-narcissus*, is smaller, with the trumpet-like tubes of the inner petals as long as but darker in colour than the more spreading outer ones. A fine point, which comes out clearly by the water's edge.

Because Farndale lies within the National Park, plants are meticulously watched and warded, pluckers are threatened with dire penalties, and the ground is largely ungrazed. All very fit and proper in its way, for gypsies used to harvest them in caravan-loads. Unfortunately the dillies have now spread to the point where they positively detract from the exquisitely hazy fresh spring green of those beckside alders. As a form of judicious control, I would turn cattle loose among them, but to the controllers of the Park the idea comes close to blasphemy.

Unfortunately, too, the stream in which the flowers admire themselves may yet put an end to the beauty and seclusion of Farndale. It rises high up in a valley which could easily be dammed. The City Corporation of Hull has for long had its eyes on that valuable commodity, and the limpid water that purls down from where the curlews call would be used to put out fires, flush toilets, and carry off sewage to the sea. As Aldo Leopold put it: few educated people realize that remarkable advances in techniques made during recent decades are improvements in the pump, not the well.

119

The story of how the ghost of a naked girl lured several young men to their death in that self-same stream might easily be dismissed as folklore founded on a fragment of fact were it not that a few years ago a local antiquarian made some remarkable discoveries about the life and death of Sarkless Kitty.

The curtain rose on that drama in the tempestuous year of 1787 when, after months of snow, the Dove twice flooded the lower end of Farndale. To reach the nearest villages of Gillamoor and Hutton-le-Hole, the local folk were obliged to ford the Dove at what is now the Lowna bridge, and then could only do so on the back of a reliable horse. To show that he had become a man, young Willie Dixon of Hutton twice waded across but, as most people knew, it was only to impress Kitty Garthwaite, and was unnecessary, too, since she had decided the previous year who should become Mrs Dixon. But she had had doubts. There were rumours that Willie had been with other lassies at times when only those courting seriously should be seen together after dusk.

In April of that year Kitty began to be concerned that their wedding should not be long delayed. There was more than one reason. But although they met together regularly at Lowna on his side of the river, so that he could carry her over to the Gillamoor road, the rumours about Willie's infidelity began to centre on that girl at Castleton who would inherit considerable property.

Kitty pressed him. He refused to give straight answers. On Whit Sunday evening in May they quarrelled. Angry words were said on both sides. Willie left Kitty there by the alder tree in the dark. Nobody saw her again, alive. What had happened to the distracted girl could be easily reconstructed from moist footprints and clothing scattered about in different fields. When they fished her body out of the pool below the ford she was wearing only her white sark, a sort of chemise.

The tragedy divided the villages. There were not a few who said that, since it was clearly a case of suicide, she should be buried at the crossroads with, if the thing had to be done properly, a stake through her left breast. Her mother, widowed only a few months earlier, could scarcely speak. She would not leave her cottage. At last she told the vicar that as by rights her daughter was already Mrs Dixon, it was Willie who would have to attend to the burying. But nobody had seen Willie since the previous afternoon.

Monday passed. And Tuesday. The unclaimed body was laid on a pile of hay at the Old Mill where a charitable soul, a Mrs Agar, after doing the last offices, removed the poor girl's sark and washed it, covering her meanwhile with some fresh sacking.

During a furious storm of rain on the Wednesday morning, Willie arrived home, utterly distracted. It seems that without telling anyone what he was up to, he had ridden to York at dawn on Monday, hoping to bring back a special wedding licence that day. He had overlooked the fact that it was Whit Monday and the offices were closed. He spent a frustrating Tuesday finding witnesses and persuading a reluctant magistrate to give him that licence. He then galloped back.

At Helmsley, twelve miles away, they told him what had happened. He made straight away for the Old Mill where Mrs Agar did her best to comfort him before she took him down to the barn. He brushed past her, ran up the steps, and then turned round to look at the old lady, astonished. The barn was empty. The imprint in the hay was clear enough, the sacks lay neatly folded, but the body itself and the clean sark were gone.

Mrs Agar was more surprised than he was – she had seen the body the previous night. But Willie, thinking that the girl's mother had somehow arranged matters, hastened to her cottage. She could tell him nothing. Nor could anyone else. Recalling that Kitty had a distant relative at the head of the dale, a half-cousin who was very fond of her, he rode there, but could learn no more. She, like everyone else, thought the body lay in the barn.

All that long day Willie, who by then was almost exhausted, rode the length of Farndale and Rosedale until, late at night, he knocked on the door of the vicarage at Lastingham, only to discover that once again he was the first to bring the news. But it was far from the end of the matter. The next morning they found his horse quietly grazing on the east bank of the river near Lowna ford, and Willie's body was recovered from the same pool, from which, four days earlier, they had recovered the blanched corpse of Kitty Garthwaite.

If the majority of the villagers thought that, like his mistress, he had taken his own life, they admitted there was at least the possibility that for once his tired horse might have stumbled and thrown him in the swollen river, and he was given a good Christian burial.

Three weeks later two young boys came home at dusk with a strange tale. They had seen Kitty sitting by the ford but, as one of them put it, 'she had nowt on'. She smiled at them and waved her sark. They were sent to bed early for making up such a daft tale.

In the autumn of that year, the riderless horse of the second of a series of victims cantered up the hill to the village just before the pub closed. It was recognized as belonging to a traveller who, against advice, had said he intended to ford the river that night. The next morning they found his body in what became known as Sarkless Kitty's pool.

The apparition appeared to others who were more fortunate. Local folk, always men, saw her at night, sometimes sitting in her tree beckoning, at other times running along the bank or wading in the water, naked, holding up her sark. It was said that animals, particularly horses turned out to graze, would not go near the ford after sundown. But strangers were lured into that deep pool; and when, over the years, ten or more were drowned there, the villagers approached the vicar of Lastingham to see whether with bell, book and candle he could exorcize that unquiet spirit in the name of the Blessed St Cedd. He confessed he didn't much like the idea. It smelt of superstition, but at last he agreed.

The service was the traditional Order for the Burial of the Dead, except that the priest stood in the shallows of the pool and after the words 'dust to dust' he added 'water to water'. It was reported Kitty 'did not trouble the company with her visible presence and the gathering quietly and reverently dispersed'.

Until the late Richard Crosland, one of the founders of the Folk Museum at Hutton-le-Hole, came across the Armadale Bible, Kitty was largely forgotten. Reports of the reappearance of the ghost were, to say the least, tenuous, but the sequel is more remarkable by far than the events which provoked it.

Among some books at a local sale, Mr Crosland bought an old leather-bound large-print Bible for a few shillings. It was inscribed *Joseph Armadale from his parents, 25.5th m. 1765*. Quite by chance he noticed a small 'x' against verse 60, Matt. 27, and at the foot of the page *x – inside back*. A closer inspection showed that something had been inserted between the end-papers and the board. It was a large sheet of paper, folded and covered with small neat handwriting, and signed, simply *H. A.*

Henry, the only surviving son of Joseph and Eliza Armadale of Rudland, the ridge above Farndale, disclosed that his younger sister Mary had died and was buried in the 'Quaker's garth', a walled enclosure about half a mile above the present Lowna bridge. They buried her on the Friday before Whit Sunday, 1787, that is, three days before Kitty's body was recovered.

On the Tuesday night, when the suicide was being discussed by almost everyone in the neighbourhood, young Henry and his mother and father, good Quakers all, sat round the table of their cottage 'up Rudland', heavy with their private grief. Precisely how the conversation went must be in part inferred from events which Henry felt should be set down clearly for the sake of his conscience. I shall relate it largely in Crosland's words.

They said grace. They ate their meal. As usual his father read a portion of the Gospels. It happened to be that chapter in which Joseph of Arimathaea went to Pilate and begged the body of Jesus. His voice paused as he came to the words

. . . he wrapped it in clean linen cloth. And laid it in his new tomb which he had hewn out in the rock, and he rolled a great stone to the door of the sepulchre, and departed.

After a short silence they all retired but, as he understood it, neither father nor mother could sleep. She said, 'That poor child under the sacks is on me mind.'

A pause, and then his father asked, 'Eliza, dost thou think Joseph left the bodies of those two thieves hanging?'

'Nay, I think he must have covered them somewhere.'

Another pause, and then, 'His own new tomb, Eliza?'

The only answer was a woman trying to control her sobs.

Then Joseph said, 'Dost thou think this is a leading?'

'There can be no doubt about it.'

Joseph got out of bed, saying, 'Then there can be no delay. It must be done at once.'

'I must accompany thee,' she said.

They rose together and dressed, and whilst Eliza stopped to take something from a drawer, Joseph brought round the old mare laden with pack-saddle, ropes, spade, and a pick.

Avoiding the few houses on the way, they crossed into Farndale and down to the Old Mill where Kitty lay. The barn was not fastened and, at a sign from Eliza, Joseph stood aside whilst she entered with her bundle. When he entered a few minutes later the body was wrapped in a clean linen sheet, and as he lifted it to carry it out a fragrance of sweet herbs surrounded him. The burden was quickly adjusted to the mare which had quietly waited and had made no noise at all, and they again took the track, this time for the burying garth.

On their arrival Eliza sat awhile with the body, Joseph going in with his tools. She could hear that he was at work, but there was no sound of the pick which surprised her. She was more surprised when she entered the garth to see her husband hard at work, opening the very grave in which their only daughter had been laid less than five days earlier.

Joseph saw her coming and, before she had recovered from her surprise, whispered, 'It could be nowhere else, my dear. His own new tomb.' So there, close above the coffin of their daughter, carefully bedded in dry leaves so that the earth and stones should not lie too heavily upon her, they buried Kitty Garthwaite.

Home from home

When anything untoward happens at Thorgill we have a convenient scapegoat; we blame the hob reputed to live under the nearby crag of that name. During our absence on a previous occasion he poured a bucketful of soot down a chimney which we thought adequately swept. A young jackdaw fluttered down too, and before the poor creature died under the kitchen sink it patterned the white-washed walls with what looked like Chinese ideograms. The hob has been known to loosen a tile at such a critical point on the roof that the rain poured in and brought down a substantial portion of the bedroom ceiling just before we turned up for a quiet Christmas. This, and much else, is the price of hobbery or, more exactly, the hazard of leaving a small place untenanted for part of the year.

Blackbirds shrieked as we approached the cottage in the eerie light of that April evening. For a songster with a limited vocabulary, this neurotic relative of the thrush could teach more tuneful birds much in the way of punctuation and volume control. In nicely modulated phrases, *Turdus merula* (meaning pure or unmixed) leads the almost-dawn chorus. In warm weather it burbles happily throughout the day, but at the mere hint of a storm, especially at dusk, the voice of the lone singer is filled with omen.

As usual we wondered what, if anything, the hob had been up to since we left. Perhaps all might be in order. But no. The key wouldn't turn. Robin Badfellow had locked us out.

After much exasperating fiddling about on the back door with a long nail, we got in to discover that something inside the mechanism of the front lock had rusted. But within the living-room all appeared in order, and as the logs began to spit and crackle in the hearth, a solitary Tortoiseshell butterfly fluttered down from the wainscot.

I still call her *Vanessa*, the cousin of one of my favourite insects, the Painted Lady, but somewhere in the courts of

125

nomenclature she picked up the generic name of *Aglais* which at least puts her among the oldest of the Graces. Within half an hour she was joined by seven or eight more. They emerged from behind the wooden pelmet, the backs of pictures and the log pile alongside the fire. They were hibernators brought out by the warmth, but I cannot explain how they managed to get in unnoticed. By the time we sat down to a candle-lit supper there were more Tortoiseshells around than could easily be counted. They fluttered against the windows reproachfully, but outside it rained with the noise of escaping steam.

Our living-room with a kitchen tucked away in a corner is of no great size, but beamy and comfortable. Though there were books and music to hand, letters to be read, and a host of small jobs to be done, we talked and talked until the candles burned low. Like that night under Hardknott it was small talk, for the most part, but for me the use of plural verbs made all seem as if the very materials of life were being turned over and properly rearranged.

Somebody who had clearly done well by the institution, probably R. L. Stevenson, once said that marriage is one long conversation chequered by disputes. Ours were of small account. They centred chiefly about how many days Madam needed to settle her affairs in a neighbouring township before we set off again, across the moors and Wolds towards Humberside. On the indisputable proposition that it depended on this and that, we snuffed the candles and left a hearth of glowing ash to the hob and the butterflies.

Soon after breakfast Katie set off in the rain. She returned before nightfall. It still rained; cold, sleety, uncharitable stuff that would have taxed the heart of a Stoic. Masochist I may be, occasionally, but not a Stoic, and until she returned I lapsed, mostly, into one of the capital vices of the Christian Church – that of *accidie* which is spiritual torpor. St Thomas Aquinas depicts it as a state of restlessness and inability either to work or pray. Lucius Cary, Viscount Falkland who was killed at the battle of Newbury fighting for the Royalists, said he 'pitied unlearned gentlemen on a rainy day'. What could be done about it? I decided to do nothing.

Through the rain-blurred window a profusion of different-coloured heathers in the garden appeared as they might to a

126

pointillist painter, or a fellow like myself who had lost his spectacles. Blobs of pink and white and the flaming red of *Vivelli* from Central Europe relieve the gold and mossy green of natives that flower only when the aliens lie dormant. In all some forty varieties have taken to a thick bed of peat scarcely twenty paces from door to gate.

There are heathers with noble names, *Praecox Rubra, Atrosanguinea, Praegerae, Elegantissima* and *Hiemalis,* and some with quite simple ones. Who were Ann Sparkes and Elsie Purnell? One can see them both in tweeds at the Chelsea Flower Show. But Ann gave her name to an exquisite little plant with reddish-purple flowers and bright green foliage tipped with yellow. She discovered that floral jewel among some quite ordinary-looking specimens of what a botanist would call the transalpine form of *Erica carnea.* I don't know where Elsie happened on her namesake, but its forebears are ling, the plant that clothes the moors.

If to all these you add a few Dabs *(Daboecia)* from the Azores, the cross-leaved heath, and half a dozen different kinds of bell heathers, the Ericas, a family of enormous variability, look fine all the year round. My own selection has been built up slowly over a decade. The flowers that die need to be cut back, but I had no mind to wade about in peat on a very wet day. *Accidie* stood between us.

Of all apologists for idlers, the industrious Samuel Johnson is surely the last to be expected on the platform of indolence but, predictably, he comes out with forceful arguments for being there. Boswell, who tells the story against himself, had suggested that we all grow weary when idle. 'That, Sir,' said Johnson, 'is because, others being busy, we want company; but if we were all idle, there would be no growing weary; we should all entertain one another.'

At times when I could most do with company I have likened the cottage to what a Highlander said of the inconvenient size of a bottle of scotch, that is, it's not quite enough for two but too much for one. When Tilly and I bought the place I drew up an inventory of my immediate neighbours, from birds and beasts down to the lowliest of insects and the most recumbent of plants. That, at least, was the plan in broad outline. In practice I didn't get very far with the flora until I beguiled that great soul, probably the best-known botanist in the north of England, to drive across the moors and help me out with the shy inhabitants of cliffs and bogs, including the beautiful Andromeda. Alas for us all, Catherine Robb is now looking for lilies and asphodel in the Elysian Fields, and no doubt her old friend Ted Lousley is with her, and perhaps Linnaeus and Albertus Magnus are of the company. Thereafter, with the exception of a keen-eyed shepherd from Egton Bridge who knew more than a thing or two about mosses and lichens, I went out on my own, ignoring what couldn't be easily looked up or pressed or pickled and sent to an authority.

Spiders outmatched me because they are, I suspect, much more intelligent than we think, but I took up with the mayflies and one in particular, the August Dun, as a man might with a mistress of long ago.

I came across her first on the Swale, not far from that ill-starred trysting-place with Hazel Brown. A delicate fly with wings the colour of a thundercloud and a body that gleams with the fire of her name, *Ecdyonurus*. With her I caught good trout. Perhaps I should have learnt a lesson from the mayflies: they go about their amatory play with unswerving resolution.

A warm evening in late July. No blackbirds sang in that month of moult. From somewhere down the Thorgill, a dipper, that aquatic wren with a white collar, remembering perhaps his courtship days, poured out his heart in one long rippling song. I felt pretty low. Tilly had died some seven or eight months earlier. In that undulatory flight peculiar to the mayflies, a procession of Duns flew upstream. With mounting warmth I recognized the August Dun and her companions, ripe for courtship. I had seen them on the Swale, the Wharfe and the Lathkill, but I saw them no more until we came to Thorgill.

> And so he conjures up the boy
> Stilled in a sudden dream, his eyes
> New-misted by the love of love,
> The force that makes the sap to rise
> The world transfigured and its sounds
> Conjoined in melting harmonies.

Another bank of insects flew upstream. They intermingled. For a moment they appeared as a palpitating spire against the

128

sky, twisting and turning in no apparent direction, and then gradually a rhythm became apparent. At first it was hesitant, uncertain, but there was a discernible rise and fall in the centre of the mass, the first movement of an aerial ballet. It increased in tempo until the whole spire lifted upwards and fell away in the concerted dance. For a few seconds isolated insects sparkled in the last rays of the light and then went out, as a random breeze might lift a dying coal to transitory brightness.

For those of us on the sunset side of the generation gap it comes as a bit of a surprise to realize our eyes are no longer as discriminating as they were; that at a distance we cannot readily distinguish between fieldfares, redwings and thrushes on the ground; but, perhaps from Old John who usually knew from the squeaks of opening doors, especially in the direction of the kitchen, what I was about, I have inherited a hearing ability which has increased in acuity as other faculties diminished.

This makes for constant entertainment in the open air but agony in towns and cities, particularly in pubs where the plop of darts and the shuffle of dominoes have long since been replaced by the demoniacal thunder of space machines, juke boxes, and one-armed bandits which, when the jackpot is breached, sound like a hippopotamus shitting bricks.

Even at Thorgill, where the sight of the moors is framed by a proscenium arch of apple blossom beyond the gate, I find it difficult, sometimes, to concentrate above the downward-falling cadence of willow warblers; and impossible when butterflies clatter on the window. I shooed them out that day, not caring how they fared in the rain. Companionship is a strange thing.

Although I have never been a cat man, my grandmother who shared Cleopatra's belief that there will be cats in heaven, often tried to palm one off on me. You need some company, she said. She may have been right. The dog is a noisy democrat, a mixer; the cat is an aristocrat, a snob, and you don't hear it stamping around the place. Helen Waddell tells how in the ninth century an old Irish scholar in the great monastery of St Paul in Carinthia took time off from his endless search for the right phrase in a translation from St Augustine to write:

129

> I and Pangur Bán my cat
> 'Tis a like task we are at:
> Hunting mice is his delight,
> Hunting words I sit all night.

As for being outmatched by spiders, a huge fellow, *Tegenaria*, one of the biggest in the country, used to emerge from behind the fire-irons but, try as I did, I could never find out where his quarters were. His custom was to come out and scuttle round the edge of the fireplace at night. If I made the slightest movement, he stopped. If I moved towards the creature, he ran. He simply disappeared. If I remained seated, we played that game known to children as Statues. When I averted my gaze, he moved, furtively, but at the slightest movement on my part he stopped dead in his tracks. No doubt his eight eyes were more than a match for my two.

Although I couldn't put a name to more than a few, we have several different kinds of spiders in the cottage; they live in untidy webs behind the pictures and in the corners of beams. Upstairs, occasionally they have to be scooped out of the bath, getting in, I believe, by way of the overflow or maybe the drainpipe. As they are rarely seen in summer, it looks as if, like the butterflies, the adults are seeking winter warmth.

Clearly the time had come to add spiderology to other interests, and I arrived at the cottage one day armed with tubes of diluted alcohol, muslin nets, and a fine book on how to identify most of our five hundred or more species. Perhaps a mere whiff of that preservative put them to flight; maybe spiders *know* when it's time to make off; for after much searching round in nooks and crannies where hitherto they had been abundant, I flushed out one or two immature creatures and several shrivelled corpses.

Imprudently perhaps, I told this story 'live' on the *Woman's Hour* programme at the BBC. Not noticing the glazed expression of the highly sophisticated young presenter on the other side of the microphone, I dwelt lightly on the courtship patterns of *Pisaura* and *Steatoda*. Spiders, I said, may be liked or disliked but nowhere can they be ignored. Some of their habits, I admitted, were not really nice by human standards and mentioned that the young of *Amorabius* sometimes started off in life by eating their exhausted mothers. I finished. She

130

gulped and then, without a glance in my direction, she said to the women of Britain, 'Well, thank heavens *that's* over,' and went on with the rest of the programme.

Katie drove back at dusk the next day, close to tears, carrying a copy of a local paper with a large circulation, the sort of paper which would be read by our neighbours. The woman reporter who had interviewed me in the Vale of Mowbray had come out with a tear-laden and essentially fictitious story headed *Bride Abandons Honeymoon Walk* and had bolstered it up with some quotes purporting to come from me. After writing a letter to the editor calculated to set fire to her pants, we did no more about it. On certain issues of a personal nature, the only way to handle the press is not to get into their hands, but it's remarkable how often I fail to profit by advice I give to others.

As to our immediate plans, it looked as if Madam would have to attend to her personal affairs for at least another week, but she was determined, she said, to walk as far south as she could manage in a day or two's time. I was bidden to try and do something useful. For my part, I said more than once that, as it had stopped raining, it was a pity we couldn't take advantage of weather which was obviously improving.

The next day it snowed lightly, and it thundered between squalls. In between times that mist from the east coast called a fret or a roke enveloped the moors, and I had nobody to argue with except myself. This is of the essence of discontent.

It will be apparent that I have more than a sneaking affection for anything appertaining to hobs, boggarts, banshees, spooks, sprites, pigwidgeons, wraiths, phantoms in general, and ghost dogs in particular. During a great mist on Dartmoor I listened in vain for the baying of the infamous pack of Yeth hounds. I could not swear that I once heard the huge dog called Barguest in Wharfedale, because it's largely wooded by the water's edge and, as every birdwatcher knows, the gruff bark of the stock dove – *wuh! wuh! wuh!* – is uncommonly like that of a dog. But there was a curious story of a ghost dog on the moors which, although I didn't know it at the time, had a tragic sequel.

About a year ago a neighbour turned up and after some conventional remarks about the weather, asked if I'd 'heerd owt aboot t'owd feller an' his dog aboon t'Eller beck'. In fact, I'd heard the story not once but several times and, within the thick of decorative particulars, the stories were all much alike, especially in respect of where the materialization was said to have taken place. Somebody hurrying across the Fylingdales section of the Lyke Wake Walk at night had seen the eerie shape of a dog and a man who either could not or would not speak to him. The place lay between the Eller beck and the cairn called Lilla Howe.

Unlike the vast majority of cairns on the moor, low mounds which date from the Middle Bronze Age, the one where the silent man had been seen was probably the seventh-century burial ground of that shrewd seer Lilla, minister to Edwin of Northumbria, or so Bede tells us.

The current tale, of course, gained some weight in the telling. The garage man's account matched my conception of the Barguest. Smaller, perhaps a wolf, in the opinion of another, who pointed out that the grave wasn't all that far from Wolf Pit Slacks, the place where the last wolf in Yorkshire was reputed to have been speared. According to the gamekeeper, the Silent Man lifted his arms slowly, whilst the van-driver from Pickering thought he wore a flowing cloak. Here were several stories about an apparition near the bones of Lilla who, some think, foretold Edwin's death at the hands of that old ruffian, Penda of Mercia: was he warning us of something undetected as yet by the radar antennae of the Early Warning System that comb the air above his grave? And, come to think of it, what was the van-driver doing out there at night? *And* the gamekeeper? After a few days it emerged that all had heard the story directly or indirectly from groups of Lyke Wake Walkers. They had been looking for something around the burial mound, they said.

What that *something* was appeared in two issues of the *Newsletter* of the Long Distance Walkers' Association. In bold type, the editor bade his readers 'Beware of the Silent Man and the Dog that does not bark'. There was no explanation, but clearly the injunction affected at least one reader. Presumably after much hesitation, a professional man from Lancashire who gave his credentials asked the editor what on earth that announcement meant. Before it appeared, he said,

132

he had seen the Man, and his friends had persuaded him to describe the occasion. But for the fear of ridicule, he would have recorded the matter earlier.

A moonlight night. He was making for Ravenscar at the end of the Lyke Wake Walk. Near the fence of the Early Warning System he had the overpowering feeling of being watched by somebody or something. He stopped and turned round. Close to the fence he had just passed, he saw a man and a dog. He hailed him. There was no reply. Thinking it might be a guard, he went back and addressed him again. Total silence, though the dog's eyes flashed green in the light of his torch. Thoroughly disconcerted, he hurried on towards Lilla Howe only to find that the Silent Man and the dog were still there, watching him. At this, he admits that he began to run. Although he later returned to the place with friends, they could find no object, neither gate nor standing-stone, to account for what he had seen. Could the editor explain?

He could. He said he had seen the quotation on a page of his desk calendar. He didn't know what it meant, but thought it might intrigue walkers who were constantly encountering dogs. My own disturbing experience at that infamous burial ground must wait until we resumed our walk.

Nowadays superstition clings to the blackamoors like mist, materializing in times of local disaster when the atmosphere thickens and the way ahead looks bleak. It might be prolonged snow, or a drought, or the fires which have reduced thousands of acres of useful grazing to carbonized peat. When this happens, it's time for the old custom of making signs, for fumbling with lucky stones, or changing clothes, putting on something outlandish to outwit misfortune. Fisher lassies with men at sea have been heard to say, 'Ah deant like t'look on them cloods an' t' winds gettin' oop. Let's gan' 'ome and turn oor sarks.'

Up to the middle of the last century there was scarcely an isolated village without at least one wise man and a competitive witch or two, who were not always the maleficent beings they are usually made out to be. Their presence might be explained in part by the decline of the Church of England at that time. Troubled folk had no-one to resort to except secular dispensers of advice. From the many stories told about them, the wise men seem to have been uncommonly perceptive and often gifted with what seem to have been telepathic powers. Famous witches were commonplace: Nan Harwicke of Spittal Houses, Auld Nanny of Great Ayton, Nanny Howe of Kildale, Bessie Slack of Wensleydale, Peggy Flaunders of Marske, Anne Grear of Guisborough, and many more.

It is likely that the Enclosures forced many old women without support into a precarious life of begging and necromancy in a hovel 'on the common'. Some witches were originally midwives who, with their knowledge of herbs, were also healers, and then through some twist of misfortune or age turned to sorcery. The cats they lived with were not so much evil familiars as their sole companions and, in part, providers. Cats brought back mice, even young rabbits which were skinned and tossed into the pot on the peat fire. Much has been made of the outlandish clothes of the dark sisterhood but, like their incantations which were largely gibberish containing some fragments of Latin and Hebrew, they no doubt added to the atmosphere of the supernatural.

Between the witches and the dispensers of wisdom there appeared, inevitably, some weird go-betweens with the uncompromising name of warlocks or oathbreakers, traitors *(woerloga)* both to God and man. Flockmasters who slapped hands on a deal on a sale or hiring and then broke their pledge might resort to a warlock who would have to be pretty careful what he said and did. Otherwise he might finish up in the village pond.

So-called magic powers are part of the underground of the occult. Whether you believe in the dark sisterhood or not, nobody who has seen the paraphernalia of local witches in the Ryedale Folk Museum can doubt they existed until at least the turn of the century, and most people who have spoken to Mr Bertram Frank, the co-founder and former curator of that treasure house, come away convinced there are still wise men among us.

One of our troubles today, says Colin Wilson, is narrowness of consciousness. It is as if we are trying to see a panoramic scene through cracks in a high fence, but are never allowed to look *over* the fence and see it as a whole; and that

134

narrowness lulls us into a state of permanent drowsiness, like being half-anaesthetized. Were it not for evocation, for weaving what is seen and understood into a much larger pattern of events, walking would be as dull as sitting in a room without a view, without books or objects that represent a much larger world. A writer lives at best in a state of astonishment.

The next morning we were up and away before Edgar had even begun to sort the mail. From eight o'clock onwards, our neighbours approach the post office for gossip and groceries, letters and newspapers, like bees to a hive. Some, perhaps the majority, live within sight of that huge sycamore which, instead of the usual spinachy pond, dominates the village green. Others, and we are among them, live a mile or more away and account the insulation providential not least because, on foot, the shortest way down to the village green is by way of a pannier trod, a line of stones sunk into a rough pasture and a high walk above the alders of the Seven beck. Given reasonable underfooting it takes about twenty minutes.

Whenever he sees us setting off with a pack bigger by far than his own, Edgar the post, a kindly man, greets us with a mildly exasperating, "Aving a bit of a break like?' He said it again that morning. I smiled a bit bleakly but, not wishing to be outdone in rural formalities, hoped his feet were in good nick. The mild joke misfired. On one occasion, when his little red van had broken down and I saw him tramping up from the village on foot, I put the same question to him and lack words to describe briefly his indignation. John Wilbraham, one of the country's leading trumpet players, a virtuoso with regular engagements abroad, once said, a little sadly, that he is often asked what he does during the day.

Occasionally I do a radio show or the like, and mention the village, which is my apology for breathing among those whose staple or sideline is getting by with a flock of moorjocks. They are black-faced sheep with mealy noses, an old and very hardy breed of Swaledales with coarse grey fleeces of value chiefly to manufacturers of carpets and stuffers of mattresses. Largely because of a lack of functional walls and gates, a few free-booters, a polite word for fodder-stealers, allow their

135

charges to graze on other people's land instead of on the common.

Since there is no way of getting through the village without acknowledging or disavowing your neighbour's notion of what you are up to, a polite nod here and there served to assure the curious that we were out for the day. Perhaps to Fylingdales, I said, although already we were talking about where we might meet up again in Lincolnshire or Norfolk.

Of all footpaths out of the village the least used by far is 'up Noddle', the name by which Northdale Rigg has been known since marauding Scots sacked the priory one death-cold night in the fourteenth century, and, as a Victorian historian put it, 'had their way with the brides of God'. The details of this rapine, one of uncountable assaults in those centuries of tumult, are lost to us except for a number of critical dates.

Edward of Caernarvon, 'destitute of any serious purpose', and his adulterous wife, Isabella of France, sat on the throne, but with no security beyond the will of the barons. His northern forces had been smashed by Robert Bruce at Bannockburn and 'roghe-footide Scottis' repeatedly pillaged the rich monastic pastures south of the Tyne. After one foray when the Celts chased the King's men to the very gates of York, they swooped down into Rosedale on their way back home, presumably to avoid the great keeps of Helmsley and Pickering. They stayed long enough to roister and wreck the priory – perhaps only one night, but much can be done between dusk and dawn. It took a year to repair the damage and reunite the frightened sisterhood.

The next we hear of the sisters is that they were up to no good, and the archbishop arrived in person 'to administer chastisements and penances'. Today the population of the whole valley has shrunk to a twentieth of what it was a century ago, when over four thousand badly paid iron-miners slept in beds left warm by those on different shifts. The steep slopes of Noddle, the tributary dale behind one of the village pubs, are lonelier now than ever they were in the past. Only two of the nine farms are intact, and in one of those, within my recollection, John of Northdale took poison, 'unable to cope', said the coroner, reluctant to probe into a tragic story.

Like no family of Lapps

Charles II stopped here

The swirling Swale

Missing man dead on moors

A SEVEN-YEAR OLD Scarborough school groundsman, when he appeared last Monday, set out to catch his missing dog, was found dead, Whitby at the ...

Little Ronald Hodgson of South-western Barms-coving, his dog, wife's Burns-coving that her wife's been ... gone returned home by the night several hours later. An extensive search by police and no sign of his ... villages found no guards of Mr Hodgson's Ard injured state.

His body was ... police arrived at Scarborough ...

Chief Inspr Jim Jameson said: "We had no idea how long Mr. He still not known on the moors. He does, not known until after today's postmortem how long he had been dead."

Wild day at Walesby

No thoroughfare

Boston Stump

Master shrimper

Wind and flint at Cley

Cohorts of conifers

Bad afternoon in Essex

Epping Forest

Journey Home

We clambered up the shoulders of that ravine, eager to get on with the long journey ahead, to straighten our shoulders on the broad track above. But it was hard going made worse by petulant showers.

I don't know whether those birds of prey, the harriers, have been given the scientific name of *Circus* because they dance in the sky, but the pairs that visit us year after year are uncommonly good at aerial acrobatics, and they were at it that morning, looping and tumbling over on their tails. Courting couples of hen harriers are marvellous to watch. The male bird swoops down, wings part-bent but still beating loosely. Within a few feet of the ground he swoops again, turning over to show off his pied costume, whilst his paramour makes as if to clutch at him as she loops the loop. Her intention of having him on her back before sundown could not be expressed more plainly. Hugely entertained by it all we trudged on, and within half an hour had climbed up on to the eastern half of the Lyke Wake Walk.

This is another old corpse road, neither better nor worse than that length from which we strayed at Farndale Head; the underfooting wet and flatulent for most of the way, but where the peat is heavily intermingled with sand the impression is of walking on puff pastry.

We glanced back to where the shapeless remains of Loose Howe appeared to be slipping below the horizon. A remark-able howe. There, nearly fifty years ago, archaeologists unearthed the remains of a man interred in a boat made of oakwood, with two smaller boats nearby. One of them had been used as a coffin lid. The vessels had curved prows and slots for the rudders. The supposition is that, like the ancient pharaohs, this chieftain of the Bronze Age had been provided with ceremonial transport for his voyage into the afterworld. No mere shepherd would have been buried with his skin cloak inside a boulder-ringed mound nearly two hundred paces in diameter.

His afterworld is now a numbered box in the vaults of the British Museum. Some gold-seeking Normans had also tried to find him: they left their broken sherds behind, but stopped digging when they came across the ashes of one of his descendants in a simple clay pot.

J.H.—7

The veneration of a boat by nomadic herdsmen during a relatively warm and dry period of prehistory is difficult to understand. Prehistoric man saw the world around him through the screen of his own culture. He had a spirit that left him during dreams, and he knew that one day it would leave his body for ever. Had the boat encased the earthly remains of one of the early Maglemosians, it would be perfectly understandable. In his imagination, at least, the crude dugout would ferry him back to his ancestors across what is now the North Sea. But that period of immigration would have been as alien, as strange, to the builders of barrows as theirs would be to the incoming Romans.

Of some thousands of barrows on the moors, few are more catching to the eye than those between the upland harbour of the death-ships and our destination that night – the moorland below the huge spheres of the Fylingdales Defensive Early Warning System. To reach that affront to the grazing rights of the commoners, we mounted Shunner Howe which has been used as a pit for fighting cocks; we peered at Blue Man i' the Moss, a freakish boundary stone on the carbonized wastes of Wheeldale; and we jumped across the Murk Esk, bridged nearly twenty centuries ago by plume-helmeted legionaries on their way to their own watchtower across the German Sea, at Whitby.

Here is history boldly displayed on unwalled moorland, with stacked turf and deep holes dug to get at the stuff of ornament and war, jet and iron. To strangers the crests of these riggs are gaunt, perhaps forbidding, but offhand I can't think of a more evocative trod. And here, as almost everywhere on these moors, the horizons are constantly changing in their relationship to one another. From the Ravenstones on Wheeldale you may catch a glimpse of the fine, pencil-drawn crest of Goathland behind Two Howes Rigg, and, behind them, only the tabular limestone to the east remains as if suspended in the air.

In the exhilaration of breezes that blow spring-fresh and fragrant, it would be easy, you might think, to portray it all in the deft strokes of water-colour, but the wefts, the patterns of the mosaic, are as elusive as cigarette smoke. The colours, changing only with the seasons, are patches of mosses and bilberry, ash-grey lichens and newly-sprung heathers in green, grouse-brown, and gold, colours which have about them the intricate lustre of oriental rugs, especially those from Sena and Khorasan which are much favoured as camel-trappings.

Of the treasure we took from the moor that day are two pygmy flints the size of a penknife blade, so perfect, so exquisitely serrated that only a highly skilled craftsman could have made them. They lay almost buried in the carbon layer of a fire which had raged for weeks not so long before. The military and the air-force had to be brought in to put it out. Though slightly burnt, the pale blue and the milky-white translucence of the flints had retained their chatoyance, as you may see it in the eyes of a cat in the almost-dark.

These flints formed part of the hunting and the kitchen gear of the invaders who came in when the ice melted. Like their clumsily named forerunners the Maglemosians and Azilians, they came originally from Scandinavia. A skull found with similar implements in the MacArthur Cave at Oban in the Highlands indicates a narrow-headed race of mankind with deep temporal hollows, much like the Australian aborigines or jungle tribesmen in Northern India.

From the midden-pits of their encampments it is known that they hunted red and roe deer, elk, bear and wild ox. Chemical tests have shown that their flints were mined in Lincolnshire and at Grimes Graves in Norfolk. Without high-grade flint they could not have survived. It was as important to them as tin and lead to the Carthaginians and Romans, and uranium to the weapon-makers of contemporary powers.

The picture, throughout the summer months, is of broad-shouldered men humping vast panniers of unworked flint along the upland trails between the great arsenals of the mesolithic. One such trail runs south-west from Norfolk to flourishing markets in the vicinity of Wiltshire. It is 'sign-posted' by so-called pudding stones, conglomerates about the size of beer barrels. Characteristically they are composed of natural flint pebbles set in a siliceous matrix like raisins in a pudding. Several have been found. They are neither in keeping with the geology of the neighbourhood nor are they

139

the remains of glacial action. To judge from the abundance of flints on our moors, this must have been a northern extension of that trail.

Without help from local guides and spearmen, the flint- and skin-traders would have had prodigious difficulty finding their way up on to these long-distance tracks, which were their only means of crossing heavily-forested Britain in relative safety. To stray below would be to invite quick, or prolonged, death. For several thousand years after the Great Melt, the human population of Britain was vastly outnum- bered by, and constantly in competition with, large wild animals. Bears are fairly good-natured animals if left alone, but a lot of bears, wolves and wild boar around the place doesn't make for comfortable portage in forests far more impenetrable than any in Europe today. They were places

> . . . where nameless men by nameless rivers wander
> And in strange valleys die strange deaths alone.

The moors are the skin of a huge plateau. That becomes apparent to incomers from any direction who find them- selves faced by some of the steepest hills in the country. But what is far from apparent is how it came about that the rocks below the blackamoors are composed of petrified mud and sandstones which were laid down in the delta of a prehistoric river. In places these deposits are now fourteen hundred feet above the present level of the sea. Far from resembling a delta, the high ridges are furrowed by dales with flanks so steep that one visitor to the cottage, standing on the slope, said it was disconcerting to find he was looking down into his wellington boots. The shape of the land came about through buckling processes over a period of time almost unimaginable to even those accustomed to thinking in terms of geological periods.

The earth is approximately four billion years old. If we compare that vast extent of time with the twelve hours on the face of a clock, three hundred and thirty million years represent one hour. The deltaic rocks of the moors are a hundred and fifty million years old or the equivalent of a half an hour. On that scale, man has been on earth for only the last ten seconds, and the era of Pygmy Flint people is a mere fraction of one of those seconds.

We gradually overhauled a group of walkers. A slight problem here since, unless you are socially inclined towards gymnasts, you are obliged to slacken speed or push ahead a notch or two above normal and pull away from those with a slower speed. Those we encountered were slower since they had started far behind Rosedale, the half-way mark. And I have no mind, I confess freely, to walk far in the company of those whose thoughts are primarily on their destination, which is what the Lyke Wake Walk has become – an obstacle course.

With a more intimate knowledge of the moor we swung off the much-beaten path and cut off a corner by venturing across an extensive tract where, five years earlier, not only the heather had blazed but, at furnace temperatures, the peat had burned deep underground. We paid for our independence.

Next to nothing had grown on the carbonized soil. At each footfall we raised swirls of black dust. I recalled that long after the fires had died down, the wind picked up so much death-white ash that the sun could scarcely pierce the murk. We came across the ruins of a fire-engine, one of several abandoned when their tyres caught fire and the machines began to sink. And we paid for our pride too.

We were rapidly overtaken by one of the finest walkers I have ever seen. Though clearly on our heels, he appeared, it seemed, almost out of nowhere. No clenched-fisted bottom-waggler. No sweaty, grunting jogger. No heel-and-toe man out for the London to Brighton road record. Like Atalanta of Eskdale, the Adonis of Howl Moor seemed scarcely to touch the ground.

When out-matched, point, game and set, I have cultivated a slightly detached air of approval. 'He's pretty good,' I conceded. Madam, who knows the ploy, enquired, conversationally, if I had any ambition to keep up with him. As the spheres of the Fylingdales system gradually inched up over the most distant horizon, I reminded her we still had seven or eight miles to cover: Fylingdales, sadly, was as far as she could go with me. We were meeting there a friend with whom Katie intended to return. She had business of her own to deal with.

141

Over the Wolds

Precisely where I spent the night in the vicinity of those shapes of things to come is my own business. Enough to say I slept badly and got up several times to piss, imagining, perhaps in snatches of dreams, that armed guards with dogs were bearing down on my camouflaged igloo. There were no armed guards, at least not near the tent, but outside all appeared through shifting veils of mist; the wind moaned like an unquiet soul and there was rain, uncomfortable rain in the wind.

For want of something better to do in that long hour before dawn I mentally rehearsed the stages ahead. With a detour towards the coast it would take me, I reckoned, at least four days, maybe five, to cover the eighty or ninety miles to Humberside. That afternoon I hoped to lunch with the man who dispensed comfort. To reach his retreat near the coast entailed a devious route through the forests around the source of the River Derwent. What time will you arrive? he had asked. Probably about one o'clock, I said, for I could not have foreseen that I should encounter a tragedy on the way and, what with time spent in calls to the police, noon that day came late.

On Lockton High Moor the Lyke Wake Walk passes within a few hundred yards of the security fence around the Early Warning System. The path stands above the Eller beck, a torrent that bubbles out of the peat below Lilla Howe where the Silent Man and his dog were reputed to have been seen. As I knew the path pretty well, the ghostly incident never occurred to me until the youths described what they had found. My thoughts were largely on the weather. If the mist thickened it would be unwise to tackle that labyrinthine path through the trees. Better, perhaps, to cling to the ridge.

Thinking I was about to turn off in a different direction, the youths shouted and waved, urgently. They were walking towards Rosedale, and had set off from the coast an hour or two earlier. What else they had to say in the confused singsong dialect of Sunderland became coldly clear through glasses. A man lay dead across the track. Nothing could be done for him. His forehead was like moist marble. That much we established. The youths were well-equipped, thoughtful, concerned, and, though strangers to the district, anxious to do what they could, but were equally concerned about getting on with a long walk in worsening weather. As there wasn't a 'phone within two or three miles in any direction, I suggested they pressed on to the busy road over the bridge and stopped a motorist whilst I made for one of the farmsteads on the fringe of the forest to the south. The distances were about the same, but they managed to 'phone the police at least an hour before I did.

The walk took on a quite irrational urgency. Ignoring the peaty driblets of water, the source of the Derwent, I plunged through a miserable plantation of conifers on a compass course. Mistake number one: rapid movement is a poor substitute for a thoughtfully planned route. The map showed the entrance to a forest ride about a mile to the west. I should have gone back. I didn't. Fences appeared. I clambered over them. Another mistake: fences usually fence off something. On the north flank of Langdale forest they marked the boundary between a gentle slope and a steep rigg densely clothed in spruce. Yet another mistake: instead of cutting across the contours I should have followed the fence.

The outcome was that, with nothing much gained in time, I reached the high forest ride painfully scratched and thoroughly at odds with myself. God knows, I thought I had got over the tendency to bust through obstacles. Clearly I hadn't. What sort of substitute activity was I engaged in? I thought, wryly, of a question put to me years ago by a road-sweeper in the old city of Metz.

Not for the first time in that long walk to the Mediterranean, I was in a hurry. With its ruins of fortification around a maze of streets, Metz has much to offer, but most of all I had a mind to see the house which was the last place known to have been lived in by that master of opulent prose, François Rabelais. It stands in a courtyard of the old ghetto, the Jurue, but it took me an hour or two to find it.

A parking-lot attendant directed me to the synagogue nearly a mile to the north, where an old, a courteous, and very well-informed road-sweeper insisted on leading me back, very slowly. With his brush over his shoulder like a carbine, he pointed out the less well-known sights of the town, making a slight detour to include the fire station and the Central Maternity Hospital. At my badly disguised impatience, he paused for a moment and said, 'Forgive me, *M'sieu*, but from what are you running away?'

What, indeed? The *reliquiae* of a stranger, for whom I could do nothing except bring words of no comfort to those anxiously awaiting news? Or was it some conflict between a sense of duty and the trivial need to change my plans when I had hoped to be in high humour? If so, I had been well scourged for it.

From somewhere below came a familiar howl. Seeing my rucksack and assuming, I suppose, that I had lost my way, it took the woodcutter a premeditated half-minute to switch off his mechanical saw. I greeted him. I asked about a telephone. He shook his head, slowly. Few of our oldsters will ever give a direct reply to the first question put to them, any more than an Arab merchant will say at the start of a bargaining session what he really wants for his wares. I told him plainly.

'Aye,' he said, straightening his shoulders, 'that'll be the feller from Scarborough. Police 'ave bin seeking 'im for two or three days.'

'A walker?'

'Nay,' he said. 'Don't think he was. They say he were out lookin' for 'is dog. A little terrier. Right fond of it he was.'

'Is there a 'phone at Langdale End?'

'There could be,' he said, cautiously, 'but chap's not often in. He'll be out in t' forest somewhere. We 'ave to work around 'ere.'

I gave up and clambered back on to the forest ride where I thrashed about, making for one farmstead after another, only to find them deserted, swallowed up by the Forestry Commission, or without a telephone. Eventually a young lad with a motorbike and an outspoken father was told to take a written message, together with a map reference, to the rural postmistress five miles away. 'Alice'll have it off in a jiff,' his dad said.

Temporarily relieved of the dull nag of conscience, I wandered down to the river which flashed bright through the wildly dancing leaves of aspen, fronds of willow, and rowan hung about with creamy-white flowers. A fine tree, 'gay in spring and autumn but sad at midsummer – *media aetate tristis*,' said Linnaeus in that great work on his native flora. There is something therapeutic about a river in its upper reaches.

Of those that flow through the Ridings, and there are many, I have traced the biggest from source to dismal conclusions. The Swale is by far the most turbulent, the Ure the most aristocratic, the Wharfe the most diverse, the Rye the most intimate, and the Derwent in places the most beautiful, flowing as she does from the moors to the very woods of Rowaleyn until, patently tired, she loses her identity among water-meadows akin to those of the milky shires to the South.

She looks too slender, too self-contained, to provide vast amounts of highly palatable water for I don't know how many millions of people. But there it was to be sampled. Her liquid capital comes from uncountable springs which, being largely alkaline, enrich good soil for crops and sturdy timber. Her old name of *Derventionis fluvius* means 'the river where oaks are common'. They were common once, but not today, at least not within the bounds of the government's foresters. You would be hard-pressed to find a sturdy specimen in the spoil of Langdale and Broxa, Cropton, Dalby and Wykeham. In a phrase which will long outlive him, a former public relations officer of the Forestry Commission said the oak is just another name for sentiment. It is a sentiment which has been effectively banished from the upper Derwent.

From two or three old folk in Rosedale, refugees from this region, it has been possible to build up a picture of what this enormous upland heath looked like before the giant ploughs and the tractors of the Commission crawled up from the lowlands and the tenants were summarily dispossessed. They were bought out. They don't pretend it was an easy living but then, at the time, they were just farm lads who received five bob a week and their keep. But if their paymasters, the tenant farmers and, ultimately, the landowners had been given as subsidies a tenth of what is now being squandered on the production of second-rate pulp, the land could have been brought to life. Thirty thousand acres would not have become an eyesore relieved only by rustic furniture for picnic parties on the perimeter of a rural slum. It's not what the public wants; it's what they are forced to endure. The pity is that a sprawl of spruce has suffocated a beautiful river.

The Commissioners and their hangers-on, the so-called commercial timber producers who snatch up farms cheaply for tax-avoidance purposes, protested feebly during a full-scale enquiry – which came to nothing – that they were the victims of circumstances. Felons in gaol for theft, blackmail or rape might say much the same thing.

The circumstances were that Britain cut down so much timber during the First World War that Lloyd George set up the Commission, offering it as much money as it wanted to do what it liked. A secret plan to devote nearly two million acres of land for the production of pit-props upset even the complacent Treasury, who cut the requisition by half. But the Commission has been squandering public money ever since.

Because the Commission is first and foremost a deeply entrenched bureaucracy backed by a powerful body of land-owners in both Houses, no government has yet faced up to the fact that it could save a great deal of money by abolishing this self-appointed squirearchy and re-establishing farms and land largely for sheep-rearing and recreational purposes.

Unfortunately softwood, especially bastard spruce, grows with gratifying speed on almost any kind of land that slopes upwards, just as fireweed will choke a garden or hide a rubbish-tip. Therefore, say the Commissioners, plant soft-wood; the more uniform, the more efficient. Cover Wales. Hide the fine breasts of the Gaels. Transmute the Border country into a stripy travesty of Scandinavia. Tear out the oak, the ash, and the rowan, and plant easy-grown evergreens screened by strips of hardwood alongside some of the roads. This is known as environmental gain. Two centuries ago the black-faced sheep evicted the crofters. Now the conifers are evicting the sheep. As a critic put it: unless the Commission and the landowners, whose forestry is tax-linked to the Commission, receive Exchequer aid for creating beauty rather than low-grade chipboard, we must expect debase-ment. It's not enough to rely on the splintered zeal of conservation groups. We shall salvage a bluebell wood and lose an entire landscape. 'Thank God they can't cut down the clouds,' said Henry Thoreau.

A poet has called spruce 'the quietest of the carnivores' which has done away with bird, beast, and man; and from desecrated Wales have come the bitter outpourings of Gwenallt Jones:

> They have planted the saplings
> of the third world war on the land
> of Esgeirceir and the fields of
> Tir-bach by
> Rhydycwerau:
> And today there is nothing
> but trees,
> their insolent roots sucking
> the ancient soil.
> Trees where fellowship was;
> a forest where farms have been.

The pattern of the forest tracks may be fairly compared with the ribs of a grilled sole. As the uppermost ride, the spine of that dismal example of silviculture, seemed to be swinging away from where I wanted to be, I turned down one of the subsidiary tracks intent on reaching a large farm that stood out clear on the opposite side of the river far below. A stupid decision. It led into a dense plantation of those very trees, that unspeakable spruce, from which I had hoped to escape. But that I didn't discover, until sheer obstinacy and a scramble down a cliff prevailed against the more prudent course of clambering back.

I have never been a climber and never could be, and this was no climb to speak of. But in the Alps and other places, the need to climb down what I shouldn't have tried to climb up has led to an aversion to heights amounting to vertigo. I find looking down verticals of almost any kind increasingly disturbing. Similarly with forests. Misadventures in the Ardennes, the Vosges, and the Jura culminated in three very unpleasant days looking for a path through the overgrown wilderness of North Maine. And my memory of it?

Silence. The utter silence. Probably the blind wilderness in the sense of seemingly endless forest must always be more fearful than

147

the open bush, the plain, even the bare desert, for the plain and the desert allow for exertion, for the resolute march that dampens doubts and uncertainty and the irrepressible voice that whispers: you are lost, you are lost. The forest is the nightmare of half shadows and the trail that leads nowhere.

The memory has persisted. It took no more than half an hour to get through that woody squalor above the Derwent, but every yard of it had to be contested.

The man who used to dispense comfort on a prodigious scale had need of solace himself that afternoon. Tom Laughton's wife had died a week or two earlier. Her gradual decline and release came as no surprise to those of us who loved her wry arguments and rumbling good humour. But a long thread had been quietly snipped, a thread that went back to those days when, as the young chatelaine of the neighbourhood, she had chased Hazel and me out of her orchard at Headingley. Tom and Isobel had been good friends of mine when I needed solace.

She was his third wife. I remembered with what pride he had dedicated the story of his life 'To my wife Isobel, who has coped so lovingly with a burnt-out hotel-keeper and brought him to life again'. Tom Laughton's emotional brother Charles, the actor, rocketed to fame and the glow is still in the sky. Tom also achieved greatness but of a wholly different, a far more self-effacing, kind – that of a grand hotelier in the mould of Vicki Baum, and that of an outstanding art collector. The two pursuits were interlocked.

In their heyday, the Pavilion and the Royal at Scarborough were justly compared with the Negresco at Nice and that expensive resort of the homesick, Raffles in Singapore. Tom tells how some of his most spectacular chandeliers and paintings, today worth millions, were acquired from the landed but impoverished gentry of the Thirties. The huge carpet for the hall and double-galleried staircase of the Royal was designed by the Italian who designed one for Covent Garden Opera House. For fine pieces of furniture and *objets d'art*, Tom quartered antique shops throughout the country. Friendship with an elderly Comtesse who owned vineyards in France enabled him, 'at one step' as he put it, to buy a prodigious quantity of fine wine for his hotels. There is a touch of wand-waving here. And only a God-fearing Jesuit child could describe dispassionately how he came close to opening a hotel in Majorca with Madge, a prosperous and exceptionally good-looking whore. Dismissing it as 'a few wild oats', he says: 'We got on not only physically but in every other way.' Nevertheless, a critic of his book* says there is 'an odd blankness' about his revelations. Without ever seeming to want to, he builds a wall around himself.

Tom seeks to justify the mask by pointing out the similarities between the life of an actor and the life of an hotel-keeper. The actor, he says, depends on earning applause, the hotel-keeper on earning appreciation. The actor's applause is given by the crowd; appreciation for the hotel-keeper comes from individuals. That applies more to the hotel proprietor than to a manager. The latter is in a different position, having first to earn the appreciation of his financial masters which can make the hotel guests a secondary consideration. No guests of the Laughtons, and they included masses of celebrities, have been known to complain of neglect.

If his brother Charles hadn't walked out of the family's hotel business at a critical time, Tom might have become a country squire, a man who both loved and understood the land. Although he came from a fairly well-to-do family, he served his time on the moors and the Wolds like any 'prentice farm lad, ploughing, grubbing out turnips, threshing, and looking after the sheep and the horses. But there were troubles at home. The restless Charles wasn't prepared 'to dance attendance on the customers' who, in the opinion of their mother, a very strong woman, 'were sacred beings who had to be satisfied at all cost'. Two significant phrases. Tom says he went back to hotel work as though it had been his natural vocation. Charles soon became one of the best-known actors in Elstree and Hollywood.

Was Tom envious of Charles's success? At first yes, he says, but not after he saw what film stardom did to a person's peace of mind. In his search for perfection, Charles rampaged through the glossy world of film-making. No script quite

* *Pavilions by the Sea*, London, 1977.

fitted his concept of what he wanted to say, or how he thought it should be played. It usually had to be rewritten, and the re-takes during filming cost a fantastic amount of money. Occasionally whole projects had to be scrapped. In bouts of depression, he cursed his good friend Alfred Hitchcock; he refused to act under the direction of that capering ring-master, Joseph von Sternberg. Charles ran into debt. His homosexuality, admitted by his wife, Elsa Lanchester, but gently brushed aside by his younger brother, cannot have done much for his equilibrium. Charles would have been at home in the Rome of Catullus and Petronius; perhaps even better on the Athenian stage where Plato said that in vain does a sober-minded man knock on the door of the arts.

Charles had a hard life, says the ever-compassionate Tom. Charles was immensely successful, but at great cost. It would have been wholly unbearable if Tom hadn't been around to pick up the pieces, sort them out, and dispense comfort. Far from looking on his brother as an egocentric defector, it was Charles, he says, who gave him the idea of employing some of the best artists and craftsmen in the country for the exotic decor of his hotels, for buying great works of art, for organizing entertainment. Always Charles. Tom, busy behind the scenes, selecting special dishes and wines for Winston Churchill who simply said, 'I leave it entirely to you,' gives the impression that he just happened to be there at the time, which of course he was, like Martha.

In their different ways, the brothers, including the youngest, Frank, a somewhat shadowy figure, were closely knit, but the picture as presented is mostly of the imperturb-able Tom looking up to that erratic figure who played Captain Bligh, Henry VIII, Rembrandt, and Claudius. In our talks and our walks together it sometimes occurred to me that Tom's 'odd blankness' was the almost transparent smoke of a smouldering volcano.

When he saw the sex life of the animals on the farm 'bursting out all over', he says he began to understand what it was all about and longed for the time when he could get some practical experience. He met Madge on the street, just as he admits he met other prostitutes. When she knew he was coming down to London she 'cleared the deck', as he puts, it, so that he could stay with her 'without interruption'. After trips with Tom abroad, and even one to the family hotel in Scarborough, she wrote to say she was getting married. Years later she sent him a brand-new Rolls Royce which he took to be a despairing gesture from an unhappy woman married to a very rich man. He sold it, and sent the money to her husband's solicitors.

At the age of thirty-eight, when he felt his instincts were failing and his judgement was blunted through philandering, he married a young girl of good family. It took them only a week to realize they were hopelessly incompatible. His subsequent marriage to the beautiful Esmé, an officer in the women's Services, had a disastrous start with public disgrace and their enforced separation for nearly a year. But afterwards, he says, it was partly through their suffering that a bond of love and respect was created that became the strongest influence on their life together.

A lofty room in the Scarborough art gallery is dedicated to the memory of Esmé Laughton. It is full of pictures, landscapes, portraits, and still-lifes from his own rich collection. That afternoon he talked of what he proposed to put in another, an adjacent, room to be dedicated to Isobel. A curious, a touching mausoleum of masterpieces for two women who brought love and comfort to the ageing innkeeper.

If the cautious paladins of the national galleries, the fund dispensers, had more vision, Tom Laughton's own collection could become part of one of the most important in the north of England. It is the personal affair of a cultivated man, a pictorial autobiography. His early life is represented by John Dalby of York, whose seascapes of the east coast might be mistaken for early Turners; there are pastoral scenes of the Wolds on which Tom turned his back, and horses by Stubbs. Tom's horizons were beginning to widen. Under the influence of Bruce Turner and, of course, Charles, he placed Landseer sketches and Gaudier-Brzeskas in his hotel bedrooms although, as he says, they were not always appreciated.

Among much else, the perfectionist bought early Constables, Reynolds, and a wholly unique work, a cartoon of Van Gogh's last self-portrait. He ventured among the great

151

moderns, Pasmore, Sutherland, and Matthew Smith, and acquired many of the flaming canvases of his protégé, Zdzislaw Ruszkowski, whose vision and abilities, he believes, are comparable with those of Gauguin and Cézanne. Later on, Tom and I became at odds with one another on the subject of remarriage, but the dispenser of comfort grasped me warmly as I struck out for the Vale of Pickering the next morning. He remarried a few months later.

There is a notion that men are like salmon who, however far they swim in the oceans of the world, are drawn back to the streams of their youth. My own would be the Swale and the Wharfe, but it was in that gracefully wooded Forge Valley on the Derwent, the very place where I walked that morning, that I first watched men catch trout with a fly. Unlike my Padre of the Rueful Countenance, they were not only un-sympathetically disposed towards a freckled lad with a stiff rod and a can of worms. They had a word with the bailiff, who gave me five minutes to get out of sight. I scuttled back to Scarborough.

The stream is still beautiful, but more democratic by far than when the polished four-wheelers of the gentry, the Derwents, the Londesboroughs, and later the Sitwells, Osbert, Edith and Sacheverell, who lived not far away, rolled along the alder-lined banks of that bright water. Today there are rustic benches for picnic parties; cars nestle among the trees; and it's not easy to hear the shrilling of wood warblers above the sound of traffic.

Shortly before we left Scarborough for the last time, Father took the four of us there in a growler, one of the many horse-drawn cabs that stood for hire at the foot of the harbour steps. There had been bitter argument the night before about whether or not I should go back to the physical and intellec-tual hunger of a boarding-school largely peopled by the sons of poverty-stricken missionaries. As I had agreed to return, reluctantly, Father asked where I would like to spend the day. With the possibility of cocking a snook at that bailiff from a position of advantage, I said Forge Valley.

Although I never saw the fellow, the day went well until, for some perverse reason, I brought up the subject of school

152

again and made the situation worse by not saying outright why I so disliked the place. Father tended to inhibit argument as keenly as Old John encouraged it. He had repeatedly enjoined me to speak out or hold my tongue.

Sir Osbert Sitwell tells a story of how, while at Eton, a classmate committed suicide. At the memorial service the headmaster asked the boys whether they could give any hint whatsoever as to why such a well-liked and highly gifted lad should have done away with himself. A moment of silence before the proverbial boy at the back lifted up his hand. 'Do you suppose, sir, it might have been the food?'

Our problems at that Dotheboys Hall near Leeds sprang largely from a grossly underpaid staff who, with few exceptions, were either timid or tyrannical. Their favourites, the prefects, were allowed to flog us and frequently did under a fagging system that encouraged homosexuality. There were no outlets beyond athletics and the food could not have been worse in a penitentiary.

Notwithstanding the corned beef, the greasy stew, the hard home-grown potatoes, the tasteless rice, the plum duff, the bread and butter pudding, the spotted dick and tart rhubarb, we were aching hungry when our tuck-boxes were empty and our allotted pocket money of threepence per week was spent. It was as much of an offence to possess more as it was to be discovered kicking a spherical ball around. We played rugger, and only rugger. Soccer was the resort of the lower orders.

To sustain appetites quickened by three hours' sport each day, we stole or beguiled food from a Victorian kitchen dominated by an old and incorruptible Scottish woman and three Amazons with big breasts who whetted pubertal fantasies and satisfied our need for sugar and cheese. Our pimp, panderer or mackerel was a youth so innocent and good-looking that he was courted by a brutish-looking classics master and provoked a fight between two prefects. The father of this young Uranus trod out the Lord's grapes in distant China, unaware, I'm sure, that the fruit of his loins could put on a wistful expression and muster up a tear as smartly as some people can wiggle their ears – an aptitude which in later life, I heard, got him three years for selling

153

bogus insurance. But he could certainly charm those breasty birds, bringing us back bread, cheese, and bacon which we used to fry on a tin lid over meths after evening prayers.

At the school he got his deserts strangely. The Amazons raped him, or at least that's how we heard the story at third hand from a prefect who found him crying in the gym with his pants torn. We never did fathom the matter, but we all felt bad about it since, in addition to our having to subscribe twopence each for the loot, the Amazons were replaced in the subsequent purge by some flat-chested wenches from the village. I think of Uranus sadly, since I contributed largely to the expulsion of us both only a week before we were due to go down decently for the last time.

An old aunt, I discovered, had an amiable lover called Robert who bade me address him as Uncle Bob and not infrequently slipped half a crown into my ready palm. It so happened that Uncle Bob turned up for prize day in a rakish-looking Singer coupé which Uranus said he could drive. I disputed this, since I wanted to try out what I had only read about in the first volume of *The Children's Encyclopaedia* – A for Automobiles, with illustrations of the shift and clutch systems. Here was a matter, surely, which could be practically resolved.

We waited until parents and guardians were safely tucked away in the Assembly Hall, listening to the choir. I managed to start the thing in second gear and, after a preliminary canter round the Great Yard, contrived to get it as far as the nearest pub about two miles away, still in second gear. There, under the influence of two large sherries, I doggishly pinched the bottom of the barmaid, something which, like driving a car, I had previously only read about. The landlord, and may Lucifer boil him for ever in the pits of hell, 'phoned the school; whereupon, before the choir had got to the last rousing strains of 'Forty Years On', the brutish-looking homosexual Latinist turned up and we both spent the night in the sanatorium awaiting fell judgement.

They sent us home the next day. Father fumed. Hazel, as always the bright cinder among the ashes, listened patiently, unsure what it was all about. Miserable as I was, for a little while I saw things with terrible clarity as a glass marble might reflect the universe. There were, it seemed, no fundamental drives stronger than hunger, curiosity, and love.

Sweet Derwent run softly till I end my song. An orphan of the Ice Age, she wandered inland when the glaciers cut her off from the nearby sea. She had a difficult time of it getting down from the blackamoors to the Vale of Pickering, for the Hackness Hills stood in her way. Sinuously, like a guileful girl, she slid round their flanks, between Mount Misery and Hilla Green, until she could scamper down into the shade of Forge Valley.

All that took place long before the Pygmy Flint people slew deer on what are now the bare moors. Before those uplands were gripped by winters far harsher than those today, the emigrants from Scandinavia trudged up there every year, anxious for supplies of meat, and antlers and bone for tool-making. With the slim chance of picking up one of these slivers of flint, I crossed the river and worked down the untrodden banks on the opposite side to the road.

A foolhardy venture. It looked as if nobody had ever been into that wild wood, and for good reason. The river is the main drain of the moors from Fylingdales to the coast. She floods whenever the sea fogs crawl inland. In the leafy depths of Forge Valley, the east bank has been raised and nicely baulked for transport. But, as I discovered too late to do anything about it, the opposite shore is indistinctly contoured, amphibious you might say. The ground sloped gradually and the river gurgled through hummocky grass and huge horsetails. There was no going on, and I felt miserly about slouching back. So up I went, through a tangle of trees, briars, and scrub so thick that in places it had to be clumsily climbed. I lost an hour but gained such a view of the prehistoric lake below that the price of exertion was more than amply repaid.

Where the ice had melted thousands of years ago, there stood an immense depression, a land of abundance, the portion of Esau between the sterile moors and the sweet grass of the Wolds. The Vale of Pickering is rich in the mud of the blocked proto-Derwent. On the southern horizon the rim of the Wolds reared up, not in a great wall but in a heave, like an advancing wave. And as a wave breaks in a sparkle of foam, the vale seemed bathed in opalescent light.

> Had I a song
> I would sing it here.

And I would sing it in praise of Ruszkowski, that hermit of a man who decided that reality lay in the mind and the imagination. Until I acquired two paintings of his for my own, I looked at his work for years, marvelling at the flash of colour but at heart puzzled, since I couldn't make out what he was saying. Was I deficient in the art of seeing? Was it permissible to look up the sleeves of a magician? Some artists might think not. When a woman told Turner she had never seen a sunset like one of his, he is reputed to have said, 'By God, Madam! Don't you wish you had?' To me, Ruszkowski's 'Spring Tide' and lake scenes seemed no more than intriguing abstracts. Could this be the man who had painted his children with such compassion and Eve with erotic fire? Tom Laughton suggested that, with the titles in mind, I should look at one or two of his landscapes through half-closed eyes.

They leaped to life. The canvases became three-dimensional. It was only later, in an essay he wrote called 'Aureolism', that I discovered that Ruszkowski had taken the courageous step of explaining what he was trying to do. As a constructional element in his painting, he was treating light as matter. He was what a physicist would call a particle theorist. He gave shape to light. He pointed out that when an object is strongly lit, it radiates upon its surroundings and appears to us bigger than it is in reality. The most strongly lit parts are the most protruding, thus altering the shape of the object.

With strong contrasts of light and shade it is possible to observe that opposing colours provoke a third element, a sort of aureole. This can be seen in the evening when the yellow light of a street lamp against the blue of an evening sky provokes a halo around the lamp. Ruszkowski makes great use of this quality in his treatment of light-splashed water and sun-fringed clouds. But, as he says, in art as in life, theories do not always work. 'They only serve to help to formulate certain thoughts and experiences. What is greatest in art can only be felt – and this is impossible to formulate or describe.'

Without knowing what aureolism was, I had seen it in water on moonless nights. Fresh from the sight of his canvases that morning, I watched the Derwent flash through the trees below as if quicksilver had been splashed on the floor of Forge Valley. Against the black clouds that mimicked mountains, a tower of light stood above the ruins of Ayton Castle, and the face of the limestone quarries on the very edge of the Vale burnt with cold incandescent fire. But magic has its own time and season. With what I took to be unseasonable timing, the black clouds masked the sun; it began to pour down, and there was no comfort from aureolism in country seen through rain-blurred bifocals.

A stern-looking woman pulled up in an old but handsome car.

'Where are you going?' she asked.

'Over the Wolds, Madam.'

'I can take you to Malton.'

'Thank you, Madam. But I'm walking there.'

'Oh,' she said, pausing for a moment as if put out. 'You look too old for *that* sort of thing.' The remark dropped like the blade of a guillotine.

It was the sort of rain associated with funerals or the Isle of Skye. Not heavy, but penetrating. I dripped through Hutton Buscel to Gallows Hill, feeling like a felon. Cottagers stared through parted curtains. I gave them some pretty sharp looks in return. People who stare deserve the looks they get. Two kids made derisory gestures. I shook my fist at them. They loved it.

I try to tell myself that on these wind-swept islands the weathercock swings about and the barometer goes up and down more often than it remains set fair. Show me the walker who can remain unaffected by prolonged squalls and, if he swears to tell me how he does it, I will pace him hard for a day. For myself, I fret through setbacks of this kind. I spend the useless time trying to think of profitable things to think about, by which time, of course, the clouds are likely to have blown away. If they haven't one can trifle with words and rhymes, or draft letters to *The Times* about the inadequacies of the Meteorological Office. Or just stare at things.

Who, for instance, lived in that architecturally mixed-up

Wykeham Abbey? I put the question to a tweedy gentleman in the Downe Arms. 'Lord Downe,' he said primly. The Sunday morning lot were looking with no affection at my dripping wet pack. Sulkily I retired to a corner, steaming gently. Recalling that Celia Fiennes had passed that way, I fished out her *Journeys*. With my finger I traced her mapped route south from Scarborough to Malton. By nice coincidence I found I had just crossed her path. Over a couple of pints I read, avidly, of what she had been up to, and then left the pub in her train. The rain seemed more tolerable.

From London that intrepid lady had ridden to the east coast by way of Cambridge, Lincoln and Doncaster. She was on her way back through Malton, York, Pontefract, Derbyshire, Warwick, and Northampton. Except for the titles of her chapters, it is often not at all clear where she is heading for, apart from calling on those ubiquitous relatives, all good Whiggish anti-Royalists. But one of her kinsmen, known to some as the 'fat Earl of Lincoln', was cold-shouldered. Could it be that Celia found him a trifle overbearing?

He ordered his servants to beat a young lad to death for having the temerity to gaze at him in the street. The coroner's jury, mindful no doubt of the wrath of His Grace if they cast any doubt on the probity of his action, promptly found that the boy 'long before was sick of a consumption and died of the disease by the visitation of God'. Times were indeed hard, the more so since that thing called public opinion had not been invented. The King's Men could brand anyone on the cheeks for theft of something worth less than a shilling, and deport them if they repeated the offence.

With her indestructible belief in the powers of medicinal springs, Celia had ridden to Scarborough to sample the waters. They were famous. She says they 'purged pretty much', but what was that by comparison with the 'stincking spaws' of Harrogate, where she could not force her horse near the well? There were two springs 'furr'd with a white Scum' with 'an aditionall offenciveness like carrion or a jakes', a contemporary expression for a bog, john, or loo. Brave Celia. She held them to be quick purges, 'good for all scorbuttick humours' and drank half a gallon in two days, having difficulty only in holding her breath to get the foul stuff down.

Quite apart from her chatter, her wit that flashed like specks of mica in granite (a mineral she was much interested in, especially if she suspected it contained tin, lead, copper or silver), Celia saw history in the making and had the uncommon sense to write it down on the spot. From the top of Castle Hill at Scarborough, for instance, she 'saw seventy sails of Shipps pass ... *supposed* to be Colliers and their Convoys'. That italicized word is significant. The year was 1697. The war with France had not yet come to an end. Were the 'colliers' warships on the way to the Channel ports? We don't know, and Celia rarely speculates. She reports only what she saw and what she heard. Scarborough had an abundance of Quakers in it and a 'few Inns for Horses only'. The accent and idiom intrigued her: '... they tell you it's a very good gait instead of saying it's a good way, and they call their gates *yates*, and do not esteem it uphill unless as steep as a house or precipice.' A pretty good example of local understatement.

After an absence of half a century I couldn't make out what had happened to the very floor of the Vale of Pickering which I had known so well. Where were the busy little farmsteads, the cowsheds, the stackyards behind intimate screens of trees? They had been razed to the ground, obliterated. A hurricane might have swept down from the Howardian Hills, leaving only a sullen river in a strait-jacket of corn and pasturage. And strangest of all, the stream which used to chatter companionably flowed in silence, like a slowly moving canal, through what seemed to be a wholly uninhabited landscape. Not a soul appeared until I approached Yedingham some four miles downstream. I wondered what Celia would have made of Ceres abounding in a place without people.

She says nothing about how she crossed the Vale of Malton, but we may be sure she chose the best tracks available. Roads were no better then than they had been in the Middle Ages. One of her contemporaries, Daniel Defoe, says that even main roads were paved only with small pebbles for a width of about a yard and a half, 'but the middle road where the carriages were obliged to go is very bad'. They would have been far worse in the vicinity of the Derwent, which he described as 'a river very full of water and overflowing its banks and all the neighbouring Meadowes, always after rain'.

Travellers were obliged to set off early in the morning to get in front of the packhorse trains which were difficult to pass on the narrow causeways. There would be horses everywhere. More than twenty thousand were employed transporting coal alone in the environs of Newcastle. In Hanoverian times, one of the commonest sounds on the road was the chime of bells from the collars of four, six and sometimes eight horses hauling massive wooden carts.

Church bells, horse bells, the gabble, the clatter of farms, the cries of carters, the call of birds – the country must have been a wonderfully noisy place, harmonious in sound though certainly not in social conditions, where stark poverty and injustice were driving cheap labour towards the towns. There the labourers soon found they were exchanging one form of bondage for another. As the pits grew deeper, coal created a new gulf between the classes. As miners spent far more time far away underground, emerging like moles, briefly, they were more cut off from their families than they had ever been before. And it was extremely dangerous work, too. Explosions due to fire-damp became everyday events. In just one disaster at Chester-le-Street a hundred miners died; many hundreds more were injured, 'besides great damage to many houses and persons for several miles round. One man was blown quite out of the mouth of the shaft, which is fifty fathom, and found at a prodigious distance from the place'.

Yedingham was the place where I recalled fishing the Derwent in the company of twenty or thirty men from the Leeds and District Amalgamated Society of Anglers. For half a crown a head the club chartered a bus for the trip. Most of us joined the bus at the city market, but the favoured few on the outskirts were picked up as it made a circular tour of the whole borough.

The driver stopped outside their houses and kept his finger on the hooter until the laggards came running out, pulling on a jacket or flapping untied bootlaces. Although it was only seven o'clock on a Sunday morning, the men in the bus bawled, 'Wake 'em up!', bringing angry faces to the windows of the stayabeds. They bundled in: fishermen in oilskins,

160

overalls, workaday suits; fishermen with baskets, bottles of beer and packets of sandwiches. There were fishermen on the dole who were going out for greater pleasure on that river than ever a rich man could find with a room full of rods. Live-baiters, spinners and champions of the float.

Even in the dead calm of winter, when the river flowed blue-black between the silhouettes of trees, the locals were about a multitude of tasks. Cottagers brought jugs of scalding-hot tea down to the rime-covered banks at midday. At dusk there were meals waiting on farmhouse tables, and the due was never more than a shilling. Yedingham seemed gloriously alive.

The river thereabouts swings south through Roman Malton and Stamford Bridge, the scene of that great Viking defeat a month before Harold was killed at Hastings after one of the greatest forced marches in British history. It marks the boundary between the North and the East Ridings, and the gradual climb up into the Wolds, a region I knew very little about. The Riding, for I much prefer the ancient name, is shaped like a half-open fan with its delicate handle at Spurn on the coast, one straight edge formed by the cliffs of the North Sea, and the other by the estuary of the Humber. I got there in three vigorous stages.

Celia trotted into Malton to visit yet another relative, Mary, who had inherited, together with her sister, Lord Eure's estate. Unfortunately, after much argument, the two sisters couldn't agree about what to do with the great house so they pulled it down and shared the stones 'exactly'. Mary supplied Celia 'with very good beer, for the Inn had not the best'. I sampled a tolerable pint at the Crown where, to settle arguments that show signs of getting out of hand the landlord points to 'the board'. It reads: *Lord help me to keep my big mouth shut until I know what I'm talking about.*

At Malton *(Derventio)* the Romans built a fort from which radiated at least seven and possibly nine roads to the moors, to signalling stations on the coast, and south to their principal link with the Continent at *Petuaria* (Brough on Humber). But Celia, who was no more interested in antiquities than she was in scenery unless it was man-made and new at that, can have known nothing of this.

161

Derventio was largely ignored by archaeologists until the nineteenth century, when layers of treasure began to be mined, sold, and scattered. Much useful work has been done in recent years, the product of which, fortunately, is now going into the local museum. Among many inscriptions, one cut into a small sheet of lead has for long intrigued cryptographers. On one side it reads: ISARES COVIS AEEO CECEX and on the other: ISVXOSIS. The letters are not Greek and they may not be Latin. The most widely held view is that it is a *defixio*, a curse. Before I struck out along the Roman road to Settrington, I copied them out carefully, thinking, with commendable foresight as it turned out, that I might have use for them.

Notwithstanding a touch of melodrama in the dark, the day on the whole went pretty well. Rolling country with some tremendous views. In theory I trod the Wolds Way. I say 'in theory' since this network of loosely co-ordinated tracks, approved of in principle by the County Council, has been disorganized by landowners whose henchmen display outright hostility to walkers. In many places the path-obliterators are covertly backed by local authorities which, when obliged by law to register and map some five hundred rights of way about ten years ago, contrived to look largely in the direction of the big house behind the trees. In short, little was done until the more recalcitrant councillors were legally prodded. As matters stand at the moment, things are improving. They will get better when the Ramblers' Association really shows its teeth, but only a niggardly proportion of the designated Way can be described as easy going. The rest is on roads, and some of them main roads at that. Members of the ultra-reactionary Country Landowners' Association and the National Farmers' Union have yet to learn that if they looked after the so-called designated paths, walkers would have less excuse for trespassing on their property.

A relief model of the Yorkshire Wolds somewhat resembles a thin segment pulled from an orange and laid flat upon a plate. The north point of the crescent is Flamborough Head whilst the south curves down towards the Humber. Some of the finest bloodstock in the country is bred on the north flanks of the Wolds, where there is scarcely a farmstead without a scampering of foals around the place.

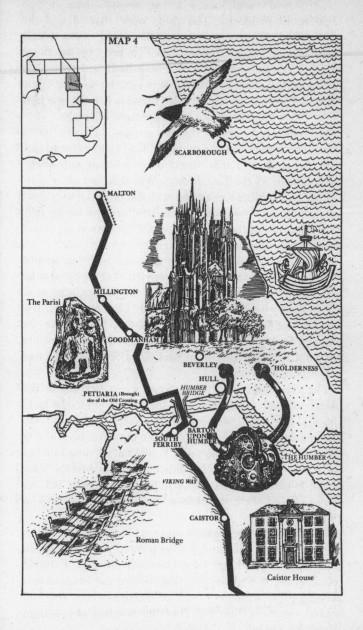

MAP 4

SCARBOROUGH

MALTON

MILLINGTON

The Parisi

GOODMANHAM

BEVERLEY

HOLDERNESS

HULL

PETUARIA (Brough)
site of the Old Crossing

HUMBER
BRIDGE

BARTON
UPON
HUMBER

SOUTH
FERRIBY

THE HUMBER

VIKING WAY

CAISTOR

Roman Bridge

Caistor House

The brood mares looked at me haughtily from behind high-fenced paddocks. The gates were chained and the surrounding plantations, I soon discovered, were thickly populated by hysterical pheasants. To keep up an air of dignified vagrancy I gave the place wide berth and tackled the railway track hidden behind the very superior-looking estate village of Settrington where every house is like the one next door. There are times when prudence pays, I thought.

Wrongly. The railway bridge over a swamp had been pulled down. In a retreat across a ploughed field I came face to face with the landowner who directed me towards one of the busiest roads in the East Riding. Was there no other way? 'Theer's nobbut the roo-ad,' he said, and he said it with quiet satisfaction. The traffic came at me hard, and but for the fairy godmother of North Grimston I might have holed up in that haven for the afternoon and walked through the night.

A frail, a gentle soul in a lace cap almost indistinguishable from her hair. Under her arm she carried what appeared to be a sizeable rook's nest. 'Kindling for me supper,' she said. Could I carry it for her? 'No,' she said, 'I live nearby but you can see me across the road.' With that fine excuse for gallantry I stopped two enormous trucks and several cars, not once but twice, since I went back for a few twigs she had dropped on the way.

The good soul of Grimston knew every footpath in the neighbourhood. She had walked them since girlhood which, she told me twice, was over eighty years ago. Could she recommend one that led up on to the high Wolds? 'Take to the old railway track,' she said. 'You're not supposed to, but there'll be nobody about.' No difficulty with the bridges? Easy in her opinion. 'And if anybody stops you,' she said, 'tell 'em you're a friend of the gamekeeper's widow. They'll know who you mean.'

We said good-bye. I gently squeezed her hand, soft but as dry as the twigs she carried. She pointed to an unmapped lane which I could not have found on my own. I turned round, twice, to find she had slowly raised her hand, as in a blessing. The stranger would be walking where she had walked years ago. She had done her courting at Wharram Percy, she told me.

All fell out just as she said it would, an embankment through trees. Mature trees, mostly birch and majestic beech that raise regiments on the crests of the chalk, but ash, too, just breaking into purplish flowers, and rose-stippled larch. Since they had been planted on – or maybe they grew naturally from – the woodland floor below, one could peer into their upper storeys as into the privacy of a neighbour's windows.

Except where the briar had raised entanglements, the cinder-strewn track ran between a shrub layer of hawthorn, elderberry, and hedge maple lightly bound together by honeysuckle and that wild clematis called Traveller's Joy, which on our northern hills is as rare as the song of nightingales. But who could want for more than the song of willow-warblers, which is as water poured slowly into a glass that rings?

On I went for mile after mile, intrigued, entranced, by the dappled light, by the clamour of birds, the excitement of the aspens. Inside, a voice kept murmuring, 'This cannot go on, this cannot go on. You will be back again on that dreadful road.' I bade the voice to be quiet. And when I scrambled around two or three cut bridges with no difficulty whatever, I said it with more conviction and inwardly thanked that good soul at Grimston.

At a highly critical point in the outcome of that day, the trees thinned and the platform I had grown so attached to swung perilously close to the invisible road above. I winced. I could hear the traffic growling like lions in an arena, waiting for another martyr. There seemed to be no escape. The platform began to disintegrate. A small road appeared. It led into a quarry. A blind alley. I took to a farm track and through glasses saw the remains of the railway track far ahead; but at my approach it dived into a tunnel, unable to cope with the upward sweep of the pastures.

Nothing for it but to strike south-west, across open country – anywhere to get away from that fearful road. The ground grew steeper. Ten minutes of trudging across rich tilth disclosed a gate like any other gate except that it stood a little higher. But it turned out to be the gate to an entirely different world. A golden gate fit for a fanfare, for there, rolling out as far as the eye could see, lay one of the great chalk basins of the northern Wolds. The vastness of it all caught my breath.

It's a bold traveller who will tell you that from one particular standpoint you may catch the very spirit of a region as extensive as the Wolds. But I trod every yard of those rolling hills from the long-deserted village of Wharram to where they plunge down into the Humber, and I claim there is no finer view than from where the good soul of Grimston went a-courting.

From crest to crest the contoured way ahead is as clear as a well-trodden mountain track. In fact, if you walk into the zenith of the sun's arc you may chuck that obscure guide to the designated paths into the first bed of nettles you come to. There is, unfortunately, a fair chance they will be growing around a sign-post which has been maliciously turned round so that it points in the wrong direction. Until I cottoned on to what I was up against, a skewed post that said *Wolds Way* cost me two hours in time thrown away. After much thrashing about in the gathering dark, I gave up all hope of finding a track of any kind and clung to a compass course that would take me to a small road some two miles to the south-west.

On that plateau of spring corn and barley, partitioned out in fields of five hundred acres or more, there are no hedges and few trees. A pin-point of light gleamed from a hill-crest roughly in the right direction. With difficulty I made for it, since it entailed scrambling down the steep earthworks of some Iron Age fort, an immense affair. To my dismay the light went out. There was no moon. There were no stars. Rarely have I walked through a blacker night, and new-ploughed earth doesn't make for easy going.

I found that building. A deserted barn and securely locked, but from it a track led down to the almost subterranean hamlet of Thixendale. A weird place. A navel deep in the belly of the chalk. Even in daylight it can't be seen from the surrounding hills. And there I stopped for the night, tired out.

When I checked on the map that purposive mis-direction, it occurred to me that I have given less than credit to those sturdy pioneers, the pathfinders who have spent years trying to persuade local landowners that ancient rights of way are precisely what they were laid down for, a means of getting from one place to another on foot.

From that hamlet to the great shrine of Goodmanham, the

Wolds Way is better posted than anywhere else. For much of the time it holds to green roads or, as geologists put it, meandering dry valleys. They are curiously narrow in places, but intimate. As you wind in and out of the clefts between those aromatic, thyme-strewn breasts of the chalk, you have the feeling that by stretching out your arms you will soon be able to touch both sides.

The chances are that the only natives you will encounter are skylarks, pipits and corn buntings, but for thousands of years those green roads were used as hunting-trails, Bronze Age war-paths, and tracks to the shielings of the first neolithic farmers. Earthworks abound on the central Wolds, and seldom admit of facile explanation. Some have yet to be excavated. They may prove to be primitive villages, field boundaries, or animal compounds. From medieval times until less than a century ago, the greater part of the Wolds remained, like the Berkshire and Sussex Downs, an extensive sheep walk, untimbered and scarcely broken by the plough. Vast areas were occupied by fenced rabbit-warrens. Today, only the green roads remain virgin because their flanks are too steep to be tilled.

In late April the Wolds are a vast patchwork quilt of greens and browns, edged with bare beech on the crests. From young pippins to old pine needles there are I don't know how many variants of green, but the eye can soon distinguish between the blue-green of the young oats, the brighter barley, and the darker winter wheat. The colour of still-bare soil also varies. Some fields are as brown as bitter chocolate, others are so stony as to appear splashed with cream when the chalk has been washed by recent rain.

Three considerable plantations and the huge estate of Londesborough stand between the corn prairies, the acres and acres of cabbages, and the church where St Paulinus and King Edwin got down to fundamental business. The two oldsters stacking larchpoles at Nunburnholme were friendly enough, but I had some difficulty in making out what little they had to say. If you don't happen to know them well, country folk are not founts of folklore, certainly not in the East Riding. That local diphthong 'eea' comes out in most sentences as, 'Ah deean't mahnd if ah deea,' meaning an unqualified acceptance of something. A still more fascinating form is the mingled 't' and 'th' which needs practice to imitate successfully, thus 'Set-therda' is the day after Friday. A child who is asked, 'Who's your father?' is likely to reply, 'Varry well, thank ye.'

There are no formal greetings beyond 'Ah do'. They said it to me and, since brevity is all, I said, 'Ahm doin' a'reight.' As it was very hot we agreed it were 'wahmish' and that I were 'gannin' on reight roo-ad', and left it at that. There are those who say fast-disappearing Wolds talk is a most ancient and authentic relic of the past, closely linked with Danish forms that steer clear of Latin roots with great ingenuity. I would call it a blend of suspicion, canny humour and cautious understatement.

The great house with its even greater grounds is Londesborough where the young Henry, Lord Clifford lay concealed among his shepherds whilst the Yorkists sought his life. Friends later spirited him off to the wilds of Cumberland. Rather curious friends one might think, since, when the Shepherd Lord came out of hiding over twenty years later, he could neither read nor write. On the failure of the Clifford line, the lands passed to the Earls of Burlington, the third of whom built Burlington House and befriended Garrick. His fussy little priest, Brian Allott, asked the great actor to give him some hints on effective Bible-reading in church. Garrick agreed. Allott ascended the pulpit and opened the Bible. 'Stop!' shouted Garrick. 'You are handling neither a day-book nor a clerk's ledger. You are handling the very word of *God. Open* it with a slow sweep of your hand and *pause* before you utter a word.' Garrick did it as if he were an archbishop at a coronation service.

The land of the Londesboroughs was sold to George Hudson, the Railway King whose slogan was 'Mak' all t'railways coom ti York'. After a spectacular career he went bust in a spectacular fashion, and so did thousands of others who thought their outspoken Lord Mayor knew more than in fact he did.

Nearby Goodmanham is quite unique. The landlady of the local pub likes walkers. She takes an interest in where they've been and where they're going. She can dispense both sandwiches and sticking plaster, and her best bitter is pumped through something that sounds like a cow in labour. On rather obscure grounds the villagers claim that their squat church on a hillock is the mother of the great Minster at York. But they have far greater claims to fame. It was owing to a sequence of events here that great Edwin of Northumbria was converted to Christianity, and the story is told by no less than the Venerable Bede.

Goodmanham was the high shrine of Northumbria when in A.D. 625 Edwin became king, ruling from the Humber river to the Firth of Forth, from the North Sea to the Isle of Man, and was overlord, the *Bretwalda*, of all the kingdoms of Britain except Kent. With Kent he made an alliance, cementing it by marrying Princess Ethelburga, who agreed to be his queen on condition that she, a Christian soul, might bring with her Paulinus, her priest, and that he would be free to practise and preach the religion of Christ.

For two years this young man of wisdom and ability could not make up his mind whether or not to adopt the religion of his Queen. Three events led to a decision: first, an attempt by an envoy to stab him to death, foiled by a friend who rushed in and received the fatal blow; second, a victory in battle; and third, the birth of a daughter.

At the time of the spring full moon, Edwin called his counsellors to his hall at nearby Londesborough to deliberate the substance of this strange new religion that advocated love and forgiveness, not hatred and slaughter. Why, from such a position of strength, should they adopt it? He called on Paulinus to speak. The man who had been sent to England by Pope Gregory spoke simply: there is an eternal purpose in Creation . . . Mankind has a special value in the sight of the Creator . . . Christ came into his own world . . . his crucifixion was a sacrifice . . . he is our reconciliation . . . the truth . . . our hope of resurrection like his . . . always present with his disciples . . .

Basic theological stuff, but it lacked the spark that achieved something close to a miracle. An aged priest whose name we shall never know stood up in the body of the hall to say that all Paulinus had said had answered his own need to know from whence he came, what his life was for, and what he might

169

hope for after death. And then, in an inspired analogy which has been recounted again and again for thirteen centuries, he likened the earthly existence of man to the flight of a sparrow which, on the dark night of a winter storm, enters through a window of a banqueting hall, warms itself for a brief moment, and then flies out again, no man knows where.

It was Coifi, the high priest of the pagan cult of Northumbria, who made the decision. 'I have known long since,' he said, 'that there is nothing in this religion we have practised. The more I sought for truth in it, the less I found . . . *this* can give us life, salvation and eternal happiness. I advise that we now burn our useless sanctuary, and who better than myself to do it!'

So saying, he borrowed a war stallion and a war axe, both of which were forbidden to him as a priest, galloped to the sanctuary, and flung the weapon into the holy place. Seeing that no ill befell him, the company, who thought he had gone mad, followed him, demolished the shrine, put fire to it, and burned it to the ground. 'This one-time place of idols,' says Bede, 'is called today Godmundingham where the priest himself, inspired by the true God, polluted and destroyed those very altars he had once consecrated.'

One of the two baptismal fonts in the present church was used as a horse trough for many years. The other one, a beautiful object from the mid-Tudor times, is inscribed, *wyth owt baptysm no saul ma be saved.* Edwin, one hopes, gained his reward in heaven, for after seven years in a state of grace he was killed by Penda of Mercia, and Ethelburga and Paulinus together with the children fled to Kent. Perhaps he was prepared for it. He may have remembered that man's existence in this world is like the brief flight of a sparrow through a banqueting hall.

Centuries before the rationalized mysteries of the Mass came to the Woldsmen from Rome, a Celtic tribe lived among these dry valleys and Ptolemy called them Parisi. He named one of their towns *Petuaria* (now Brough on Humber) and gave both its latitude and longitude. But why, without knowing anything about their customs, he should have called them Parisi, suggesting they were adventurous emigrants from the lower Seine, I have never been able to make out. But for all

170

that, contemporary archaeologists admit in their cautious way that the burial rites of the Yorkshire Parisians 'are to be compared with rites found on the continent, particularly in eastern France'.

Filled with curiosity I struck south-east from Goodmanham, making for Arras Wold, an elaborate fold in the chalk where over a hundred characteristically square barrows of the Parisi have been excavated. Very successfully, you might think, since there is next to nothing to be seen there today. The site is not even marked on the Ordnance Survey map. I came away thinking that the reputation of our Yorkshire Parisians has been somewhat undeservedly exceeded by that of their poor stay-at-home relatives, who gave their name to the French capital and so gained an easy place in the pages of history by sheer lack of enterprise.

Some of the barrows contained what are usually referred to in quotation marks as 'chariots'. Far from being the battle-wagons of the dead, they may have been dung carts, Celtic fire-engines, hay carts, or hearses built in the style of their decidedly more warlike neighbours, the Brigantians. Apart from that sop to vanity, they were a down-to-earth people. In what may be the prehistoric source of that revered Yorkshire custom of serving ham for the funeral tea, the Parisian burial-chambers often contained a leg of pork.

When the Romans arrived, they became a client tribe, remarkable for their wheat and their leather, two commodities much in demand by the legionaries. Fortunately for the Romans, they were a peaceful people who could be sealed off when the legions were busy trying to subdue the bloody-minded Brigantians who ranged the whole length of the Pennines to the west.

Cartimandua, consort of the restless Brigantian king Venutius, seems to have been an ambitious woman with an eye to the luxuries the Romans could provide her with. In the opinion of the late Sir Mortimer Wheeler, she married beneath her. She certainly put her foot in it when she handed over her fellow countryman, Caractacus, to their arch-enemy, the bronze-helmeted *Princeps* of York. Her tribe revolted and she had to be rescued by Bolanus in A.D. 69. Tacitus says their troops 'finally succeeded in snatching the queen from danger. The throne was left to Venutius, the war to us.'

Sir Mortimer, who dug into the site at Stanwick where the forces of Venutius were routed by Petillius Cerealis, the new governor of Britain, has a more imaginative comment. He says, 'The Cartimandua-Venutius *impasse* is more easily intelligible if Cartimandua be regarded as an exile from southern lands of cakes and wine, married incompatibly to a skin-clad rancher of the North, who became thoroughly tired of unmitigated mutton.'

How did the Parisi stand in all this? The answer is that, with their backs to the sea and the Romans all around, they were bottled up. And until raiders started crossing the German Sea, they did pretty well out of their good relationship with the Romans.

On I went, through Deepdale which is precisely what it says, a narrow cleft in the chalk which might have been clean-cut by one blow from a gigantic battle-axe. The rift opens out into the ups and downs of Forestry Commission property unique in its diversity, and beyond lies an emptiness of fields as large as any in the Wolds. The squalor of the manscape is made worse by the tattered remains of blue and yellow fertilizer bags which, tossed about by the wind, clatter from the branches of dead trees like Tibetan prayer flags, but with no such piety of purpose.

The clipped accents worsen in the villages that stand above the Humber. The farm lad who told me his father had gone off to shoot pheasants said, 'Ees art shuttin' fer fezzies reet nah,' but a kindly lad, concerned that I should find my way to the topmost point of that last mile of those Wolds. And there I looked down on an estuary unlovely in the glow of the westering sun.

Hundreds of pylons pierce the smog of Broomfleet, Ellerker, and Brough, now a factory for warplanes. Through glasses I focused on the wide strip of muddy water that, twenty centuries ago, divided the thickly soldiered lands of *Lindum coloniae* from the bleak wastes of the north. In my mind's eye I saw that chain of flat-bottomed boats which, in the year A.D. 71, Petillius Cerealis ordered to be anchored across the Humber.

Brigantian resistance from the Swale to the Upper Derwent was about to be broken and brought under the heel of Rome. It had to be done. Cerealis had been given orders from Vespasian himself. It was to be his reward for breaking the Batavian revolt in Holland the previous year – no less than the governorship of Britannia.

Cerealis had brought a cohort of Batavian auxiliaries with him. Originally Rhinelanders, a clan of that great Germanic tribe the Chatti, the muscular Celts were renowned as bridge-builders and tough fighters. And over that bridge which it had taken them a month to build marched five thousand men.

They spoke many languages, for among them were Hamian bowmen, Balearic slingers, black Numidians, Nervians and Tungrians from Germany, Dacians and Moors. The only Latin they knew was short sharp words of command. They hated, they feared, they respected, their centurions.

First across were the artificers – the smiths, the masons, the carpenters, and the men who handled the catapults, for they had to make hoists for the horses. Then followed the surveyors, the clerks, and the cooks, for Hispana had been promised a feast that night. Then, proudly, behind their black eagle held high by Aquilifer, the legionaries marched into the shire of York.

Plogsland

At Barton on the Humber's southern shore I bought a particularly fine pork pie and a can of beer, and set out for where, a local told me, the Viking Way began. I found the signpost that was to haunt me for days – the symbolically horned helmet of a Norse marauder – on the edge of a reedbed, and there I sat between a roofless shack and refuse dump and looked back across the estuary.

Traffic poured over the great bridge and disappeared south, down a motorway which, cynics say, leads to nowhere in particular. Barges butting the tide left a soapy-brown wash. Planes took off from a nearby airport. Sand-martins fluttered north across the wind-flecked water. Everything seemed to be on the move, going somewhere, purposively. As for myself, I felt that my store of energy, like oil in an over-heated engine, had grown thin and shrunk. It wasn't physical tiredness so much as a curious diminution of drive. This, I know from past experience, happens at intervals of about two hundred miles.

A long-distance walker's daily activities are governed by circadian rhythms to which he gradually accommodates himself. Mine include one or two short naps, no matter whether on a mossy bank, haystack, or with discretion at the back of a pub parlour. Ten minutes will suffice, for in ten seconds I can usually drop off to sleep. The more extensive rhythms are strongly influenced by destinations. I thought, warmly, of Shap Fell and of our return to the cottage and our native dales. Humberside had become merely a staging post to what on the map seemed the edge of the habitable world, the marshes of Fosdyke on the Wash. I felt as remote from what lay ahead as from a receding galaxy.

Well-disposed friends in the tortuous politics of footpath preservation had warned me what I should be up against in Lincolnshire. Stark hostility on the part of the landowners, they said. Worse than anywhere else in the country. They referred to certain sections of the Viking Way as Plogsland,

174

which means 'ploughed land' in an old Scandinavian dialect.
And a very good word too; but not in a place where, when a
man talks about farming two or three, the chances are he is
talking about thousands, not hundreds, of acres. Their
ploughs and their bulldozers, I was told, have already destroyed more than 100,000 miles of fine footpaths and
hedgerows. Plogsland can't be outflanked easily. It is the
south-eastern extension of the Yorkshire Wolds. Anyone even
casually acquainted with that great chalk ridge could point to
something I missed. But I am wholly unrepentant. My
understanding of Sod's Second Law is that it's better to get
through obstacles at some cost and learning something, than
regret not having been there at all.

The reedbeds that fringe the shore-line are a ready-made
bird sanctuary but, if I understand the situation aright, some
of the shack-dwellers have their minds on more venal attrac-
tions. They hope to be bought out by an entrepreneur who
wants to build a suburban golf-course thereabouts. With
surprising candour, one of them admitted he had tried to set
fire to the reeds but had been threatened by a clandestine
syndicate of duck-shooters. The forces and counter-forces of
conservation operate in curious ways.

At a point where the chalk quarries give some indication of
what lies deep underground, I swung south and began to
climb up on to the ridge, encouraged by the Viking sign, a
black helmet on a ground of mustard yellow. Until I referred
the matter to an historian, I thought the term 'Viking' was a
misnomer when applied to the Lincolnshire track. Shouldn't
it be Danish Way? Not so, he said. It seems there is
distinction today only between the land-hungry Norse who
largely settled in the west of Britain, and the rest of the
marauders. As for those fictitious horns on their helmets,
there were some protuberances on their headgear in the pre-
Viking period, but the horns as generally depicted are a bit of
romantic old hat dreamed up by Victorian painters. But we
have learned to live with them. You might as well introduce a
child to Santa Claus without whiskers.

On the northernmost rim of those Wolds, on the airy
uplands of Horkstow, there are great decisions to be made.
With confidence the walker can press straight along a little

road that connects what are called spring-line villages, long narrow hamlets set about a mile apart, each with its own wells in country where water is almost as scarce as in Arizona. Or one can take a chance with that hazard-beset abstraction, the designated path. I chose the latter, and I pray that Gabriel in whose books, God knows, there is little to my credit, has noted that I kept at least a degree of cool among displays of downright vandalism.

By dumping barbed wire in critical places, by throwing signposts into the ditches, by ploughing up age-old paths to within a few inches of stone-built walls, by shaking their fists at incursionists, the get-rich-quick farming community has reduced parts of what I trod into something resembling the thoroughfare of Carthage when Scipio Africanus had done with it. The farmers don't sow salt, but Amazon M40 pelleted sugar-beet seed treated with organo-mercurial fungicide and methio-carb insecticide dressing probably has more serious long-term effects. In a vain effort to keep strictly to the path, it took me three hours to cover less than six linear miles. As Tibullus, that obstinate lover of nature, said, the first two leagues were beaten out with flails.

Far below, the estuary flashed like a sabre held at the ready. No wild flowers caught the eye. A narrow strip of bare soil between the barley and the fenced-off motorway had been heavily doped, but above that sterile scene a mile-long concourse of sand-martins clung to the telephone wires like notes on an enormous sheet of music. They were coming in from the south-east, from that great river of migratory bird-life which each spring sweeps up the coast with tributary streams breaking off to the north-west; and, providentially, since there was little else to look at, I had cut across such a stream. To the west, smoke the colour of diarrhoea plumed the sky from the foundries of Scunthorpe.

The martins fluttered about unsteadily, spending most of their time industriously grooming themselves after that long flight from their winter quarters in Africa. I tried to remember from where, but could recall only that touching story about how, at the beginning of the thirteenth century A.D., the inmate of a Cistercian monastery in Germany conducted one of the first experiments in bird ringing. Noticing that the same

176

swallows appeared to be returning to the eaves above his cell year after year, he captured an adult bird and attached a fragment of parchment to one of its legs, with a dab of red wax. On it in Latin he wrote, 'Oh swallow, where do you live in winter?' The following spring it returned with the answer in scholarly Greek, 'At the house of Petrus in Antioch'. In times of stress I try to think of matters like these.

Through copse, spinney and unmistakable enclosure, the track, if such it can be called, swung away from the engulfed motorway. It still climbed, gradually, and from a Golgotha of blighted elms I looked back on the fast-disappearing towers of Super-span, a beautiful thing, an engineering triumph, but a bridge that abounds in paradoxes. From most economic points of view it leads from nowhere to nowhere. It took eight and a half years to build instead of four, and cost three times the estimated cost of thirty million pounds. It is neither the tallest bridge in the world, which is the Golden Gate at San Francisco, nor is it as long as the Mackinaw which crosses the strait between Lakes Michigan and Huron. But the single central span, stretching for almost a mile, sets a world record. This span is so enormous that the engineers worked out that the curvature of the earth makes the distance between its twin towers nearly an inch and a half greater at the top than at the bottom. I kept turning round to look at it until, on the bridleway to Barnetby, the topmost tip of the last symbol of the north slipped down behind Wootton Wold.

Until the boundary-spoilers divided up the counties a few years ago, Yorkshire ranked as by far the biggest, with Lincolnshire second. Today, a considerable slice of both counties has been annexed by an amorphous thing called Humberside, leaving thousands of Lincolnshire men with nothing in the way of regional identity. The new boundary is crossed somewhere near Bigby, a handsome place with houses unhedged and unfenced but shaded by huge trees. The church, a restored thirteenth-century affair, houses among other fine things an effigy of Sir Robert Tyrwhit (1581) and his wife, Lady Bridget, on a bed of alabaster. Not inappropriate, perhaps, since this runaway maid-of-honour to Queen Elizabeth bore him twenty-two children. One wonders how she ever had time to get off it. An epitaph to Edward

Naylor, rector of that parish, leaves much to the imagination when it describes him as a faithful but 'painefull minister of God's word'.

In country which began to look more cared for I strode, progressively, through the hamlets of Somerby, Searby, Owmby, Grasby and Clixby. That suffix *by* denotes a variety of Scandinavian settlements from a prosperous borough to a single farmstead. There are close on a thousand in Eastern England. In Lincolnshire they cluster like swarming bees. On the Yorkshire Wolds the word *thorp* means a dependent secondary settlement.

These place names point clearly to what lay behind the Viking invasions. Calculations show that between forty and sixty per cent of the names ending in *by* in Yorkshire and the East Midlands contain a personal name. In Denmark the percentage is only about ten. The Danes wanted some land of their own, and to get it their fearful ships crossed the German Sea.

The hard-begun day took on dignity towards nightfall, but whether only because I abandoned that badly bruised track and clung to small lanes, or because Lincolnshire takes on character to the north of Caistor, I cannot say. Small farms and trim hamlets look the better for people who cheerfully return your greeting. But there were six miles still to be trod, and in that time, because I wasn't sure where I could find a bed, I quietened a host of thoughts, some of them not of the best, by noting what birds sang until the dusk was left to the owls.

Although that avian insomniac, the blackbird, is generally supposed to lead the dawn chorus, followed by the thrush, the wood-pigeon and the robin, this I contend is wrong. The lapwing or peewit calls before all the others, and settles down long after even the swifts are silent. It called, plaintively, as the lights of Caistor appeared on the crest. There, quite unexpectedly, I fell among friends and without so much as a glance at the Roman camp or the place where Egbert of Wessex mauled the Mercians, I fell to gossiping in the most hospitable house in town.

Madame la Directrice came from the Valkenswaard. What with talk of the last falconers I had met on that Dutch heath,

178

and the good cigars they make there, eleven o'clock had struck before some Flemish folk came in. They had lived in the Belgian Congo, and the magic carpets of memory were unrolled yet again.

Overnight it poured down for hours and hours. Unknown to me, fortunately, villages in the flood path of rivers had been warned by radio and patrol cars to put sandbags around their doors. It came out the next day that part of the substantial township of Horncastle lay deep under water. Crops had been literally washed out of the soil. Much stock had been drowned. A county agricultural officer described the situation as catastrophic. Towards dawn the walls of Caistor shook under a cannonade of thunder. I winced, but took heart when, like a surly dog, the storm growled away to the west and the sun sneaked out cautiously between fleets of billowing clouds. Innocent of what had happened, I ventured out early to find the world new-made and shining, but everywhere wet.

As I quartered the outskirts, looking for that elusive path, I hailed a young Plogslander and asked for some directions. I provided him, I suppose, with a story he has retold several times. He didn't answer for a moment and then said, 'You'll find a notice over there'. With difficulty I rounded two waterlogged fields only to be confronted with a large board that read: *Beware of the Bull.* Simple rustic humour, perhaps, but fairly typical of the prairie farmers' attitude towards walkers. When in doubt for the rest of that day I kept to a compass course.

The path wanders up into the narrow valley of Nettleton, intimate in its prospects and bestrewn with shy flowers. The swollen beck plopped and gurgled, becoming faster as I climbed between furrows of landslip, of soil plainly on the move, the product of bygone mining made worse by the previous night's storm. Several furrows gaped, ominously, as if about to slither into the water, which in places overlapped the path. Beneath the surface one could see the eyes of forget-me-nots like litters of Siamese kittens.

The woman with the screaming peacocks on her roof looked mildly horrified when she saw me taking notes. She hoped I wasn't going to write *anything* about the Viking Way for the newspapers. It came out that some *dreadful* man on the radio had talked about the path and the next weekend they had to put up with *hordes* of walkers. How many? I asked. It seems she had seen about a dozen. They left litter lying about. Curious this, since, except where farmers had strewn their ditches with empty plastic bags, I had seen no litter whatever. And, of course, they left open gates. Within my experience, those gates were mostly festooned with barbed wire and tied up with twine.

The stream dropped into a sheet of placid water where I sat down to watch a contemplative heron and two families of coots with their flotillas of fluffy cootlets. Quarrelsome birds. In some dispute about territory, they yelped and flew at each other so aggressively that the heron, apparently tiring of it all, made off on majestic wing-beats. Whilst the argument continued, one family of chicks cruised across the pond, line astern, intent on rejoining their parents. All made it successfully except one laggard. It was scarcely half-way across when from behind a rat appeared, gaining on it rapidly, its head arrowing the water. Without so much as a squeak, the cootlet disappeared in a vortex, as a mayfly does to a rising trout. Moral: don't quarrel in front of the children.

The beck skittered about in wanton fashion, swinging between the ironstone and the chalk, which made for slippery going but displayed a profusion of early orchids. I crossed and recrossed that angry little torrent several times, before I came to where she gurgled out of some underground caverns and left her, regretfully. With no way-marks to speak of, this entailed a laborious uphill trudge to the highest plateau in Lincolnshire.

By our northern standards, Normanby-le-Wold can scarcely be called mountainous. It stands somewhere between five and six hundred feet, but all around are prairies of corn, and away to the south are the mount and turrets of Lincoln. As if tired of supporting the church tower of Normanby for seven centuries, the arch leans wearily and I rested awhile under the curious corbel of a man apparently in the throes of toothache, one hand being raised to his head and the other holding his mouth wide open. Then began as strange a couple of hours of changeable weather as ever I have experienced.

Apart from a thin but extensive layer of stratus just above

the horizon, the sky was cloudless, but even as I strode down the mile-long slope from the church, that layer began to rise. The lower edge became blobby. Owing to some cooling influence below the cloud, the stratus turned to cumulus of a kind known to meteorologists as mammatus, clouds like huge pendulous breasts, goat-like. They filled the sky. But not a drop of rain fell. Even as I marvelled at this, the breasts became more rounded, the nipples more pronounced. The air had become ominously still. From far away came the reeling of invisible larks and the call of whitethroats which is wet and juicy. Flax and meadow-rue, mullein and milkwort, that exquisite little lapis-lazuli flower of the chalk, abounded underfoot, but I had eyes only for the sky.

> Instead of this or that fictitious woman,
> Marry a cloud and carve it in a likeness.

Though I have no liking for the current demystification of the female bosom, when two beautifully-shaped clouds, slightly pendulous yet firm, detached themselves from that great array of moisture and air of different temperatures, I thought, warmly, of Hazel and Monica who, in their wholly different ways taught me, as Tom Laughton put it, what it was all about.

I was shy. I was timid. Until Monica came along I got nowhere. If I had realized that a bra could be unhooked more easily than a trout, the Catterick affair would not have ended in a flurry of frustration and hurt pride. For all my bright talk then, I knew absolutely nothing about the callisthenics of intimacy; nor, I suspect, did Hazel. But Monica did.

An ardent Roman Catholic, she had been happily married for six or seven years when her husband died suddenly, of a heart attack. For months she had less life in her than a sack of potatoes. She didn't go to Mass, hitherto an unimaginable thing. She refused to see the priest. She refused to let him in. God, she said, was not just unjust. He was cruel. She dropped all her charitable work.

Temporarily defeated, the Romans sent in one of their shock troopers, a young Jesuit. Perhaps they knew what they were doing. Perhaps they didn't. He not only managed to talk to her, he stayed the night; not just once but, until they promptly transferred him, several times. The next week, she told me, she went to a town miles away for her first confession after the death of her husband. Miraculously – yet why set miracles apart? – she became more of what she had been, a passionate Christian, and it was about that time I had the good fortune to meet her.

An Irish lass with a bosom she was proud of, she was probably eight or ten years older than I was, but in rich, uninhibited sensuality older and wiser by far. What distinguishes the foregoing only slightly from countless other initiations is that she would not include mechanical methods of birth-control among her confessed deviations from rectitude. She taught me alternatives which to start with made my hair stand on end. And with that I have kissed and told as much as I intend to. Anyone who attempts to write of sexual experience directly must anticipate failure. Even the best are betrayed. They write about the plumbing, not of the spirit. Monica often said that one day I should meet a younger woman, and would remember her, she hoped, always with love. She said love, not affection.

In the sense that, like Scheherazade's insatiable bedmate, we all want to know what happened next, the sequel to our association is, unlike a novel, in part predictable. I volunteered for a regiment of field artillery. She taught at a school for the blind in the north. I married for the first time, wholly incompatibly. She remained a widow. After the war I saw her only once, but she looked as I remembered her: radiant, and at peace with life. For some people events fall out better than they do in most modern novels. Monica, I'm pretty sure, is one of them.

For quite different reasons, Hazel was another. As for myself, what with a long-delayed divorce and the aftermath of a much-loved wife, with one outstanding exception women friends came and went with increasing rapidity. That exception, an extremely graceful, warm-hearted woman with more talents and more delusions than anyone I have known intimately – and for longer than many people have been married – had something in common with Blanche du Bois in *A Streetcar named Desire*, in that facts and fancies alike were what she thought they ought to be. There were times, I

182

suspect, when Pépé, as I called her, didn't know whether she was making things up or had accidentally told the truth.

During the blackest period of my life I owed something close to sheer survival to her enterprise and imagination, and even when I despaired of what she was up to we gambolled on the wilder shores of love; we worked together for certain operations, as bandits sometimes do, without mutual confidence but with love and professional esteem for each other.

That afternoon, those bosomy clouds, so firm to begin with, started to sag and shred and reform until one great thunderhead towered above the crouching Wold. I could see the rain coming as plainly as a squall at sea flattens distant waves. It raced up the hill to the accompaniment of a sudden clap of thunder:

Baccharentur in aethere

Aldhelm, Bishop of Sherborne forged that tremendous line in his description of a storm on the Cornish coast to show that, when it came to phrase-smithying, the schools of Canterbury could outpoint the barbarians. It has about it the very rip of thunder, and the louder you say that first word, the better it sounds. I recalled it in the church of All Saints, Walesby, where, wet through and not at all pleased with the village below where I could obtain neither food nor drink, I sought sanctuary.

A strange church. Robert Burton who wrote *The Anatomy of Melancholy* is said to have been rector there, and well I could believe it. Notwithstanding recent restoration, the roof leaked. With its priest's doorway, double piscina, and strange altar, there is much treasure there, but a cold place. Stretched out uncomfortably on a pew, I slept briefly, only to be awakened when, after a grinding noise from machinery in the tower, the clock struck two.

From notes I have kept over the years, it is apparent that the delicate qualities of spring, the infinite gradations of green, usually come to a violent end with a series of storms. As the flowers of trees become fruitful and the branches heavy with foliage, virginity is lost. Woodlands gradually become much of one colour. This usually happens between

183

mid-May and the beginning of June. In late April I was unlucky. The weather changed from hour to hour. Over-bright sunshine was followed by furious rain with sleet in the wind, and at one point it snowed. Heavy stuff, too. The kind of storm you may see in miniature by turning one of those old-fashioned glass paperweights upside down. When the sun reappeared, guiltily it seemed, the rooks' nests in the crowns of whitened elms looked like blobs of frogspawn. All this would have been tolerable but for the infernal barbed-wire and ploughed-up paths which have turned parts of the Viking Way into an obstacle course.

In the corridor of the County Hall at Lincoln there is a large wall map 'Respectfully dedicated to the nobility, the gentry and the clergy of the county'. The map is a hundred and fifty years old, but throughout Lincolnshire a great deal of this exaggerated regard for the rights and privileges of a quite different generation of landowners, many of whom are up to their necks in borrowed money, remains today. Members of the National Farmers' Union and the Country Landowners' Association dominate the County Council and all the important committees. The county suffers from not having a university or any base of power other than agricultural interests. And the Quality.

At Bayons, that is on land first owned by Odo, Bishop of Bayeux, half-brother to William the Conqueror, I got unceremoniously chucked out of a wood by a gamekeeper with a gun. The Way passes through that ancestral estate, at least that's what it showed on a pamphlet printed by the County Council. But the way-marks came to an end where, I suspect, the signpost had been pulled out of the ground.

'Get out,' he said. 'It's private.'

'But where's the Way?'

'Down there,' he said, pointing to where for half an hour I had trudged up through the mud. Peevishly I hung about until he drove off, and then went on to where the path plays hard-to-find in a series of unmarked loops.

This Bayons was picked up by Charles Tennyson, uncle of the poet, who built a historical mock-up of something I suspect he had read about in the Waverley novels, a castellated mansion complete with moat, drawbridge, gateways, and artistically ruined keep. He then called himself Tennyson d'Eyncourt, though his claim to noble ancestry was more than dubious. A snob of a high order, he once described his literary nephew Alfred as a hog, and asked, 'What can you expect from a hog but grunts?' The Arthurian-minded Alfred despised Charles but coveted his title and, when offered a peerage towards the end of his life, applied for it. The College of Arms turned the application down. What with a family background of epilepsy and alcoholism, the poet's generation had much to put up with in the way of its genetic inheritance.

I settled for the night in a pub within bowshot of the ancestral estate of the Heneages. A sultry night. Misty, oppressive. A night for intrigue, knavery and venality. After three hours thrown away in avoiding rivulets which had turned into torrents, and rivers that flowed across roads, I felt dog-tired. Since the coming of the juggernauts you hear little talk about the niceties of farming in the ale-houses of Plogsland. But owing perhaps to the meagre population of labourers and the isolation of their cottages, local folk seem prepared, almost compelled, to talk to strangers, and intimate talk some of it is. A good soul told me what she intended to do when her fifteen-year-old daughter came home with her baby. 'It's like that nowadays,' she said.

When, after some casual talk, I asked a partly crippled man whether he lived on the estate, he said yes but not there. In the next valley. That might have ended the matter except that in a wholly unexpected burst of confidence he said, 'For years and years, me and me missus sweated our guts out to build the house, and then she buggered off with me best chum.' I didn't know what to say. Outside it began to rain, heavily.

I thought of that wall map in the County Hall when I heard how my Lord Monson, eleventh in his line, allowed neither pub nor Methodist Chapel, chimney pots above a certain size nor even a letter-box of which he didn't approve, in the village he owned. When this baron contrived to rid his villagers of the pastor they were fond of, in large white letters on Good Friday they painted *Who crucified the Vicar?* in several prominent places, including his own front wall. This I know, since I saw the incompletely obliterated notice of their disapproval. Plogsland is one of the last resorts of the squirearchy.

185

Farm name-boards on the concrete tracks that lead from the road to the owner's house often have '. . . and Sons Ltd' appended to the name of the farmer. On paper the properties may well be worth millions, but not, usually, to the men who run them. Big banks, insurance companies, Sun Alliance, Pearl, the Prudential, and Pilkingtons Pension Fund, have invested heavily in land which, to repay borrowed capital, has to be thrashed to the last acre.

The story of how Old Henry, a farm labourer, clung to his bicycle whilst George, the son of the boss, grew up to live like a lord has become part of the folklore of Plogsland. The two grew up together, they were about the same age, and for years they did much the same work. They were friends, too, so that when George wanted to go off courting in Lincoln one Saturday, he asked Henry if he could borrow his bicycle. But as the back tyre was flat and they hadn't the price of two inches of valve tubing between them, Young Henry, as he was then, wheeled it down to the local garage where he traded in a couple of eggs for the tubing. Eggs were part of his perks as a labourer. And off George went.

The years passed. George's dad died, and the lad who had borrowed a bicycle began to collect cars. First, that Mercedes Sports which he had always coveted; then, as he grew older, a Rolls, more in keeping with the image of a country gentleman. He bought a Range Rover, too, which put him back about fifteen grand, and he gave his wife a gleaming Riley for their wedding anniversary. Old Henry sees them purring past his cottage every day. He gives the impression of being quite content. He still has the bicycle and he keeps a bit of valve tubing in his weskit pocket. He will show it to you if you ask him.

More storms that night. More trudging along almost invisible paths across wet barley the next morning. But, worse by far, this proud walker acquired a couple of blisters of which he felt as ashamed as a priest with pox. In the hurry to get away I had not adequately arranged my toes before pulling on damp socks and boots. Little toes tend to play at piggyback; they are apt to curl over the ones next to them, and I limped down to the valley of the Bain, guided only by the great TV transmitters ahead.

The Bain is a beautiful valley, made the more mysterious that morning by swirling mists that hid the full extent of the flooded pastures, though the high-water mark of the river showed what havoc had been wrought by the storms. Among a sorry assemblage of bales of straw, tomato boxes, and plastic sacks were the swollen corpses of sheep and poultry. It looked as if the moles had had some premonition of what they were in for and had moved up on to higher ground, where more than a hundred hills could be counted in as many paces.

Moles are downright quarrelsome creatures at any time and normally have a well-defined home range. One could imagine the subterranean fights that went on when the riparian population invaded the territory of their more prudent neighbours. It would be actively resented, for a mole's tunnel system is not only its home, but its food shop, its store cupboard, and its dining-room.

In Donington-on-Bain, an out-of-the-way village with no evident signs of prosperity beyond the poshed-up water mill, I came across a most hospitable pub, patronized that morning only by locals who went out of their way to welcome a muddy and inquisitive stranger. It could scarcely be described as an unspoiled place, since there wasn't much to spoil except the goodwill of Mary, the lady of the house, and her regulars.

As she clumped down from some business upstairs, one of them warned me what I was in for. 'She'll say she won't serve hikers,' he said. 'But let her go on a bit, y'know.' And he closed one eye, heavily.

She went on at some length. On the day they opened the Viking Way, twenty of 'em in bloody great boots trampled all over the chrysanthemums. No, she'd done with *that* lot, she had. At this I affected to look downcast and walk out slowly. Mild consternation on her part, and chuckles all round. Good rustic humour.

During the ensuing gossip it came out that Lincolnshire had more prematurely retired people to look after than anywhere else in the country. Jobs were desperately scarce. The old-style farms of two hundred acres had meant work for seven or eight men. Today the same number were employed on farms ten times that size. As one of them put it, there were no ladders, no chances of advancement for their sons and

187

grandchildren. Farming had become a deal in the City. What did the fellers rushing about in their bloody great Mercedes care for the community? Farms were run by people, and people had to be cared for. They hadn't even got a village bus. They were up to their asses in a system they could do nothing about.

The talk turned to the floods, and I got in a word about the moles. One of the company said his uncle had been the last mole-catcher in the district. At sixpence an acre he'd made a fairly comfortable living out of it since he'd upped the price of a halfpenny an acre which *his* father got. In addition, uncle sold the skins for up to sixpence each, to merchants who cured and dressed them for the trade. In a season that lasted from after harvest-time until June the following year, he often caught up to three thousand moles.

An abundance of molehills didn't necessarily mean the animals were abundant. There was probably a shortage of earthworms. They were having to work harder, for they ate up to fifty or sixty a day. Uncle used barrel traps, which were nooses buried underground and triggered off by a steel spring. It knocked 'em off at once. Strychnine? That was what they used today. Rotten stuff! It killed the worm bait, and moles wouldn't eat dead worms when they could get live ones. And had I ever seen an animal dying from strychnine? He described the writhings, the contractions, and I decided I didn't want to.

A grim feature of the valleys that run through the chalky Wolds is the number of deserted villages encountered, a legacy of the take-over of the land for sheep. Or of the Black Death. Or both. The plague reached Lincolnshire in the middle of the fourteenth century and within three weeks 'it waxed day by day more and more, insomuch that church-yards will not suffice for the numbers that die . . . no such pestilence has been seen since the beginning of the world.'

From isolation and unemployment the present villages are thinning out, and those that live in outlying hamlets are curiously suspicious of strangers. From a flash from a cottage window, I saw through glasses that I was being watched through glasses. I waved and walked on.

Until I came across a book written by a quite remarkable

American, I thought the wholesale uprooting of hedgerows was a relatively modern practice. Not so. In July 1863 a Mr Elihu Burritt of New Britain, Connecticut set off from London on foot, convinced that his fellow-countrymen 'would profit much' by learning more about British farming practices. In four months he had reached Caithness. The next year he wrote *A Walk from London to John O'Groats.* * A signed photograph of the author in my treasured old copy shows a gentlemanly figure in top hat and frock coat. He carries both a cane and a furled umbrella which, held over his shoulder like a rifle, serves as a hook for 'a small bag of necessities'.

More urbane by far than Celia Fiennes, he is less interesting, but everywhere thoughtful. In Essex, for example, the elegant enquirer noted that the fields were larger and fewer than he had seen elsewhere. 'This feature indicates the modern improvements in English farming more prominently to the cursory observer than any other that attracts his eyes. It is a rigidly utilitarian innovation on the old system that does not at all promise to improve the picturesque aspects of the country. To "reconstruct the map" by wire-fencing it into squares of a hundred acres each, after grubbing up all the hedges and hedgetrees, would doubtlessly add seven and a quarter per cent to the agricultural production of the shire, and gratify many a Gradgrind of materialistic economy, but who would know England after such a transformation?'

What he would have said of the destruction of over 130,000 miles of hedgerows in ten years can be imagined. The facts have been well-aired and the consequences seen through the whirling clouds of dust which have swept across East Anglia like the twisters of a tornado. But even in mercenary Plogsland there are signs of change. In the brick-village of Goulceby, where I went in for some blister-pricking, they had planted whitebeam at intervals of a hundred yards alongside miles of wire fencing. In Scamblesby, known as sleepy hollow since they were by-passed, they told me in the Green Man that they were thinking of doing something – wasn't right, a ploughman said, to live in a damned desert. At Salmonby, if nowhere else, some genius has reintroduced hedgerows in

* London, 1864.

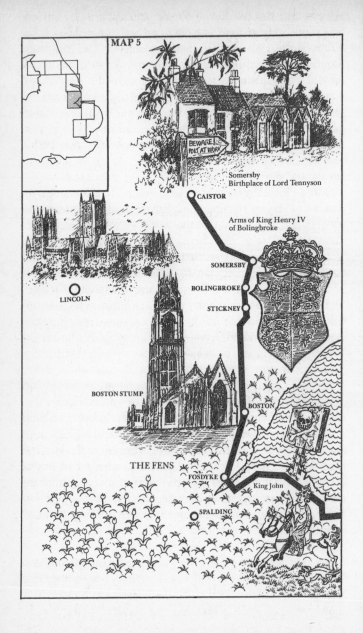

MAP 5

Somersby
Birthplace of Lord Tennyson

BEWARE POET AT WORK

CAISTOR

Arms of King Henry IV
of Bolingbroke

SOMERSBY

BOLINGBROKE

STICKNEY

LINCOLN

BOSTON STUMP

BOSTON

THE FENS

FOSDYKE

King John

SPALDING

190

embryo. Acres of barley, the size of airfields, are surrounded by seven-inch-high seedlings of hawthorn, the mayflower or quickset, the cuckoo's bread or the shiggy. The plant has dozens of regional names. For some reason I can't fathom, the Puritans abhorred it. Possibly because the stale-sweet scent of its flowers, the product of trimethylamine, stinks of sex, sweat and putrefaction. But a wonderful shrub that harbours most of the wildlife of open country. The pity is that those 'little lines of sportive wood run wild' they grubbed out might have been there since the barons shoved Magna Carta under the nose of King John.

Salmonby lies close to the quietest, the least populated, literary shrine in Britain. You might walk up from the babbling brook and past the rectory to the old greenstone church without realizing the Tennysons had anything to do with Somersby. No cafés, no guest-houses, perpetuate the name of Maud, Arthur, or Merlin. No plaques indicate, no boards point to, where the slightly mad family lived behind 'the seven elms, the poplars four'. Even before the onset of the Dutch elm disease, the trees had disappeared. But this does less than justice to a hamlet of twenty souls who live in a handsome cluster of houses almost entirely hidden by trees.

Mr Fluck, the rector, says many visitors turn up during the summer months and he is grateful, for, without their alms and the memorial services, he doubts deeply whether he could keep the church going. He knows a great deal about ghost parishes. In that deserted country he looks after nine others. I hadn't the heart to ask him whether he was a Tennysonian himself. In a nicely respectful pink pamphlet for visitors, he says: *Despite a troubled childhood due to his father's ill-health, Alfred was happy here.* Frank Kermode puts it more directly:

Tennyson's father was the eldest son of a tough Lincolnshire business man who accumulated a great fortune, but he was early disinherited and made into a clergyman, though wildly unsuited to such a career. Noisy and ungovernable from earliest youth, he was, as father of a family, morose, drunken and idle; one of the nicest things about him was that he rose in the late afternoon and then played the harp, but he was also violent and spendthrift. His wife was odd in more agreeable ways and their twelve children exhibited a great variety of eccentricities, ranging from downright insanity to opium addiction, alcoholism and every kind of psychic instability. Edward entered a home for the insane at nineteen and died there sixty years later. Charles went in for opium, Arthur for alcohol. Septimus would introduce himself to a stranger by rising from the hearth rug where he had been lying, extending a languid hand, and saying 'I am Septimus, the most morbid of the Tennysons.' The daughters were noted for their strange manners; Mary, very beautiful till savaged by a mastiff, took to Swedenborg, Spiritualism and Mesmerism; Matilda was never quite right after a fall into a coal scuttle as a child, and would embarrass Emily (who had been engaged to Arthur Hallam) by raising her umbrella in church to keep off the draught.*

As for the man who became the first Baron Tennyson, the hero-maker of my school days, the marvels are, first, that he managed to get away from the family without going right off his head, and, second, that this fundamentally naïve man did so well. An aspect of it is the unexpected. Amid all the boom, clash and bow-wow of those knights in iron clothing, we come across some absolutely golden lines. Two in particular fascinated Gladstone. They are about a guardsman at Arthur's court who is told of a dreadful event when chewing a gobbet of pork.

> He spoke: the brawny spearman let his cheek
> Bulge with the unswallowed piece and turning, stared;

Only Tennyson could have turned out such stuff because he had no idea how it might be taken. Matthew Arnold thought it provincial because it lacked high seriousness, that quality which Arnold had invented as the Great Criterion. Not so Tennyson's doting friend Lord Dufferin. He told the future Laureate that his poetry had shown him what poetry was all about. Until then he had never been able to make anything of it. And on that judgement, at least, the country was solidly behind Dufferin, not Arnold – nor Henry James who, after meeting the poet at some grand affair, had it borne upon him 'sadly' that Tennyson 'was not Tennysonian'. That didn't matter to those who clamoured to buy *Maud*, all fifty pages of

* *London Review of Books*, Nov. 1980.

it, as if it were the first edition of *Lady Chatterley's Lover*. Together with Dickens, the Lincolnshire lad represented the peak of popular achievement. Like a contemporary pop star, he brought the crowd in. And the money too. In 1850 he regretted, sadly, that he was only making about £2,000 annually. 'Alas, Longfellow receives three thousand and there is no doubt that Martin Tupper makes five.'

No matter that he bored his friends with endless recitations, that he tippled cheap port, smoked shag, and had a habit of putting his foot in it on right royal occasions. From the Good Queen downwards, they loved him; and as for the old wizard himself, he thought his own lyrics finer than Shakespeare's, but it's to his credit that, after careful consideration, he added, 'To be sure though, I've really nothing to say.'

On those high Wolds the landlords and their flunkeys, the estate agents, the tenant farmers and gamekeepers, gave me as bad a time as I have experienced anywhere in Britain. This I shall never forget. A few were the avaricious scions of old Lincolnshire families, the Yellow Bellies both high-born and simple. But the majority, I suspect, were outsiders, in for whatever they could get at whatever cost to the land. It is a frightening thought that Marion Shoard, who held a senior position on the Council for the Protection of Rural England and in Agricultural Research, the government body, considers that, although few people realize it, much of the English landscape is under sentence of death. Indeed, she says,* the sentence is already being carried out. The executioner is not the industrialist nor the property speculator. It is that figure traditionally viewed as the custodian of the rural scene, the farmer.

The English countryside has become a tax haven. Not only do farmers and foresters enjoy very considerable tax concessions from central government; they also flourish on complete relief from local taxes, that is, rates. And they can pick up more or less what grants they want, whether they are rich or poor. This monstrous state of affairs is upheld by extremely powerful lobbies in the Houses of Parliament. Farmers'

* *The Theft of the Countryside* by Marion Shoard, London, 1980.

means are not examined before they receive a grant as, for example, are those of citizens seeking legal aid or rent rebates. A visiting delegation from West Germany – where capital grants are only given to farmers who could not otherwise afford to make improvements – asked officials at the Ministry of Agriculture whether they would have given a grant to Paul Getty if he had applied for a grant to increase the profitability of his land. The British officials replied, yes. Yes, they would, they admitted.

If I hadn't encountered that carp fisherman and his friends in a village not far from Boston, it is likely that I should have dealt even more hardly with the woollybacks, those high Woldsmen who used to ward sheep before they discovered how to live more profitably on European dole for barley and wheat. But that good fellow enabled me to distinguish reasonably clearly between ridgers and marshmen, fen-dwellers and a particular type of Yellow Belly in the Spalding area who, he claimed, would sell strangers a glass of water as they watched the Tulip Parade. But then, as he admitted, he was a bit mixed up himself, being conceived if not born on a pile of stones at Revesby which is a glacial moraine. He brightened me up no end.

The diversity of Lincolnshire became apparent as soon as I walked from the chalk to the Wolds of Tennyson country. They are of sandstone with a relatively sour soil, deep fretted by streams down to the clay. It was a region intensely settled by the Danes, remarkable now for small parishes, poor churches and friendly folk – when they are native, that is – who speak with broad double vowels which gather more lilt and burr the nearer you get to the fens. 'Them folk gits pike on lumps o' fat beácon an' eáts 'un.' They call a path a 'pad' and use 'ah' instead of 'I' as in 'Ah'll see yer termorrer'. They seem grateful to be alive and in what is almost a benison you will hear them say, 'Ah'm short of nowt ah've got.' What a fine expression.

The closer you get to the sea, the less people seem to open their mouths when talking. Some say it's because of the strong winds. In Old Bolingbroke where I spent the night, the rector told me that one way of detecting the difference between a Woldsman and a fen-dweller is that the latter can

194

hold a pipe between his teeth without it affecting his speech. I met that worthy cleric in his local pub.

In Boston they were putting up the stalls for the May Fair at the foot of that great tower, the Stump, which can be seen for thirty miles. Celia Fiennes by-passed Boston on her way north from Ely, but she had good cause to remember the fens. 'I had froggs and slow-worms in my roome,' she wrote, but charitably assumed they had come up with the firewood. She came close to falling into one of the 'fendiks' which 'are deep ditches with draines' when her horse all but pitched through the planks of a rotten bridge. She escaped 'by a special providence which I desire never to forget and allweyes to be thankfull for'. She thought the region an ill place in which to live. Writing in 1635, a Lieutenant Hammond found the fen people drinking 'unwholesome Crowland sacke ... which they hold highly convenient and necessary to avoyd the divilish stinging of their humming gnats which is all the towne musicke they have ...'

The carp fisherman put it more simply. His grandfather, he said, had bidden him at an early age to ''ave nowt ter do wi' them owd lodunum eaters'. At one time they took large quantities of opium to relieve pains from the ague and the screws. But the old man was equally suspicious of those who favoured the Wolds. In his opinion, 'them there woollybacks were a rum lot'.

From the topmost turret of the Stump I looked down on a vast panorama of land and water. Toy boats cruised across the North Sea. To the south, beyond the marsh, I could just make out Fosdyke on the estuary of the Welland, where I hoped to spend the night. It looked the hell of a long way. To the north-west the Wolds were enveloped in a mist, pinkish in the falling light. And even as I stared, more and more of Plogsland began to disappear from view. No time to waste. I scuttled down from the tower and out through the docks of a town which, in company with Hull before Goering got at it, used to have much in common with the Hanseatic ports.

The policeman who pointed out the way to Wyberton Marsh wanted to know why. I made a facetious remark about them laudanum eaters, which I had cause later to regret. Out on those saltings the sunset was extraordinarily vulgar and the silence profound.

An hour passed. And then another. Time, as philosophers and geologists understand that word, is nowhere more provocative of thought than on an immense marsh with no visible bounds. In my imagination I saw that forerunner of the Rhine of the pre-boreal era, with the Thames, the Ouse and the Trent for tributary streams, a huge river that laid down the sands of Dogger Bank. All that most of us can ever know about any place or portion of space that we pass through is that it stirs within us emotions unlikely to be matched anywhere else. It comes from solitude. And that night I thought I had the marsh to myself.

But I was wrong. Through glasses I saw two figures bent almost double, at the foot of the sea wall. Each carried a shotgun. They were stalking something. Geese, I thought, and watched. The older of the two suddenly straightened up and fired both barrels into a small field of tulips. Immediately the air seemed filled with rocketing pheasants, maybe a dozen or more. The pair swopped guns and the man fired again, bringing down a high flyer and missing another. By this time the lad had reloaded the first gun with the dexterity of a Sandringham keeper, and handed it over. More firing, and then silence as the last pheasant squawked off into the gathering dusk. The man had managed to knock off six, or maybe seven, birds. But far from taking pride in his achievement, the tulip-grower shouted with rage.

He said them bleeding pests were picking the heart out of his crop and he'd poison the sods if it wouldn't do in a lot of other creatures too. He knew, because he'd tried. The man was clearly ill-disposed towards the Phasian bird.

He told the lad to pick up the birds. He was cross because they couldn't find one which had made off, winged I suppose. He looked at me. I shrugged my shoulders. What was I doing there? I told him. He shook his head. Some people, he implied, were daft. 'Better come along and have a drop,' he said. 'You've five miles to go an' it's gonna be a dirty night.'

In his cottage, over a very respectable malt, he told me much about marsh life, but he kept returning to them bleeding birds. It was clearly an obsession, but I couldn't make out how much damage the pheasants actually did. And I suppose there's much to be said for a scapegoat. Or bird.

Some talk about what the storms earlier in the week had done to the sugar-beet and the tulips was interrupted by a peremptory rap on the door. He went out. After some muttered talk he returned with a policeman, cap in hand.

'Ahum,' said the Law, addressing me. 'We 'ave instructions from Boston to ask what you be a'doing out here like.'

'Walking to Fosdyke,' I said.

'Then what you doing on Kirton Marsh?'

'Because I prefer to get my feet wet than be knocked down by dam' great trucks.'

He sniffed. In short, if I couldn't produce what he called 'full and proper means of identity' he would have to search my pack. For some of that laudanum I suppose. Small jokes are apt to misfire.

Now it happened that I had very proper means of identity. Five years earlier I had set off across the Apennines for what turned out to be an abortive walk to Rome with a letter written by my solicitor. It begins: *As his legal adviser, I hereby attest that the bearer is a man of the utmost integrity who ... etcetera,* etcetera. It gives my solicitor's home telephone number, *and that in the Inns of Court within the City of London.* On the opposite side the whole thing has been translated into flowery Italian, with stamps and seals fit for a papal courier.

With studied nonchalance I took it out of a side pocket of my pack and handed it to him.

Instead of the deferential response I expected, his jaw dropped. He blinked and looked up. 'What the 'ell's *this*?' he said. His eyes had fallen on: *Come legale del latore della presente attesto che John Hillaby e' un uomo di assoluta integrita ... egli e' presidente del ... ed e' un noto scrittore, biologo e viaggiatore ... ha attraversato ...* hum, hah and ho!

I turned it over. He smiled. We all smiled. And as he made a note of the telephone numbers for that goddam sergeant in Boston, I broached my own small store of excisable liquor, a bottle only for use in dire emergency. And we had a pleasant hour.

But outside it had begun to rain, hard. And it was nine o'clock before, wet through, I met the Linehams of Fosdyke.

197

The lonely shore

Of all the families that deserve the name of the Fen Tigers, the Linehams of Fosdyke are unique. They have managed to survive. They are still at the top of the local peck order. And because they have lived on the pickings of The Wash for more than two hundred years, they know what they are up against. As a means of livelihood, there isn't much that can be netted in that treacherous inland sea except shrimps, cockles and mussels, and they are getting pretty thin. Gone are the days when, for some of the thirstiest members of that thirsty clan, one good haul of fish meant a month on the beer. Pollution from the heavily sprayed land means it's not worth even trying for sprats and smelt. Even the dabs have been reduced to dollar-sized dablings. The air is still noisy with wildfowl, especially huge flocks of Brent geese. Seals bask and wallow on the sandbanks but are no longer legitimate prey. Only two boats now cruise out of Fosdyke, and the Linehams own both of them.

All this and more I learned when, dripping wet, I walked into The Ship feeling thoroughly out of sorts with the habitat of Hereward the Wake. Instant conviviality. No juke-boxes, no space-machines. The customers were talking to each other. Youngsters in the back parlour; their elders and no betters in the front: dyke engineers, marshmen, tulip-growers, truckers and thirsty Linehams. The walls were hung about with stuff which had been used: nets, ships' wheels and the signboards of marine chandlers, dominated by an old punt gun as long as the bar.

Val, the woman of the house, a trim soul like a hovering tern, had a word for everyone including John Lineham, her husband, who somewhat resembled an old bear in a pensive mood. He hadn't washed up some pint pots, but she modified the reproof, putting her head on one side and smiling, looking even more like a tern. They hadn't been married very long.

Until far into the night and during much of the next day –

for John took me out fishing – I learned more about life on the marshes, about seals, and codworm, and the daily ups and downs of that fidgety little creature, the common shrimp, which he knows so much about. That one man in a boat, alone, could shoot his nets and boil the catch at sea struck me as remarkable. But as an aspect of survival it pales beside the story of the tragedies, the deaths, the injuries, which have beset that closely knit family. Old Harry, the reclusive Godfather of the Linehams, keeps out of the way nowadays. He has much to think about.

John lost a leg in a motor-cycle accident. Riding a similar machine, his brother Terry was killed on his wedding day. Uncle Norris was drowned in the Humber. After a marriage that came to pieces, Uncle Spratty took his own life. Cousin Tony lost an arm feeding a rope on to a power-driven capstan, a dreadful story. Uncle Tommy, a licensed seal-shooter, died from a sudden heart attack.

Pointing out the paintings of ships on the wall including one of his own fishing smack, the *Terence*, named after his brother, John related all this in a dispassionate voice. The company had gone home. Above the slow ticking of the clock the pub seemed enormously quiet. John reckons he can't handle the boat on his own much longer. Would he retire? He shook his head. Could he live anywhere else? He shook his head again.

Fosdyke lies four miles up the river that flows into the most westerly armpit of The Wash. The *Terence* lay moored, just afloat, at the foot of some towering piles. A trim smack made to measure by Scottish shipwrights, but, after years of being thrashed, a smack with a distinctly asthmatic engine. A young lad, Alf as I shall call him, came with us that morning before moving on to another job. He could do most things but, once aboard the *Terence*, only did what John told him in picturesque language.

'Get that sod going,' John said. But she wouldn't go. John swore and tried himself. Two coughs and an explosive bang, and not another sound. What they did with injection fluids and a new lead, I don't know. But if the plugs wouldn't spark, John's sustained blasphemy had some sort of electrical effect and, with a noise like two skeletons making love in a dustbin, we cast off and headed for the Black Buoy Sands.

The smack is, by any standards, strictly utilitarian. The fo'c'sle is just high enough to kneel down in to make tea and other things. A shrimp-boiler, like a small dustbin, stands just aft of the mast, opposite that ominous-looking winch. The furled net with its heavy raised head and long beam is lashed to the deck. The echo-sounder is fairly modern, but what John calls the auto-pilot must have been an innovation in Phoenician times. The tiller can be jammed in any position by two iron pintles, which means that, when sailing by himself, John can leave the helm and go for'ard.

On a fine day The Wash looks like an immense lake with shimmering horizons, but when the wind gets up and banks the tide, the channels between the sandbanks become sluices in which a cockleboat has no more stability than an empty matchbox in a flooded gutter. Half an hour before low water, the tide races out as if someone's pulled a plug out of the sea. Craft can easily be marooned.

The Wash has been partly filled with clay, silt and peat from the richest soils in central England. If all this were dredged out, the sea would lap the walls of Lincoln, Peterborough and Cambridge. This is what the region must have looked like in prehistoric times, but since the Romans put the natives to work, a succession of engineers have not just resisted the sea, they have invaded it. John said crops were now growing where, as a lad, he had helped his dad, Old Harry, to shoot their nets.

On we went, first between banks of samphire, salicornia and softly purple sea-aster, that salt-loving Michaelmas daisy, and then mud, just mud, until we saw afar off, looking like slugs on a yellowed cabbage leaf, seals basking on hummocks of sand. John said that years ago they rarely saw more than a dozen or two in a day's hard fishing. That day we saw two or three hundred. Altogether there are probably about five thousand in The Wash, which has become the metropolis of the common seal in England.

Overhead a solitary tern, that most elegant of sea-birds, the swallow of salt water, wheeled around us, hovered for a moment head down, and then dived, emerging with a tooth-pick-sized smelt or spratling. 'Lucky bugger,' said John. 'I didn't know there was one left.' The tern flew off. 'One good tern deserves another,' I murmured, but he didn't hear.

He had his eye on the first of a line of bell-shaped buoys through which the North Sea foamed. Though I had no idea of what they were up to, there began a process of sampling the stock below, of looking for elusive shrimps by trailing a small try-trawl. Imagining it to be the real thing, I felt the economics of the business were really precarious when, among feathery sea-wrack and small crabs, up came fewer than a dozen shrimps in the purse at the rear end. The second try produced even less, but with the addition of some eel-shaped garfish and young squid which vomited ink. Things began to look up when, at the third or fourth try, he shook out about a jugful on to the coamings. He looked at them with something between scorn and sorrow. He nodded. 'We'll have a go here,' he said, and swung the *Terence* into mid-channel.

Alf threw a loop of rope around the winch I didn't much like the look of. A kick with his foot and it started to revolve. Up went the heavy beam-trawl and out and overboard until, gently, some thirty feet of netting were lowered on to the floor of The Wash. For an hour thereafter it was a matter of cruising up and down what John hoped were the shrimpiest parts of the channel that morning.

Fishermen distinguish between brown shrimps, the commonest kind, and the 'pink 'uns' that live in deeper water. As John described it in rather too much detail, shrimps will live on almost anything, from worms as big as themselves to the bodies of poor souls who go down to the sea in ships and don't come up again. As I was munching a plump specimen at the time, I managed to cut short his account of how, long before putrefaction sets in, shrimps attack the soft parts of the skin behind the ears and under the eyes. 'And if you have to fish out a poor sod that's been in for a long time,' he said, 'you'll find that . . .' I held up my hand and tossed the shrimp overboard. 'Tell me what they do during the day,' I said firmly.

He pointed to a strip of water indistinguishable, as far as I could see, from any other. 'They're off now,' he said. I blinked. He began to spell it out, slowly. 'Shrimps burrow into the bottom during the ebb, but as the water rises they start to go up on the marsh to feed.' I looked even more puzzled. I had visions of hordes of them, hopping out of the water. No wonder the seals were restless.

It slowly dawned on me what he was getting at. To a marshman, the marshes are what are disclosed at low water. Shrimps feed on the newly covered banks. Otherwise they would have nothing to feed on, for the channels themselves are lined with sterile clay. Shrimp-fishing starts when the banks are covered with five or six feet of water. 'Then we know where the little bastards are. Otherwise,' as he put it, 'we should have to go looking for 'em all over the bloody Wash.'

John could judge the state of the tide by looking at streaks of foam behind the black buoy. He suddenly stopped talking as if at a sign from on high. 'Alf!' he shouted, 'turn the wick up.' Alf dutifully lit the boiler. John glanced at his wake and swung the helm over. A rope was thrown around the ominous winch and the catch was hauled up. It came in, at first, slowly, as the trawl-heads cleared the bottom, and then at full speed to rid the net of its burden of debris. Lines were lowered, the beam came aboard and, with the *Terence* on the auto-pilot, the men first stifled and then brailed up yards and yards of netting until only the cod-end, the pay-load, swung in the air. Among the weed were enough shrimps to fill three plastic sacks. They were poured out on the deck, hopping wildly.

This is commonplace to offshore beam-trawlers everywhere, but to me, an onlooker, it came not far short of marvellous to realize that for years John had been handling the whole bag of tricks on his own. As soon as they had emptied the net they shot it again and got down to the laborious task of sorting out, cleansing, boiling, cooling down, and bagging the hard-won catch. Shrimp-cleansing is a skilful operation in itself. Like a miner panning for gold, John leaned over the side, perilously, and whirled them round and round in an open sieve to wash away all the unwanted stuff. We were followed by a spire of screaming gulls.

After six hours of sampling and trawling, the total catch weighed less than a hundred pounds, say forty kilograms. In times of plenty, times which have gone for ever, the day's haul might easily have been five, or on good days even ten, times that weight.

As we chugged back to Fosdyke, the home of the Godfather who would sell the shrimps, John talked of the day he had knocked off well over a hundred wildfowl in one shot from the punt gun that hung in the bar. It belonged to his great-grandfather. He recalled the morning when, in less than an hour and a half, he and one of his cousins dredged up a third of a ton of mussels. Not for the market. They were for re-stocking purposes. Under a gentleman's agreement, the Linehams had their own beds. John kept his eye on his own seventy acres, but there was a lot of poaching because, as he put it, 'they're not all gentlemen around here'.

The channels between the Mare Tail and the Boston Deeps are pretty well cleaned out. Yet from the mudbanks skeins of Brent geese began to take off in their hundreds, wavering and undulating in a distinctive and graceful manner. Their confused babbling attracted other geese feeding on the drifting beds of eel-grass. The skeins united until, turning and twisting in the air like columns of smoke, a concourse of a thousand or more drifted away towards the Norfolk shoreline.

The black and white birds, so unlike other geese, were assembling for their long flight back to breeding-grounds in the High Arctic. Those that flew over us, low, were talking to each other intimately. *Grunk, grunk,* they called, adding a variety of guttural chuckles and whistling sounds. Ornithologists have no idea what this means. And nor have I. But it is likely that the Sea Indians, with their affinities with wildlife, understand them perfectly well.

With food packed by the ever-attentive Val I set off early the next morning, the first of May, to walk round the seaward edge of the marsh into Norfolk, to meet Katie near King's Lynn. With that pleasure to look forward to at the end of the day, I ambled along, marvelling at the solitude, the sheer immensity of those unbroken saltings.

Beyond The Ship, the track dwindles into a narrow path and the path to a raised embankment to which I clung, venturing even closer to the sea where the going seemed firm. Saltings are unique in that they change not only with the seasons and the daily weather, but with the hourly movements of the tide, when land becomes water and water dry land, with an ever-shifting boundary that is neither water nor land. As for the feeling of exhilaration on that great marsh, I cannot better what has been said of it by Edward Storey, a man who is both a native and a considerable poet. He describes it as:

... not unlike being in some strange and almost mythical domain. The lungs inhale and exhale more deeply. The fresh air penetrates into every fibre. The eyes, lips, cheeks, hands, all feel different. The silence works through the mind, dispersing clinging worries like dandelion seeds blown from their stalk. You feel yourself, more alive, more aware. Suddenly every nerve and cell is responding again to the power of the landscape, to its magic and challenge. It's like entering a theatre, you have to dispense with belief and let the unreality of the occasion lure you into a new reality, a new experience.

More than anything else in nature, he says, he searches for silence – meaning, I presume, the absence of the fearful noises of our super-machine age, especially the roar of traffic and of low-flying aircraft. I have experienced almost complete silence only in the desert where for hours and hours the creak of the loads roped to the camels and the strangely hypnotic *whoomp whoomp* of their feet striking the sand were the only distinguishable sounds. On the marshes, a profusion of waders, especially the pied oyster-catchers, the gulls, and the geese, were almost never silent; and as for the sea, from a distance it spoke in whispers, like the wind in the reeds. Without those gentle noises the marshes would become a fearful place.

What makes the marshes around The Wash more remarkable than those anywhere else is the sheer extent of the unbroken horizons. They are divided fairly evenly between Lincolnshire and Norfolk. I doubt whether the marshmen who live close to the boundary care much which county they belong to, but I didn't get the opportunity to ask them. With the exception of a brush with an irascible security officer, I met nobody during that day-long stage.

Towards midday I tackled a pint of John Lineham's shrimps, which, together with ale cooled in a dyke and samphire sandwiches, couldn't have been bettered as marsh fare. A shrimp, I recalled, should be pushed, not pulled apart. The common custom is to peel off the segments, like shelling peas. This is rarely successful and usually results in the crunching-up of gritty bits that refuse to be parted from their occupant. The technique is to hold the creature's head and tail firmly between forefingers and thumbs, and *push* the segments into each other, wiggling them backwards and forwards until the salty morsel emerges from its articulated plates. This should be written above every shrimp stall in the country, although I must say it's not as easy as I have made it sound. The meal over, I dozed in a hummock of sea-lavender, wondering how far I lay from where King John is generally reputed to have lost his jewellery. From the most credible account published a few years ago, it was some two or three miles inland.

As a contemporary historian puts it: the manner of the unfortunate monarch's death 'has become part of that assorted collection of irrelevant incidents which makes up what every schoolboy and many adults know about the history of medieval England'. John Lackland was more unfortunate than most. He was detested by the people for his tyranny, despised by the nobility for his deceit and cowardice. He provoked the Anglo-Irish barons by his arrogance; he plotted against his father Henry II, his brother Richard Coeur de Lion, and was deeply implicated in the murder of his cousin Arthur of Brittany. When he died at Newark Castle on 18 October, 1216, possibly from poison, he was extremely hard up and a considerable French force had landed in Kent. Documents attest that John, with his baggage train, was at King's Lynn on the eastern side of The Wash on the eleventh of that month. There, already a sick man, he heard that his garrison at Dover was considering surrender to French invaders. He set off that morning to cross the dangerous estuary of what was then called the Wellstream, now the river Nene.

These are attested facts. By far the most dramatic and improbable account of the sequel was written about ten years after the event by Roger of Wendover, who made the disaster total. 'He lost all his waggons, carts and pack-horses with his treasures and precious vessels and everything which he loved with special care . . . the ground opened in midst of the waves, and there were bottomless whirlpools which engulfed every-thing, with men and horses, so that no man escaped to tell the King of the disaster.'

The story has been retold several times with, latterly,

varying degrees of scepticism. Today, I suspect, most historians would go along with Professor James Holt of Cambridge who doubts whether John lost anything of great note; even if he did, his journey west was scarcely interrupted and he had enough money to pay his attendants and the advance wages of three hundred soldiers after the so-called disaster.

This view has been pieced together by a re-examination of contemporary documents and a physical examination of where the crossing was probably made, now an inland village. Professor Holt considers that what really happened was that, once dead, King John was robbed, like his father before him, by members of his household who looted his goods and left his body without even decent covering. All this was told to a writer at Coggeshall Abbey, who gave his account of the affair before Roger of Wendover launched his fiction. This holy man had it from an eye-witness, a clerk who had met men loaded with their booty as he entered Newark, intent on keeping watch by the dead King's body and saying Mass for his soul.

Another hour slipped away serenely. The tide crept up into the saltings. The distant outlines of King's Lynn appeared through a heat-haze. But, alas, every silver lining has its cloud. As soon as I heard the roar of planes and saw red flags fluttering from poles on the embankment ahead, I knew what I was in for: a bombing-range unmarked on the map.

By keeping to the foot of another wall on the landward side of that embankment, I reckoned that at least I couldn't be seen, and walked on. It wasn't a pleasant walk. At irregular intervals the planes dived down from a great height to drop flash-bombs on targets not far out to sea. The fearful sound of their engines culminated in a series of supersonic bangs. From the map it looked as if I could reach a track that led inland by half an hour of hard walking, and I was more than half-way there when an irate fellow in a Landrover headed me off.

The dialogue was in part predictable.

'Hey! And what the devil d'you think *you're* doing?'

'Walking,' I said.

'But this is a defence area!'

206

'Not marked on the map,' I said.

'Then what do you think those red flags are for?'

I looked up at those fluttering pennants. I had the calendar on my side.

'Why, it's May Day,' I said.

When we set off on this walk, one of my ambitions had been to explore the possibility of a reasonably comfortable trail from the north-west of England, the Lake District, back to London by way of East Anglia and the Home Counties. Looking back on what had already been done as I struck inland from the shores of The Wash, I felt that the outlook was fairly promising. It seemed that the frustrations of paths which had been maliciously interfered with lay far behind me. But if there is one section which turned out not only difficult but downright dangerous, it is that road from Sutton Bridge which carries heavy traffic between Lincolnshire and Norfolk. It could have been avoided by going back to The Wash, but that would have added another ten or fifteen miles, and I had arranged to meet Madam on the outskirts of King's Lynn that afternoon. Except to recall the fact that there are hosts of ridiculous gnomes in suburban gardens, I shall say little about that fearful day.

Without mentioning that she'd nearly been knocked down herself, Katie said she'd discovered a path to the Lynn ferry about half a mile up the road, and if we walked behind each other we'd be there in no time. She's pretty good at cooling me down. The trucks still hurtled past us but, somehow, they seemed less dangerous, less noisy when we could make small jokes about them. And when we turned off into a little lane, quite an ordinary lane, it seemed one of the quietest lanes on earth.

As we wanted to reach the coast of Norfolk the following day, we decided to set off that night, late, and settle down in the igloo somewhere along the way – experience has shown that it's not easy to leave even the best pub in town at six o'clock in the morning. Consequently we saw little of the handsome quays and courtyards, the alleyways and cobbled lanes of Lynn, that splendid gateway to the lands of the *Nordfolc*. However, to make it something of an occasion, we

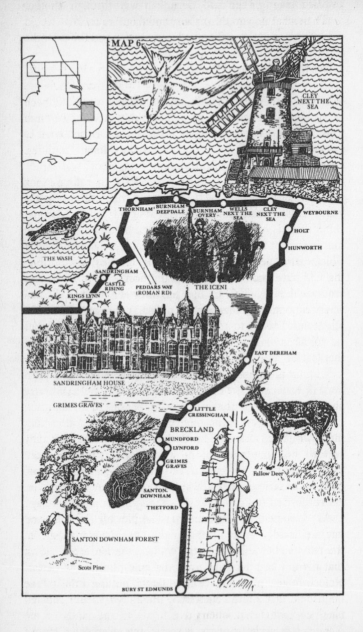

MAP 6

CLEY
NEXT THE
SEA

THE WASH

THORNHAM BURNHAM BURNHAM WELLS CLEY WEYBOURNE
DEEPDALE OVERY NEXT THE NEXT THE
SEA SEA

HOLT

HUNWORTH

SANDRINGHAM

CASTLE
RISING
PEDDARS WAY THE ICENI
KINGS LYNN (ROMAN RD)

EAST DEREHAM

SANDRINGHAM HOUSE

GRIMES GRAVES LITTLE
CRESSINGHAM

BRECKLAND
MUNDFORD
LYNFORD

GRIMES
GRAVES

SANTON.
DOWNHAM

THETFORD

Fallow Deer

SANTON DOWNHAM FOREST

Scots Pine

BURY ST EDMUNDS

208

dawdled over dinner and were half-way through another bottle before we agreed on a roundabout route that would take in the coast where we had had such a good time at the expense of that television company.

Our proposed route through the southern shires would entail returning to a place only a day's walk from where we were sitting that evening. The coastal detour would add well over a hundred miles to the whole journey, but we were undecided only on how best to reach the sea. By yet another designated Way? Or by one of our own making? As things turned out, we chose well.

North Norfolk lies across the north-eastern end of by far the most famous prehistoric track in Britain, the Icknield Way. The full extent of this Way is wholly unknown, but the central portion, the Ridgeway, is clearly defined by much trampling. It starts within sight of the great stone circles of Wiltshire and comes to a semi-colon rather than a full stop in the Chilterns near Aylesbury to the north-west of London, crossing the Thames between Streatley and Goring. Somewhere among the Breckland, those sandy heaths of Suffolk, the prehistoric track re-emerges as Peddars Way and makes for the sea close to where we intended to walk round part of the Norfolk coast. But we didn't want to spend much time looking for a track that might prove no more substantial than the Viking Way. We were out, we agreed, to enjoy ourselves, and affected to take no notice of a distant roll of thunder.

A sultry night but with any luck, we hoped, the rain would hold off until we reached the outskirts. It began gently enough, but soon was pouring down. By that time we were close-hauled and ready for it, but even the best of rainproof clothing under a full pack becomes oppressively hot.

We hurried on, dismayed by the sight of massive storage tanks, gasometers, and factories behind high fences and guarded gates. No suburban greens, not even a vacant lot where a tent could be discreetly pitched. We had reckoned on making no more than three or four miles, but not in rain of almost tropical violence. It pelted down, putting a misty haze on the surface of the darkening road. No shelter, not an overhang, not even a solitary tree.

After half an hour of wet going, a few dilapidated shacks

and a caravan appeared alongside a gated drive. Thinking that at least one of the tenants could scarcely refuse to let us use seven square feet of their ground, I knocked on one door after another. No response. No footprints, no wheel-marks, on that gritty drive. The place seemed completely deserted.

We paused outside a sorry-looking caravan. The door stood very slightly ajar. We first knocked, loudly, and then peered into the retreat of a solitary who had not used it for at least a month. Everything dusty, the windows cobwebby, and a green patch of algae under a slow-dripping tap. With something of the apprehension of the Babes in the Wood, we edged in and took our packs off; just until the rain stopped, she said. In our state of need I would cheerfully have crawled into the stables of Sandringham, just up the road. As evidence of good intent we spread out the igloo in the kitchen annexe, ready to be put up outside.

But the rain didn't stop for hours and hours. It hissed down on the tin roof with the noise of someone breathing heavily into a microphone. Looking round for something to do, Madam found an old brush and began to sweep the floor. This done, she cleaned the windows.

At her insistence, in the light of a candle, our candle, we polished and swept, scoured the sink, and managed to fix the dripping tap and the catch on the front door. During these penitential chores, a car pulled up outside the gate and sprayed the drive with a fearful searching light. This, I thought, is it, and blew out the candle.

A man got out of the car but left the engine running. He put a chain round the gate. He locked it and, to our tremendous relief, he drove away. I felt a bit disappointed about not being able to trot out a rehearsed tale of woe.

Locked in, yes, but a child could climb over that gate. We were divided, temporarily, Madam and I, on the issue of whether, once entered upon, the issue of trespass was compounded by staying another few hours. On being put to the vote, the matter came out so evenly that I, with Solomon-like judgement, thought it only proper that our double sleeping-bag be placed in the space between the two slightly mouldy bunks, where one of us slept so soundly that, towards dawn, I awoke with a start, wondering what the hell was making such a curious noise below the floor.

First a deep-throated chuckle, and then an ominous series of clicks and scraping noises as if someone was trying to turn a key in a rusty lock. Cautiously I opened the door. To my relief a covey of partridges flew off like a flock of startled hens. They had been scratching about for grit under the caravan.

Sleepily, we packed up. Between prodigious yawns we gave the place a final polish, clicked the door behind us, and set off in that pale blue light which is the mother of the dawn.

The royal road to Sandringham passes through the gardens of a vast housing estate, remarkable chiefly for more of those plastic gnomes. But not far beyond lie the great woods of Wootton which, at that early hour, throbbed with birdsong. Blackbirds and robins vied with redstarts and nightingales in such glorious confusion that we struck across a patchy common the better to appreciate the more thinly spaced-out soloists.

I suggest that, to those of us out and about simply to enjoy ourselves, it matters not at all that birds sing best under stress of competition, of a threat to their territories. I am not interested in the structure of that sound-producing organ, the syrinx, that minute voice-box unique to birds alone. It can be both seen and heard that the dunnock, the so-called hedge sparrow, the bird with the beautiful name of *Accentor modularis*, sings most ardently in the brief throes of avian copulation. But does he sing the better for it?

That morning the song prize went to two wood-larks which rose and fell to the ground in ever diminishing spirals, pouring out music which ended, as the nightingale does, in that liquid *tee-loo, loo, loo*. Callas could not have bettered them with her *Lascia, lascia mi piangere*. Amid this clamour, we swung along in step.

Castle Rising is all its name proclaims: a more than handsome village draped around the echoing arches of a fortress on the crest of a hill. Since the village slept and we were hungry, we laid out our gear on the green, discreetly, behind an enormous and aromatic lime between the church and the almshouses called the Hospital of the Most Holy and Undivided Trinity. Whilst Madam prepared breakfast I slipped

211

into the church of St Lawrence. A marvellous church with piers that soar and columns and arches all lozengy and zigzag in the grandeur of Stamford stone. I went back to take over the chores, that Katie might see it too. In the days when a tidal river brought ships almost to the doors of that church, Castle Rising, they say, far exceeded the importance of Lynn.

Rising is still all of a piece except, perhaps, that grim keep on the hill. It was there in 1328 that Edward III imprisoned his mother, Queen Isabella, for consenting to her husband, Edward II, being tortured to death. And no quick death at that. After he had spent months at the bottom of the great *oubliette* on foul bread and ditch water, she brought in those who specialized in the *gravissima*, the slow engines of torment. We prefer to recall how, just before we left, a frail hand waved to us from one of the upper windows of that ancient almshouse where everything except the collared doves seemed so quiet.

It is not easy to explain to overseas visitors that, while there are the best of reasons for Buckingham Palace and Windsor, for Holyrood House and Balmoral, the royal family live at Sandringham simply because they like it. The Big House has always been more of a country gentleman's seat than a monarch's castle. George V often referred to it as 'dear old Sandringham'. His son, Edward VIII, said his father's affection for the property 'had defied the encroachment of time' for 'there in remote Norfolk his private war with the twentieth century was fought out victoriously'. Had he his grandmother's name in mind?

What little of the towers and turrets of the sprawling mansion can be seen through an immense screen of trees suggests an illustration for a Gothic novel. When Albert Edward was Prince of Wales he bought the property from Lord Palmerston's stepson, and soon found he had acquired 'a voracious white elephant'. It's been done up several times under a succession of sovereigns, but thoughtful guests usually pack woollen underwear, even in summer. The screen of trees, or rather the forests that stretch for miles and miles, are, like those of Balmoral, examples of as well looked-after woodlands as you may find anywhere in the country. They contrive to hide the coaches and picnic parties as well as the royal family.

The belief that Norfolk is as flat as O'Dooley's cat when the house fell on it is not even half true. The boulder clay, the aftermath of glaciation, has had a flattening effect, especially around the lonely coast, but inland the surface is undulating, rising up to some uncommonly fine and well-timbered Downs. A mile or two beyond the unsignposted perimeter of Sandringham, we swung up the first hill I had encountered since I turned my back on Boston Stump. From that breezy summit we looked down on a vast arc of sea from the nearby Wash below to the north-easternmost stretch of the saltings beyond Hunstanton.

Like Wymondham and Cirencester, that noisy little place is not pronounced the way most people think it should be. 'Hunstan', we were told at least twice. 'Not a bit of it,' said the landlady of the Royal George. 'It makes outsiders feel a bit superior and us a bit folksy-like. We call it Hunstanton.'

On the way down from that hill a fine dashing sparrowhawk burst out of a coppice and strafed a hedgerow, turning rapidly from side to side in its efforts to flush out the occupants. It struck at a small bird, probably a finch or a robin, but failed to clutch it. Up it went, up and up in an almost vertical climb. Two larks ceased their babbling and dropped like stones. And then a marvellous thing happened. In an incredibly tight loop, that master of manoeuvrability flew underneath one of them, upside down, disclosing his pallid underparts. He snatched at it, but missed again. Not perhaps the raptor's best flight of the afternoon, but it helped to make ours.

Only the rolling Downs of Ringstead stood between us and the coast. They are composed of chalk. As 'clunch', that chalk can be used for building. Like the cob or daub of the West Country, all that clunch needs, they will tell you, is a proper hat and good boots, meaning an overhanging roof and firm foundations. And for centuries quarried chalk from characteristic pits was burnt to make lime and marl to put the land in good heart for corn and beef. 'Mountains of roast beef,' said Horace Walpole. 'Roughly hewn into the outlines of human form like the great rock of Pratolino, I swear I see no difference between a country gentleman and a sirloin.' Since he did precious little for the family property in Norfolk, that hall at Houghton where his father, Sir Robert, held prime-ministerial court, the gibe is undeserved.

As I've said quite enough about designated paths which don't live up to expectations, it's a matter merely for the record that a fair stretch of Peddars Way beyond Ringstead isn't posted. Local folks went to some lengths to point it out to us, but by that time we were fast bearing down on the sea on a track of our own and thoroughly enjoying it.

The Way, presumably, had been used long before the Romans arrived. But in their methodical fashion they made the most of it during the suppression of the natives after the bloody revolt of A.D. 60.

A man I talked to in London years ago spoke in what I took to be a warm Cockney voice. Was he, I asked him, born within sound of Bow bells? 'Now Guv', that I wasn't. Proper Ickney I am.'

Ickney? He smiled. 'That's what they call us.' He came, he said, from a village near Norwich. Which one I forget, but it must have been within – if not at the very centre of – the kingdom of the Iceni whose Queen Boadicea, or Boudicca, came close to putting an end to the Roman domination of Britain.

Like Cartimandua of the Brigantes, this spirited lady was almost certainly the power behind the throne, but unlike the woman who, some think, married beneath her, Boudicca married Prasutagus, a rich, sophisticated philo-Roman. After an abortive revolt among the East Anglians, it looks as if the Emperor Claudius regarded him as a reliable commander of a client tribe, which may be fairly compared with a contemporary satellite government. Claudius allowed him to mint his own coins and Prasutagus, not to be outdone in generosity, a Celtic trait, declared, thoughtfully, that half of his considerable wealth should eventually go into the coffers of Rome. He wrote it into his will. No doubt he had in mind the favour of the Emperor, but what he could not have foreseen was that Nero would take the lot.

After the death of Prasutagus in A.D. 59 or 60, the tribal area was overrun and, to quote a local historian, 'loans were called in, the tribal aristocracy was stripped of its inherited wealth and reduced to slavery; the residence of Prasutagus was plundered, his daughters were raped and his widow, Boudicca flogged.' The ensuing revolt could scarcely be called unexpected.

Under the command of that enraged woman, the Iceni joined forces with the Trinovantes of Suffolk. In a series of furious attacks, they first sacked the enormous wealth of Camulodunum (Colchester) and Verulamium (St Albans), and then advanced on Londinium which they fired to the ground. The 'Boudiccan level' of charred wood has often been disclosed by excavations in the City.

Their victories were short-lived, for they took place when the bulk of the Roman forces were engaged in North Wales. Suetonius Paulinus, the Governor of Britain, promptly marched back and inflicted an overwhelming defeat on the armies of Boudicca who, though an inspiring leader, was no military genius.

Nobody knows where the final battle took place, nor what happened to the Queen except that, as a symbol of freedom, her statue stands in her battle-car alongside Westminster Bridge. But the aftermath was the almost total subjugation of the Iceni for at least one generation. During that period of bondage the Romans built a signal station at Thornham at the coastal end of Peddars Way so that, in the event of further trouble, they could bring in the legion stationed at Lincoln.

We soon ran into trouble there ourselves but, for reasons I have already mentioned, I shall say little more than that the ironing out of the short-comings of these long-distance paths is long overdue. Thornham and Titchwell are cheerful little places, with quite a number of houses built of chalk and a history that goes back to Boudicca. Unfortunately, walkers are obliged to keep to the busy coastal road which is downright dangerous, or must wind through paths on the saltings which are regularly flooded.

The retired mariner at Thornham who sells postcards and popcorn told us, without rancour, that he could name five good men and true who would cheerfully chuck the path-planner into the marshes if they ever met him again. They were fed up with paddling out to those who got trapped by the tide. Been up to his arse several times, he said.

Thus warned, we ventured among the samphire and the sea purslane cautiously; we were quickly deterred from further venturing by what we saw, and we hopped, skipped, jumped, and plodded back to where, with no regard whatever for the recommendations of the Commissioners of the Management Plan for the Heritage Coast, we eventually settled down for the night. As this entailed outright trespass on several occasions, I have no intention of disclosing how we wove through the sea-girt gardens of the gnome-fanciers, but by judicious stealth we went undetected.

The Seven Dwarfs and a variety of gnomes and pixies peered at us shyly from miniature lawns, bath-sized ornamental ponds, and reedbeds. Could it be that this obsessional regard for pixilated ornaments stems from some folk memory of days before the marshes were drained, when Will o' the Wisps, the so-called lanterns of the Little Folk, were often seen where marsh gas seeped out of the silt? The notion is, to say the least, tenuous, but at least it gave us something to think about in our search for a bit of dry ground that wasn't too far from a pub. All went well thereafter.

For three sun-lit days, and nights enlivened by sand-hoppers, we held to those marshes, never venturing inland for more than a few hundred yards. The path that started off so badly found its feet a mile or so beyond our first uneasy pitch and behaved pretty well for many miles. For much of the way it clung to the break between the saltings and the sea-wall, and there we saw almost nobody at all.

The commercial life of what envious traders inland refer to as the Gold Coast is nicely confined to a number of attractive townships, the resort of beach-loafers and weekend sailors in distinctive togs. Naturalists flock there too, but quickly make for the sanctuaries between Scolt Head and Blakeney Point where there can't be much in the way of solitude during the bird-migration season. As for the sailors, they are in a class of their own.

To be really acceptable among them, says David Yaxley, a native with an exceptionally keen eye, one has to be seen 'in an expensive fisherman's knit polo-neck and natty sea-boots, touching up the immaculate paintwork of a dinghy. The air over the foreshore at Overy Staithe or Brancaster is thick in summer with the fine sea-oaths of weather-beaten old tars from deepest Berkshire or Solihull. For much of the time, of course, the water is so far away that it's hardly worth the trouble of launching the boat; but some mighty fine sailing goes on in the bars of Brancaster, Burnham Market, Overy Staithe and Blakeney. The damned trippers, thank God, prefer Hunstanton and Wells.'

In the Norfolk Hero at Burnham we sat among them, briefly and respectfully, at two-pint time, which is about half-past one on Sunday afternoons. A minor pilgrimage, this, in its way, since Horatio Nelson, born in the local parsonage, is both Norfolk's hero and one of mine. His popular fame rests largely on those last hours aboard the *Victory*. But there is much else to him. He could not do the impossible, any more than other men. He was only more ready to try. This included his deliberate choice of the role of hero.

In ill-health and despair at the age of twenty-two, the man who was constantly sick at sea thought about throwing himself overboard, but decided that as things didn't much matter anyhow, he might as well end his life serviceably. 'I *will* be a hero,' he confided to his life-long friend, Thomas Troubridge. That a man who lost an eye, an arm, and part of his guts in the way a child goes through mumps and chicken-pox should take up with a simple-minded beauty is perhaps less surprising. Horatio had a somewhat simplistic view of the arts. He thought that Italy, the land to which he resorted with his beloved Emma, was an intolerable country, fit only for violinists, poets and scoundrels.

As for Emma, Ortega y Gasset, that cartographer of the passions, says that however desirable she may look, an extraordinarily beautiful woman is an obstacle to the advances of men of fine sensibilities. They tend to keep her at a distance in order to admire her as an aesthetic object. In his view, the only ones who fall in love with 'official' beauties are fools and drug-store clerks. Beauties are public monuments, curiosities. In their presence one feels like a tourist, not a lover.

Emma pulled off the extremely difficult feat of living happily with two men, because they had dominating passions of their own and she was an actress. She was satisfied by social occasions, and posing, and being talked about. She had married a man nearly twice her age. At night, his official duties done, William Hamilton, the ambassador at Naples, was far more interested in his famous collection of antiques

217

than in going to bed. That could be left to her licensed lover, and there seems to be no doubt that Sir William was extremely fond of the hero of the Nile. As for Horatio, he had not done with heroism, yet.

The pity of it is that, in terms of being able to enjoy the fruits of ambition, Emma came out of it worst. After Trafalgar she was reduced to utter penury. Lord Nelson's brother received an earldom and an annuity of £5,000 from a grateful government. Seldom can a man have collected more for doing less.

Our second day on the Gold Coast brought us to the enormous sands that surround Holkham Hall, home of the Coke (pronounced *Cook*) family. Here, as elsewhere on that coast of inlets and outlets, the day's stage didn't amount to much in the way of linear mileage. We were beguiled by beds of sea-lavender, dancing butterflies and bird-life until, too late, we discovered that the shifting dunes had a grain of their own which made walking difficult and led too often to where the tide, racing in, looked dangerous. In places it advances and retreats for over a mile.

Apart from a handsome herd of Friesians which took a fancy to Madam's bouquet of sea-grasses and insisted on following us down to the water's edge, the atmosphere here is one of utter isolation – so much so that when that great agriculturalist, Thomas William Coke, who became Earl of Leicester, succeeded to the huge family estate he claimed the King of Denmark as his nearest neighbour. The wall that encloses the park alone is nearly nine miles long.

We could do no more than glance at the famous avenues of Corsican pines, planted to stabilize the sand dunes, an early and highly successful example of land reclamation. There was too much to grasp on the infinite gradual slopes to the sea. It came as a surprise to find that the older and more rounded dunes have provided wind-protected bowers for such unlikely plants as dog-rose, privet, hawthorn, and honeysuckle, with delightful drifts of pyramidal orchids in the sandy lanes between them. From their nibbled leaves, these appeared to be much to the taste of hosts of rabbits. One warren of some thirty burrows amid a dense mat of bramble might have been the back entrance to Watership Down.

218

The plants thin out towards the line of the distant sea, a line, it seemed, drawn with chalk at the bottom of a prodigious skyscape. There, under hovering tern, appeared the embryonic dunes, faintly shadowed with couch grass. Once this agent of new properties by the sea has set up a solidly rooted business, its more cautious compatriots, marram grass and floppy sea-rocket, that little salt-tolerant cabbage, move in. Life goes on in little heaps everywhere. But the conspicuous flower-bearers, rosebay willow-herb and butter-yellow ragwort, bide their time.

Nearing the point of Holkham we found we had been indirectly cut off by the tide. The holiday-makers were becoming progressively more densely packed as waves pursued happily shrieking children up the beach. This is a national nature reserve, and the right to toss a ball about on the windy waterfront is an important aspect of it. Everyone seemed to be having a whale of a time.

The pine woods planted by the son of Thomas William Coke are gloomy, the haunt of our native red squirrels and rare plants including an orchid, *Goodyers repens*, which may be loosely translated as the tresses of the repentant lady. It looks as if they arrived there in the soil of those pines introduced over a hundred years ago.

Before the methods of Charles 'Turnip' Townsend swept the country, there was not an ear of wheat grown from Holkham to Lynn. The land was poor, short of manure, and best suited to rabbits, which in some places were given hay during the winter. Coke, taking over two farms which had fallen on bad times, started an agricultural programme that lasted sixty years. He gave body to the sandy soil by extensive marling. He manured it heavily, too, saying, long before Yorkshire folk popularized the phrase, 'where there's muck, there's money'. He developed stall feeding, and was one of the first to use ground bone as fertilizer.

Coke carried out trials of livestock best suited for local conditions, and settled for Devon cattle and Southdown sheep. He even developed grass-seed selection by giving local schoolchildren lessons in what he wanted and encouraging them to scour the countryside for the best they could find. As for his tenant farmers, he offered them incentives, that is long

219

secure leases, if they would sign and observe a high-cultiva-
tion clause. Not surprisingly, he soon managed to raise his
rent roll from £2,000 to £20,000 a year.

Wells-next-the-Sea is now two miles inland, and if a Coke
hadn't dredged the channel and built a long embankment
from the quay to the Point, 'one of the most incommodious
sea-ports in England' might have been wholly silted up. David
Yaxley tells an entertaining story of how, in Elizabethan times,
the inhabitants tried out a social project well in advance of its
day. They chose for one of their parish constables Robert
Jarye, 'thinking therebye to have somewhat restrained him
from his former unrulyness in gaming and using the ale-
houses. But now perceyving that nothing at all it avayleth but
rather that it doth incourage hym to bolster out both his owne
loose behaviour and also the ill demeaner of others', they
sacked him.

We found the place tripperish and friendly, but not good
for a meal more imaginative than deep-fried fish and chips.
We settled for cold cuts and a bottle of wine, and bore them
off to the marsh.

One of the many advantages of the igloo is that, once
erected, it can be lifted up from inside and moved about like a
tortoise with its legs withdrawn, or, perhaps more accurately,
in the manner of a pantomime horse. With its view of the
marsh at sunset and the flighting duck, we could not have
chosen a more spectacular pitch, but sea-wrack and pebbles
are not the best stuff to lie on and we were obliged to indulge
in much horseplay before the thing was finally pegged down.
And then the sand-hoppers began to make an infernal noise
under the groundsheet. We ignored them, and slept until five
in the morning when the lapwings woke me up. Katie can
sleep through a thunderstorm.

Recalling that John Lineham had said that with brown
bread and butter and sufficient ale he could live on samphire
for ever, I went off to collect a couple of handfuls for
breakfast. Curious stuff. It looks like emaciated asparagus. In
Lincolnshire, samphires are called 'pissers' which is not as
vulgar as it sounds since the word comes from *perce-pierre*,
that which breaks up the stone.

Madam, engaged in frying bacon and mushrooms, said

they would come in fine as an appetizer. They didn't. They tasted like gritty grass. We were not aware, then, that pissers have to be boiled and served in melted butter.

Until the mist fell around us like breath from the pit, we walked for six or seven hours. The seemingly endless beds of salicornia are relieved by faintly purple mists of sea-lavender and tufted thrift, which is like walking on soft rubber that has miraculously burst into flower. The oyster-catchers probed and preened. They are indolent birds. When the incoming tide overtakes them they try to ride it out, standing on one leg, not bothering to remove their bills from under their striped wings until some small wave threatens their equilibrium, and they run before it, piping indignantly.

Stiffkey (pronounced *Stewky)* is renowned for the beauty of the village and, for those old enough to remember the affair, the indiscretions of its late vicar. Mindful perhaps of the Magdalene, this indulgent priest ministered unto groups of whores until he was defrocked himself. A showman exhibited him in a barrel on Blackpool Pier for sixpence a peep, whereupon, as if in fulfilment of some dreadful prophecy, he was literally worried to death by a lion in an adjacent booth. The villagers affect not to recall the matter.

The birdwatchers were making their way to that shrine of ornithology, Blakeney Point, where they would have to queue up for limited spells in the observation huts. Through powerful glasses, seals appeared as black dots on the sand-banks, but two obligingly looked out of the water. Not at us but at each other. Suddenly they began to thrash about, appearing and disappearing in playfulness or aggression. It seems unlikely this was a preliminary to mating, which takes place towards the end of September.

From the steep cliffs of Shetland, two observers, Ursula and Pat Venables, are among the very few who have watched seals' wildly erotic courtship. They roll over one another in the water, 'writhing and twisting in almost continuous contact ... mouthing each other's heads and necks, yelping and snarling, and slapping the water with their flippers until the sea foams'. Then they sink to the bottom, and each blows a fountain of bubbles until they float up together on the tail of the bubble stream. The play is reported to go on for a long time, and ends with complete coupling in a few fathoms of water.

Among professional fishermen there is no room for more than one opinion about seals. They hate them, vehemently, in the way that gamekeepers' eyes narrow at the sight of a sparrowhawk or a weasel. Their argument – which is irrefutable – is that seals not only eat fish, they transmit a particularly unpleasant-looking parasitic worm that infects cod to the point where commercial catches are sometimes almost unmarketable. What bedevils perfectly good arguments about seals' right to live is that scientific investigators, over-emotional conservationists, and fishery officials can't agree what constitutes a balanced stock of seals – that is, herds large enough to maintain their numbers but not so large that they grab more than their share of rapidly diminishing stocks of fish.

In Blakeney they tell how the village ne'er-do-well regretted trying to capture a young seal pup stranded by the tide. With hopes of selling it to a circus or a zoo, he managed to carry it off upside-down in a sack slung over his shoulder. In the process it bit his fingers, and then bit its way out of the bottom of the sack, and then, before he knew what was happening, it bit him in the bottom.

The story about the gnome that escaped from a garden and went off to see the world is so fragile that even to enquire about it deeply is perilous. But it deserves to be told, not least because the landlord of the tavern on the waterfront assured us he knew the owner, who couldn't make out what had happened to it.

This man, he said, had been collecting gnomes for years. They came in all shapes and sizes, but by far the best was not one of those mass-produced things from vendors of suburban garden furniture. It was an impish-looking creature which had been chiselled out of some fine-grained stone. The rector thought it might have been a corbel from some old church. And then one day it disappeared. 'The chap wasn't half mad,' our informant said. 'He thought some tourist had nicked it. But not a bit of it. A fortnight later he got a little postcard from Rome which simply said, *Looking up a few friends* and was signed *your gnome*.

'And then, true as I'm here, during the next month or two he got three or four of them little cards, all from the gnome. They come from Florence, Venice, and somewhere else. Could have been Vienna. They was all signed the same way.

'But the really odd thing was the gnome came back! Yes, it did. Chap couldn't believe his eyes. It was in just the same spot and behind it, in the rockery, was a suitcase about the size of a matchbox. All covered with little travel stickers it was.'

Our chances of reaching Sheringham that night dimmed appreciably when, after an hour's elaborate detour, we scrambled up on to an immense wall of shingle to find that on all sides the horizons were rapidly closing in. To the north, almost immediately below us, the sea broke sullenly. A strange sea with no outer bounds. The waves appeared out of a mist of such opacity that we might have been walking on a platform through the clouds. And to the south all the half-seen features of that great marsh, the huts, the dykes, the reedbeds and the windmill at Cley, were being progressively blotted out by swirls of vapour. Within minutes we were completely isolated.

Madam suggested we should go back. Go back to what? Going back meant going down into the marsh. Better by far to cling to our modest elevation. No waves could reach us. We knew precisely where we were. We had three hours of daylight, and we could always pitch down on the shingle. Not for the first time, I blessed the tent and the invaluable feeling of security it gave. And the murk, as I saw it, would soon blow away.

An hour passed. The visibility had closed to about thirty yards in all directions, and I reckoned we had crunched along for less than three miles. No sound except that *crunch, crunch* and the distant waves. From the marsh some bird called, but so faintly and so infrequently that the sound emphasized the silence, the solitude.

Ahead of us the map showed the steep cliffs of Weybourne some five or six miles away, and a path inland to which, I hoped, the shingle bed would lead us. For the second time I timed our crunches. They were slowing down, slightly. About seventy to the minute. Time for a rest. Five minutes, maybe.

223

No more in that damp and chilling air. We crunched and slithered down the shingle to where I probed the marsh.

Through a trellis of reeds, a dank sheet of water steamed eerily. Two ducks squawked off into the gloom. No road there. I returned, and together we crunched up to the top and, since there was nothing else to do, we crunched on.

An enforced trudge on flint pebbles has something of the dream-like quality of that sequence in which Marcel Marceau walks on the same spot in slow motion. It's like walking on glass marbles. At each footfall the nodules of flint are crunchily depressed; they are pushed backwards to that point where propulsion is most needed so that, until you get into the swing of it, each step gained falls short of what was intended and the outcome is both frustrating and abnormally tiring. When that solitary bird called again, I had the feeling, momentarily, that, under cover of the mist, all the regenerative forces of nature had ceased and that, very gradually, the world had started to run down. Or it could be that after walking for more years than I cared to think about, my own store of energy, of drive, which I had sometimes thought to be illimitable, had begun to run down? Perhaps it was just those damned pebbles.

I hadn't much liked the look of them when Katie and I had tramped along the ridge, briefly, the previous year. Earlier, much earlier, in 1953, the year of the great Flood, I had flown up and down that coastline on one of my first assignments for an international newspaper.

Ten years with what was then the *Manchester Guardian* had convinced me that, with two young children and a difficult marriage to handle, I needed something more than prestige. The liberality of that paper did not extend as far as the wages of its correspondents. They paid niggardly, and bickered about expenses. When I discovered that pieces of mine were being syndicated to the *New York Times*, I wrote to the editor of 'All The News That's Fit to Print' and suggested that he should buy his corn direct from the mill. I rewrote that letter two or three times. To my surprise he agreed to a probationary year, which lasted until I set off for Central Africa in 1961.

During the first night of that disastrous North Sea surge in 1953, the sea broke through the coastal defences in many

224

places including that shingle ridge, flooding thousands of acres inland. The bureau chief of the *New York Times* in London told me to get there before the agencies, and to hire a plane and then tour the coast for eye-witness accounts. More than two hundred people were drowned, and a warden told me how without warning he had been washed out of bed.

Over the years I wrote several accounts about how scientists marked the pebbles with paint and tracer elements in their efforts to find out how they moved, where they came from, and what, if anything, could be done to avert further disasters. To their credit, scientists admit that the ridge is still much of a mystery. The waves exert a sorting effect on the sand, the ground-up shells, and the pebbles, but what they call the problem of supply has not yet been solved.

The thought was of no comfort to us that evening, but before the cliffs appeared through the mist and soon afterwards the little road that led inland, I had come to a decision. We had done with coasting. We had been walking for a month. Time we set off towards home.

Through Breckland

To make the best of what lay ahead, we drew a thick red line across one of those huge gas-station maps that leave absolutely nothing to the imagination except where roads might be most easily avoided. Since this is largely impossible between Norfolk and where we live in north London, we struck out for the heaths of Breckland and the less well-known tracts of Suffolk, even if it meant making some elaborate detours.

This is the very reverse of how, years ago, I set about a walk to Scotland. I tackled it from the south and not in the opposite direction because, principally, I wanted to get into the swing of things before the big hills hove up, and also because in our high latitudes it's easier by far to walk with the sun on your back and not slap-bang in front of your eyes.

In terms of exertion, Britain is nicely graduated from the Channel to the Hebrides. It might have been tailor-made for north-bound walkers. By that I mean that the Welsh border country is higher than the Quantocks and Mendips of the West Country; the Peak District is higher still, but less strenuous by far than the broken jaws of the Pennines; whilst the Western Highlands make all that has gone before seem puny.

On this walk, we started off in a fashion befitting a nuptial occasion, for among mountains you may expect miracles to happen. The views from the Cumbrian fells had something of the quality of a bugle-blast, and the bright days came as a bonus. But what one of us had not foreseen was that, thereafter, we could be likened, unromantically, to two flies walking down the neck of a bony horse. We had now inched across the ribs, in a series of ups and downs, and were close to the tail. It would show both lack of spirit and enterprise to jump off on to something mechanical, but we had no mind to dawdle.

Yet there came much to catch the eye that morning. In its unexpected variety, Norfolk is a land apart from its neighbours, a place that people love even more than they admire it. The vigorous air of the high-standing heaths, the silence, the shimmering ribbons of the distant sea, the little lanes with their chintzy patterns of small flowers, these are but the ingredients; they are not the *genius loci* behind such places as Little Snoring or Corpusty, and along our route from Kelling to Holt, Hunworth, Briston and Bintree. David Yaxley, the county's proud historian, lists a series of furlongs whose names, as he nicely puts it, are a mixture of the practical, the allusive, and the poetic: Olde Hilles, Foxholes, Cockywonge, Minkte, Hanging Barrow, Slophow and Lark Dehaunt.

Madam, a deft crossword-puzzler, made sport out of the local signposts, reducing the names of villages to anagrams and the stuff of incantatory verse. I bade her cease and desist. Would it not be more profitable to tease apart the subtle rhythms of sedge-warblers which were more common than sparrows thereabouts? Had she no *feeling* for the very soul of Nature? But she, knowing that deep questions deserve only frivolous answers, said, 'High Holkham', and we left it at that.

To judge from what contemporary novelists have to say about the subject, marital harmony is not only an uncommon but an unfashionable commodity. Or could it merely be that writers are fascinated by difficult women? With more experience of that class than I care to own up to, it came as an enormous pleasure to discover that Katie and I shared so much, both out of doors and in. The relationship has been built up, slowly, over a period of several years, and we see no reason for it to change. A little smug, you think? Possibly. But then we laugh at the same sort of things. We come from not dissimilar backgrounds. We speak the same language.

Mr Yaxley, I feel, deals hard with those whose accents, like ours, differ from what he calls that 'fine, expressive, humorous, and perfectly intelligible accent' of his fellow countrymen. Nowadays, he says, their homely talk is being replaced with 'the horrible screwing tang of the Home Counties, the flat mispronunciations of the Midlands, and the uncouth grunts of the north'. We caught little of what he complained of, and then mostly in towns through which we passed at a fair pace.

From the coast to East Dereham, half-way across Norfolk,

we covered over twenty-five miles that day, and with a sense
of urgency too, since Madam had to get back from Dereham
to King's Lynn to retrieve the car. There were friends of old
standing and places to be revisited in the Military Zone of
Breckland where I had manoeuvred as a young soldier. And
since the route entailed little in the way of mapwork and path-
finding, we watched pipits parachuting out of the sky, tiger
beetles vaulting over patches of sand, and noticed how the
rhododendrons had invaded the huge heaths which isn't
perhaps altogether surprising since the rhododendron is at
heart a huge member of the heather family.

Those Jaguars and Mercedes so common on the Lincolnshire Wolds were inconspicuous, if not rare, among the lanes
of Norfolk. The quality has kept to the horse, and when the
second or third rider gravely doffed his cap to us, it occurred
to me that the rumpus about fox-hunting, the scuffles at
meets and so on, has little to do with the well-being of the fox.
It stems essentially from the age-old antagonism between the
pedestrian and haughty equestrian. For there is no doubt
about it, a man on a fine hunter looks and behaves and *feels* as
if he is a superior being. Since one declining ritual deserves
another, we wished them good morning respectfully. Madam
lowered her head, slightly, and I touched my forelock in
proper fashion.

Towards sundown, the trim countryside began to look
shabby in the vicinity of small factories and housing estates.
There was no room at the inn. Huge truck parks and garages
were not places to put up our plastic tent in private, or so we
thought until we asked the advice of a man clipping his hedge.
That sympathetic fellow promptly offered us the liberty of his
small plot of grass. We cooked in his outhouse and woke up
between the shrubbery and a fine bed of wallflowers.

A lazy river, the Little Ouse, reed-flagged and fish-full, marks
the common boundary between South Norfolk and North
Suffolk. It flows through the very heart of Breckland, an
enormous tract of country some four hundred square miles in
extent, which, until a substantial part of it was annexed by the
Forestry Commission and the military, meant precisely what
it was called: the brecks are tracts of heathland broken up for

228

cultivation from time to time, and then allowed to revert to waste.

That morning, alone again, I struck south-west for twenty miles before venturing into the huge man-made forest that surrounds the neolithic flint arsenal of Grimes Graves. I say 'venture' deliberately, since, although you can get to within a few hundred yards of those prehistoric pits on a track, a light mist hung about the glades of the woodlands. There, forty years earlier, I decided that as soon as I got out of the army I had done with the humdrum life of a general reporter. I wanted to travel. The mist added a touch of other-worldliness to a landscape which for once was all that, and more than, I hoped it would be.

'There's the wind on the heath, brother; if only I could feel that I would gladly live for ever.' The heaths that delighted the heart of Jasper Lavengro are somewhat patchy today. They lie around the forests between Mundford and Thetford. They have been trampled down by an ever-advancing army of conifers. You see them first in patrols. The approach roads are lined with Scots pines at least twice the height of those I recalled, their crowns bent and wind-thrashed. Hard on that initial sortie come irregular platoons of the Caucasian species, with Douglas firs in the rear until, as if at a word of command, the pines and the firs outflank and protect great armies of larch.

Much of this forestland, perhaps a quarter of the whole, has been taken over by the Ministry of Defence – a place where bored-looking lads in berets and military motley are for ever being driven in and out of zones marked *Danger*. From the stutter of light weaponry and the boom of the heavy stuff, it was audibly clear what they were in for but, though I daren't ask, I would bet that few of them knew why. We certainly didn't in 1940 when, as gunners without guns or ammunition, we took to whitewashing the trunks of trees to mark the sacrosanctity of the officers' mess. And we had known even less when, a little earlier, we were sent to France after the evacuation of Dunkirk.

From what could be seen from the deck of a south-bound transport, France was on fire. Black plumes of smoke appeared to be rising from the entire landscape from Le Havre to Cherbourg. This is an exaggeration; a gross exaggeration. But then everything was exaggerated at that particular point in time – everything, from what the Second British Expeditionary Force, about half a division, was expected to achieve, to the extent of the support we should get when we landed.

Most of us thought we should never land. The Panzers were said to have crossed the Seine and swung west, deep into Normandy, with the idea of isolating Cherbourg. The radio was no help. Germany said Weygand had surrendered. France was a babble of voices, agonized, poetic, patriotic, utterly confusing. The BBC said our allies, whoever they were, were digging in, and fresh forces, including the Foreign Legion, were coming up from the south.

We munched army biscuits, the first we had ever tasted, and watched the smudge of coastline getting nearer and nearer.

About five o'clock in the afternoon our three transports, two of them former cross-Channel steamers, hove to within sight of the squat fort on the eastern wall of the entrance to Cherbourg, whilst a seemingly endless procession of ships chugged past, all of them sailing north, back to England. France, it seemed, had given up the struggle and everything seaworthy was getting out fast. Light naval craft glided through lines of trawlers; cargo ships were crowded with soldiers and civilians. There were also hospital ships, and an antiquated carrier with half of its bridge missing, carrying a burden of old biplanes. A destroyer dipped flag and swung towards us, signalling madly. Was it saying the game was up? For a minute we hoped it was going to act as escort and we were off home again, but as if despairing even of the gesture, it left us to whatever we should find within the harbour entrance.

At seven o'clock we inched in, nervously. Dense plumes of smoke were still rising to the east. A few planes droned inland like tired bees. As the anchor chains rattled out I think the majority of us would have welcomed a few shots from the shore. By this time we were convinced that Cherbourg was in German hands. What massive guns did the forest conceal? Half a dozen shells would have finished us. But it grew dark without disturbance. Fishing boats pulled out, most of them with masthead lights, and were soon netting whiting.

We were field-gunners, a Territorial regiment from Sheffield. Although many of the men handled steel for a living, and some had even forged the pieces they fired at annual camps, it was clear even in 1940 that the laborious business of getting batteries laid and co-ordinated on distant targets was not the most efficient method of stopping an onrush of armour.

My own service extended over a period of three and a half years, and my recollection is of an infinity of boredom and chronic discomfort, marked only by good companionship and a few incidents that stand out like punctuation in a long sentence. One of them, an exclamation mark, occurred in Cherbourg harbour at about two o'clock on the morning after we had arrived, which makes it 14 June 1940.

There was an explosion. A bloody great bang. The rumour went round that our ammunition boat had gone up, and by the time the card-school scrambled up from a lower deck, prepared to leap overboard, the bits of a fuel-tanker, some burning, were falling all around.

The small-arms sergeant bawled, 'Man the Lewis', but he bawled in vain. It was not that men cowering behind lifeboats and peering apprehensively skywards were by nature cowards, it was just that we hadn't seen the gun for months. Even cleaning it as a fatigue duty had had to be abandoned when those who took it to pieces could rarely put it together again.

The old sergeant, the only man who knew how the thing used to work, crouched down and, aiming at nothing in particular, blew away part of the rigging and a portion of the funnel. There was in fact no visible target, but this proved no deterrent to any man behind a weapon in Cherbourg, ashore or afloat. For five minutes the sky was filled with tracers, star-shells, and aerial bursts of ack-ack, and two French airmen hurriedly took off in a seaplane, apparently convinced that if they left it moored it would be sunk by fall-out. The machine, a flimsy affair of canvas and wire, returned in a quarter of an hour, fussily, and then began a practice of taking off and returning at irregular intervals.

Precisely what happened between disembarkation the next morning and the chaotic retreat about ten days later is blurred. Everything happened; yet nothing happened; at least nothing that can have been of much military comfort to the despairing French. Liaison officers would turn up on bicycles and try to explain, tearfully, that we should have been two hundred miles to the east eight days earlier. At least one of our gallant captains turned to drink, an exercise in which he was matched only by gunners at eight shillings a week, who soon discovered the paralysing effects of Calvados.

Within three days it was apparent that not only were German units operating on both sides of us, advancing, it seemed, on St Nazaire, but they were also moving in between our irregular lines of inter-battery communication. One of our dispatch-riders rode south and was not seen again for three years, when he escaped from a prison camp.

When I tried to buy cigarettes from an impassive shop-keeper, the old woman behind the counter said she had sold out her whole stock that morning to the Germans. In a wood late one night, when our guns were miles away, we heard what appeared to be several combine-harvesters advancing across a cornfield. We assumed blithely that the French were getting their crops in under cover of darkness, but the harvesters were, of course, tanks. Theirs, not ours. With the exception of some Algerian cavalry, nothing military seemed to be on our side.

We encountered the Spahis on the fourth, or maybe the fifth, day. They were improbably decked out with cloaks and sabres and mounted on exuberant stallions, and they insisted vehemently that they were our allies and refused to go away. If we hadn't taken the precaution of mounting a gun open-sighted on a distant crest one night, it is possible that they would have been with us for the duration of the campaign. They were delighted with the gun and camped around it. Shortly before dawn the 25-pounder was fired by a nervous sentry, uncertain about something advancing down the road. The shot scraped a peasant's cart laden with hay and scared the daylights out of the Spahis' chargers. By the time they had rounded them up, we had left.

By the seventh day we had criss-crossed the greater part of Normandy and Brittany, receiving occasional orders which were usually countermanded before they could be put into action. On several occasions we were told to abandon the vehicles and scatter. The gunners refused to sabotage their guns, but as petrol was being eaten up by the Bren-carriers, the drivers unscrewed the plugs and threw them away. Within a quarter of an hour, another distraught liaison officer pedalled up to say that all light armour had to be kept intact, so we waded into the alien corn and managed to recover a few of the jettisoned plugs. At that point three black Stukas raced overhead, presumably in search of targets more military than a line of upturned bottoms.

The mystery was that we never received more than a few desultory bursts of fire on any occasion, but later we understood that the German intention was to keep the roads open for the oncoming German armour. Hence our continued existence. When one German column was reported to be sheltering in a village at night, a barrage of rapid fire from our battery annihilated the village. But, we were told afterwards, not the enemy. They drove off before the bracket of shells closed in on them.

War was far from what I had imagined it to be. A Breton farmer continued to scythe his field, oblivious, it seemed, of a horizontal hail of tracers. The Germans were advancing between rapid bursts of fire. Opposing them were tired-out English infantry with only a few rounds left. They were retreating, but in no disorder. Some of them drove into our bivouac in a glade that night. They staggered out of khaki-painted buses so full that when the seats emptied, a few men remained swaying like marionettes, still hanging on to the straps, fast asleep.

Whenever we stopped, villagers pressed armsful of honey-suckle and pots of cider on us, but for the most part we kept away from habitation, uncertain who the inhabitants were. There was also the problem of refugee congestion on the main roads. They all wanted petrol. A dignified Frenchwoman drove out of Granville behind the wheel of her Mercedes hauled by a very old horse. 'How much?' asked a gunner, holding up a jerrican. 'You can have my maid,' she said.

After ten days of futile manoeuvring from positions that were never taken up, the orders came to the separated batteries to get to the coast and get out.

Cherbourg was still burning. Engineers who had labor-iously placed mines under the dockside cranes soon found it was easier to destroy them by setting fire to adjacent warehouses, reasonably certain that the flames would soon attract low-flying bombers. Looting parties ravaged the waterside restaurants. Everyone was hungry and tired. So tired that when the little coaster into which about a hundred of us were packed moved away from the wharf still tied up at the stern, the jolt as the cable broke went unnoticed by the majority of the sleeping men.

Katie arrived at Mundford, the little Breckland village where I had once been stationed, almost exactly on time. Remarkable, this, since it had entailed a cross-country journey by infrequent buses to pick up the car and drive it further south, towards home. And then get back, so that we could continue the walk the next day.

What is even more difficult to explain is how, after such a long interval, the Breckland looked even more attractive than I remembered it. On the face of it, a venture predestined to disappointment. An ex-serviceman and his wife make an elaborate detour to see the place where he was once billeted, where he had slept in Nissen huts in the woods, where his life had largely been ordered by NCOs and trumpets – bugles are for mere infantrymen. The place should have been completely unrecognizable. It wasn't, but of course it had changed a great deal.

The trees had grown immensely. Most of them, like ourselves, were youngsters in the early days of the war. The heath and the patches of marsh among the conifers were shrubby and bright with flowers. The rivers, especially the winding Wissey, looked well cared-for, and the little villages such as Mundford, where at night the gunners had crowded into small pubs, were now isolated by wide roads and looked much the better for it. By sheer good luck I had been billeted briefly in a vicarage where the priest had a well-stocked library behind glass-fronted shelves of rosewood. Finding me reading one of my own small store of books, possibly W. H. Hudson or Gosse, he asked if I knew Gilbert White, saying I might well find some parallels between that account of a corner of Hampshire and the surrounding Breckland. *Selborne* came only little short of a revelation.

Much of White's appeal to those he calls 'nice observers of natural circumstances' lies in his use of words of classical origin, akin to those in the Authorized Version of the Bible which were already archaic when the translation was made in 1611. They invigorate lines that would otherwise be unremarkable. 'Anecdote', for example, is something published for the first time; a bowl containing goldfish is a 'vivary'. The 'imbecility' of birds, meaning their physical weakness, would now mislead many, but we know precisely what he meant when in the autumn he found little parties of ring-ouzels 'cantoned' all along the Sussex Downs. He deals with one correspondent 'peremptorily'. He sounds a little cross, but he isn't at all: the word carries a Latin root for 'definitely'. The snipe's bleat is 'ventriloquous'; Timothy the famous tortoise had an 'arbitrary' stomach, and swallows and house-martins discover the 'greatest address' in building their nests. To his ear, the nuthatch 'chatters'. Today we might liken that staccato call to amplified morse-code, but his notion is unquestionably the prettier. Likewise the 'crink' of the field cricket and the 'clamour' of stone curlew echo those sounds nicely. Gilbert White is a man for all seasons, and, like the sight of geese in flight, he carries his readers along into seasons yet to come.

During those long summer evenings in the woods of Didlington and Cranwich, stone curlews, field crickets, and fern-owls (the old word for the night-jar) became our familiars. Gilbert White I read and reread, decoding his most curious words from the dictionaries at the vicarage, and learning something from every page. Until I borrowed some powerful field-glasses from the signal sergeant, I had never before heard or seen a goldcrest, that 'shadow of a bird', at close quarters: they foraged in troupes in the crowns of spruce and pine. I searched for long for a harvest mouse feeding its babies, 'administering a teat' to each.

When the word went around the camp that I could identify plants and animals, the gunners began to bring in specimens. Often it was to settle a bet about what a particular creature was. We were said to be infested by scorpions. This arose from a regimental order that the litter on the forest floor around the Nissen huts had to be swept up before the daily kit inspection. It mattered not at all that the trampled-down pine needles were blown about by the lightest of breezes. It gave bored and unoccupied men something to do between man- oeuvres. In the sweeping-up exercise men claimed to have been bitten by black scorpions. They brought me a headless specimen of a Staphylinid beetle known as the Devil's Coach-horse, a ferocious-looking creature which can bite pretty smartly. Another mangled 'scorpion' turned out to be the grotesque larva of the Lobster moth.

Late at night the guards heard and duly reported diabolical screams. They were stone curlew. I heard them myself. Since there didn't appear to be very much else I could contribute to the war effort, I got the temporary unpaid post of an assistant to the medical officer, a promotion confirmed when I reg- ularly caught trout for the colonel's breakfast.

Before we struck south through the forest together the following morning, Katie and I made a determined effort to solve a mystery which had long intrigued me. A picture as valuable as a Velasquez, you would think, could not disappear without some questions being asked about it, but we could learn very little of what had become of it at Lynford Hall.

That rambling old place with its courtyards, turrets and towers lies close to Mundford. It used to be a military hospital for cases waiting for treatment elsewhere. It is now a motel and a country club. Before my regiment left Breckland, the medical officer despaired of treating my acute dermatitis with gentian violet and methyl blue. So he sent me there. 'It's those goddam insects of yours,' he said.

When I turned up, both looking and feeling pretty blue, Lynford Hall had been requisitioned from its owners only a few days earlier. Many of the owner's fine collection of pictures were still there. Some had been vandalized. Daubs of paint emphasized the sexuality of a Greek statue and two stucco angels by Della Robbia; a dart-board had been placed alongside a huge painting of a Spanish infante on a rearing horse, which had been pierced by several darts. Before he sent me off to another hospital, I mentioned the matter to a harassed young officer. It was none of his business, he said, and he implied it was none of mine. This annoyed me.

The old gardener who was also packing up to leave gave me

236

the name of the agent in the village. I 'phoned him and evoked such an indignant response that I hung up. No, I said, I wasn't going to give him my name.

All this we related to the present owner of the Hall. He knew the building had been used as a transit hospital, and had heard about the pictures. But as the property had changed hands several times, he had no idea what eventually became of them. What had made me think the boy on the horse was so valuable?

I related, briefly, a tale of coincidences as strange as any in the pages of John Buchan. On the evening of 16 June 1957, two men who had never met before introduced themselves in the bar of the Royal British Club in Lisbon. They had arrived there by plane that afternoon, one from the Canary Isles where he lived, the other, myself, from Brazzaville in the Congo. We were both bound for Paris but the incoming plane had been delayed and there were no flights out of Portela until the following morning.

It came out during the course of the evening that my companion lived on one of the islands in semi-retirement. For years, he said, he had made a comfortable living as a picture-restorer. He had just finished his last commission, the restoration of a masterpiece damaged during the War. By bombs? I asked. No, he said. He didn't know all the details but, as he understood it, the picture had been damaged in a Norfolk mansion occupied by soldiers.

There should be pause here. A lengthy pause. I remember only that I said nothing until he described how one of the darts had pierced the eye of the youth on the rearing horse. A very sensitive place. By using a binocular microscope he managed to piece together a mosaic of paint fragments some of which were recovered from the back of the canvas. He admitted he had been well paid for his work, for the picture was a Velasquez. I told him he owed me a drink.

'I think I owe you both one,' said our host at Lynford. We spent the night there.

When Corot used to go out painting early on misty summer mornings, he always knocked off work about nine o'clock, saying, 'Everything can be seen now, and so there's nothing to see.' For him the half amounted to more than the whole. As soon as the elements of a landscape began to emerge from partial obscurity, he wanted no more of it. And we were at one with Corot that morning.

By some fine balance between the temperature and the precipitation point, the forest was only partly obscured by mist, and even as we struck down one glade after another, keeping strictly to a compass course, great shafts of lemon-coloured light swept up the most opaque of vapours as lightly as a feather duster and left in their wake a sprinkling of diamonds among the dewy grasses.

Fallow deer, nicely camouflaged by splashes of light, scampered ahead, stopped and turned with one leg raised, before scampering on. Birds sang, timidly, awaiting the full dawn which in a thick woodland is often an hour or more after the sun's first showing. And all around and above were trees of weight and cathedral majesty. These are trite observations, but surely the best part of experience is the discovery that what a thousand poets and prosers have said before is shiningly and exhilaratingly true. An intriguing difficulty, in returning to a place after many years, is to distinguish between what is literally seen and what the memory process has imprinted.

Because of its location in Snake Wood about a mile to the north-west of Grimes Graves, I could point out where, for lack of anything else to do, we had guarded the wreckage of a Wellington bomber, one of the many that had almost limped home, high-octane fuel pouring from its bullet-ridden tanks. The River Wissey, unpolluted by time, prattled on. The prehistoric flint mines, probably the most extensive in Britain, the centre of our first export trade in kitchen utensils and weaponry, were heavily fenced off. Perhaps it was as well since, notwithstanding an abundance of barrows, we were heading fast for Bury St Edmunds and had little time for the neolithic that morning. And yet I cannot resist quoting from the report of a nineteenth-century excavator who, examining a skull found among some amber beads and gold ornaments, described it as 'remarkably thick and, speaking phrenologically, displayed a large development of the animal passions as also caution and love of approbation'.

The forest thins towards Thetford. Farmsteads lie in sandy clearings. A keen ear may detect a change in the accent of friendly fellows who lean over gates, prepared to discuss badgers or bees for which the district has been famous since the Domesday Survey, probably on account of the thick heather. But though we crossed and recrossed the county boundary three times between Santon Downham and the disused railway that runs south to Bury, there is little distinction between Norfolk and Suffolk thereabouts. We were still in the engaging grip of Breckland.

To the south of Bury you may come across the church of St Mary remarkable for having all the letters of the alphabet set into the flint of the flushwork. For centuries, pilgrims on their way to the tomb of the Blessed St Edmund gazed on those letters. They recalled their errors. They crossed themselves and hastened on, 'in God's grace much comforted' a chronicler said. But he didn't say why. And until somebody found an explanation in an old breviary together with a couplet in Latin, the potency of the indulgence was lost. The couplet ran:

> Per hoc alphabetum notum
> Componitur Brevarium totum

which is an even shorter way of saying that those who had omitted to say their daily office could, on that occasion at least, take comfort from the fact that the alphabet contains, potentially, all that it is possible to say.

As our time was running out even faster than the pages I have left for Suffolk, I shall, by the grace of St Mary, alphabeticize a great deal. Otherwise I should be going into what actually happened to the bones of King Edmund, beaten in battle and martyred like St Sebastian by the Great Army of the Danes in A.D. 870. There are five theories, including that one put out by Lady Patricia Ward who cherished an unshared conviction that the coffin came to rest in a passage under her front lawn. I should like to say a requiem for the last Great Bustard known to have bred in Britain. It came to a violent end in 1832, not far from where the dying King commended his soul to God. But, with more than a thought for both, we slept at Bury within sight of the great Norman tower. In an excellent pub. Celia Fiennes also had had no time for the martyr, but excused herself on the grounds that she just happened to be 'passant'.

In a trick commonly practised by film producers and cameramen, you can square off the landscape ahead by holding your arms out at full length with upturned fingers and only the thumbs touching. On our way down to a certain village between Bury and Clare, we did this several times in an effort to get a glimmering of what Constable might have made of its rural intimacy. For Suffolk has no stage effects. Its beauty is tranquil and elusive, but with a vignette at almost every turn. It has managed to absorb the twentieth century, as you may see it in a moated Tudor manor-house functioning as a farm, tethered to present-day reality by a chain of modern pig pens and aluminium chicken coops.

Of the great trees that Lady Ward wrote about with such affection, the elms are slain of the beetle and the deadly infection it carries. Like vanquished Titans left to rot, they lie about in ditches, unburnt. The survivors, especially the truly gigantic oaks and the ash, are an independent lot. They refuse to march in order along the edges of a road but go wandering off singly or in pairs, across a field or hedgerow, like bored children at a dancing-class striking unauthorized attitudes on a self-chosen part of the floor.

As with the trees and the higgledy-piggledy, high-gabled, different coloured cottages, so too with the people. They are noticeably independent or, if you prefer it, politely self-contained, not much given to small talk with strangers unless it should be about flowers, for they love their gardens with pride and passion. The phrase 'silly Suffolk', meaning that the natives are more prone than most to do 'summat right daft', is an unfortunate interpretation of the Anglo-Saxon word *sely* (German *selig*) meaning blissful or blessed, which is understandable in a county remarkable for the number and the quality of its churches.

But for all that, the lads and the lassies and their elders and no-betters get up to some strange tricks. And their wives too. There were those members of that Women's Institute we passed who, at first undecided about where to go for their annual trip, settled eventually for an instructive day out in the local slaughterhouse. In pubs you will hear oldsters arguing,

240

quietly but with heart-felt conviction, about the best time to plant marjoram or dahlias, or whether that lovable workhorse, the Punch, looks best from the front or from behind.

People love Suffolk for many reasons, not least because most of the roads are too narrow for City shuttlecockers. It's a place in which naturalists settle down as industriously as wild bees in secluded burrows largely of their own making. For this reason I'm not saying where the Matthews live. I doubt deeply whether Leo would sting me if I did. We have known each other quite a long time, but he can emit a sort of throaty bumbling noise which inhibits the importunate as effectively as his, 'Oh, do you think so?' which means he is not at all of your opinion. And as for little Dolly, his wife, one of *Les Girls* who played at *Les Folies Bergère*, she knows more than a thing or two about repelling unwanted attention. They met at sea nearly sixty years ago in RMS *Andes* homeward bound from Buenos Aires.

When Leonard Harrison Matthews became Director of the Zoological Society of London it was said of him that naturalists who come to sudden fame seldom seek it. For if a naturalist is a good one, he spends more time tending the garden of his research than in talking about it. And when the fruit of his work eventually ripens, he is sometimes more surprised than everybody else.

Up to that appointment he had been very much of a wandering albatross, the title of one of his books, which showed that the study of whales in 1920, when precious little was known about them, was a highly adventurous as well as an important business, especially in South Georgia when, as he puts it, 'it blew quite a lot'. Beyond Cape Horn and the Roaring Forties the wind blows like hell for weeks on end, driving icebergs the size of Suffolk ahead of the blusters. Only the albatrosses and the mollymawks feel at home.

Leo is very much of a naturalist's naturalist. Whereas scores of his fellow Fellows of the Royal Society are invited to join that scientific priestcraft for work of a highly specific nature, the man who sailed south on the *Discovery* began his career by exploring a whole world of organisms from the minute to the immense. The world of the sea. This is the particular privilege of that élite corps of internationalists, the oceanographers. As intellectuals, they are probably neither better nor worse than characters confined to conference halls, lecture-theatres or laboratories, but in the matter of getting pleasure out of what they do, I reckon them infinitely more fortunate.

From the structure of whales, what they fed on, and how fast they grew and reproduced themselves, Leo turned to the plants and animals of South America, the predators and scavengers of East Africa, and the sprats, seals, and basking shark of the high latitudes. This is where, on a speck of an island off Skye, I came in contact with him, marginally, through the late Gavin Maxwell. Then more intimately as my mentor, and for many years as a friend. That's why we tramped up his secluded drive that afternoon. That's why, until far into the night, Leo and I set the world to rights over more than a dram or two. We wonder, often, how it goes agley in between times.

Talk has none of the freezing immunities of the pulpit or the platform. What you can get away with on a page such as this is a throat-clearing exercise, mere practice for the cut-and-thrust of intimate conversation. There is in it, too, a competitive element. Talk flows the better when one of the party, in this case myself, knows that he is likely to be unhorsed if he gets too deep into vertebrate zoology or marine fauna with or without a backbone. The trick is to draw the elusive Albatross into the narrower, the more esoteric, fields of speculation and enquiry. This isn't easy, since for years Leo has teased, chided, questioned, and pointed out fresh paths to a roving reporter who, until he got the feel of the tropics and the tundra, hadn't really seen much beyond his familiar heaths.

It must have been somewhere around two o'clock in the morning when, with an uneasy look at what was left in the bottle, I asked the Albatross if he remembered what he had said long ago, before I took off for the Congo. This I knew to be a conversation-stopper. Most people would answer 'no' and leave it at that. But Leo doesn't trade in ordinary answers. He lifted an eyebrow. Just one eyebrow.

'Not precisely,' he said.

What I recall him saying was, 'When do you intend to write

242

up your notes?' For this was in those days before every field-tripper in search of a Ph.D. went out laden with tape-recorders, tachometers and movie-cameras. When I said, 'Each night, of course', Leo merely breathed a 'H'm' which is another of his expressions of deep disapproval.

His advice, so simple in retrospect, so important in fact, was to make a note of whatever was seen the moment it was seen. Within forty-eight hours I had the opportunity of putting it into practice alongside the Stanley cataracts above what is now called Kinshasa, on the great river. During that four months' trip I filled five notebooks, and wished, later, I had filled more.

That opportunity for almost unlimited travel in the Congo fell into my lap at an international meeting of zoologists in Denmark. I had been interviewing Victor van Straelen, the president of the Institut des Parcs Nationaux du Congo Belge about the fate of the mountain gorilla among the volcanoes of the Virunga. Would I care to see them? he asked. Before I could even think about the possibility, he went off into a reverie the substance of which was that the great apes were the inhabitants only of the fringe of the rain forests. To appreciate how they had parted company with their lowland relatives, it would be necessary to see something of the pygmies of the interior and also the game plains of Ruanda. It would take two or three months. Could I leave London fairly soon? A geologist from Yale would accompany me on the ascent of the Ruwenzori, the Mountains of the Moon. It would facilitate the *mission* if they could arrange porterage for us both at the same time.

Before I flew back to London, somewhat dazed by the turn of events, the president's *chef du secrétariat* had drafted a schedule which for exotic variety offered more than the combined resources of Thomas Cook and American Express. And I was to be paid for the trip. The Institut wanted a report on a proposal to admit tourists into regions which up till then had been devoted to scientific research. I nodded judiciously. It seemed unwise to mention at that moment that I had never been within a thousand miles of the tropics.

From Khartoum south the course of events as set down in those notebooks still seems curiously unreal. It began with a

243

flight over an orange-red desert that had no beginning but after hours and hours came to an end in enormous banks of cloud. The clouds above the rain forests. 'The trees are always breathing,' said the Sabena pilot laconically. He made the trip twice a week, and dreamed of buying an apartment in the suburbs of Brussels. He didn't much like Stanleyville (Kinshasa), describing it as a *blanchisserie*.

For me, with a private plane at my disposal, I seemed to be constantly on the move between places out of Conrad's *Heart of Darkness*, the sweaty forests, the great plains, and those hill residences of princely proportions, the up-country headquarters of the *conservateurs*.

From dusk to dawn the steamy air of the great river was literally punctuated by Lokele message-drummers, incessantly sending out news of births and deaths and markets and invitations to feasts. Naked black women, as lithe, as beautiful, as Chinese brush-strokes on rice paper, poled their *pirogues* between trumpet-shaped fish-traps some twenty feet in diameter, woven from osiers. We encountered pygmies in the Ituri and gorilla among the volcanoes. One almost conical peak, Nyiragongo, obligingly blew its top and oozed a mile-long stream of acrid-smelling tar whilst we were at the base camp below. Weeks slipped by rapidly in the company of game-wardens, plant-hunters, tsetse-fly investigators, and a man who, among much else, literally pursued large and poisonous snakes for the extraction of material for anti-venenes. In my diary I wrote:

Drove down a track in the gallery forest ten miles north of Garamba. Tall trees, mixed, on one side; scrub, mostly *Euphorbia* on the other. Gaston became excited. A large green mamba, about ten feet in length, swung towards us. Three feet were on the ground. The rest at an angle of forty-five degrees thrashed, purposively, from side to side. It seemed to be going fast. It looked cross. Gaston swerved away, gave me the wheel, and got out his bamboo pole with the wire noose at the point. 'Chase it!' he said. Nobbled it in second gear when the mamba going, I suppose, flat out can't have been doing more than four mph. So much for the speed of deadly snakes.

But for excitement all paled beside our ascent, to a height of about fourteen thousand feet, of snow-capped Margherita, one of the Mountains of the Moon. With the help of twenty Banisanza porters with headloads, it took five days.

A characteristic of tropical peaks from the High Andes to Central Africa is that at a certain critical height, a number of plants such as heathers, lobelias and groundsels *(Senecio)* grow to a truly gigantic height that is upwards of thirty feet. I thought we had done with high drama when olive-green bats skimmed round our camp among the bamboos, and round-eared elephants appeared against a background of blinding white snow. For the beds of sphagnum moss and the giant plants had emerged, it seemed, from an entirely different world.

The reaction of a newcomer is likely to be more emotional than that of a seasoned plant-collector, but this is how Patrick M. Synge, a man who for many years edited the publications of the Royal Horticultural Society, reacted to the Mountains of the Moon:

A grey mist made a fitting background for the most monstrous and unearthly landscape I have ever seen. Vague outlines of peaks and precipices towered around us. Here were plants which seemed more like ghosts of past ages than ordinary trees and herbs. They appeared as a weird and terrible dream to me, a botanist and hunter of strange plants. It all seemed so unreal, like some imaginary reconstruction of life in a long past geological age, or even upon another planet. Our own familiar and common herbs seemed to have gone mad. Although not lunar in fact they well lived up to that name in appearance. On the ground grew a thick carpet of mosses, some brilliant yellow, others deep crimson in colour. Every shade of green was represented and the tree trunks were also clothed in thick moss, often tussocked into the semblance of faces. It is good to be able to escape sometimes from the ordinary world; this strange mountain carried us into a dreamland which was often a fairyland, occasionally a nightmare . . . and a little ahead there was permanent snow and ice.*

Most journeys end far more abruptly than they begin. That trip was a shining exception. In Congo the return flights on the monopolistic air-service, Sabena, were booked up for weeks ahead. It said on both my ticket and *carte de matriculation* that, under pain of unspecified penalties, I was obliged to

* *In Search of Flowers* by Patrick M. Synge, London, 1973.

present myself at the airport at a certain hour on a certain day. I looked at the ticket with growing distaste. Like a schoolboy who does everything he can to delay going to bed on his birthday, I 'phoned, I cabled the All-Highest in Brussels. Nothing happened.

I said to hell with Sabena and booked a passage on a dirty riverboat, down to Leopoldville. It took nine days. The ITB *Lieutenant Lippens* ran into beds of an invasive water weed called the Devil's Lilac *(Eichhornia)*, and broke down twice. We had to be towed for the last thirty miles.

There were no available flights out of Leopoldville. I crossed the river to Brazzaville and switched to Air France where, with some difficulty, I reached Rabat in Morocco. After a night in the airport lock-up (I had no visa and the Moroccans were at war with somebody), the American consul managed to get the representative of the *New York Times* on to a Portuguese flight to Lisbon. The British consul had been plain damned unhelpful. In Lisbon I met the man I mentioned earlier, the restorer of damaged pictures, and realized, as I did again at Lynford, that some journeys never really come to an end.

Suffolk took hold of us from the start but left me to make what I could of it on my own. Not from choice. Madam had gone off with Leo to retrieve the car, a piece of domestic machinery we often felt we could have done without. But since this is an honest account of how things worked out between us, conscience impels me to ask, first, how we could have done the whole walk without the thing and, second, how it came about that I had not gone a dozen miles before I felt sadly in need of someone to talk to. This worked up into quite a personal argument.

For years I thought I had Hazlitt on my side. He said he could not see the wit of talking and walking at the same time. In my defence of freedom to the uttermost, a phrase not far from the Book of Common Prayer, I trotted this out to a scholarly priest in a pub at Clare, not far from the border between Suffolk and Essex, but he came down ace on king by recalling Hazlitt's intense delight in his long walks in the company of Coleridge.

As I trawled about in my memory, unsuccessfully, that Jesuitical fellow diplomatically offered a little solace by quoting C. E. Montague: 'Immense as our admiration must be for all who can talk to magnificent purpose about their own uncommon selves, one may admire, too, the magnificence of the unbroken silence of others.' And after that there wasn't much to be said.

Clare stands a little to the north of the Stour, a Celtic word meaning 'the vigorous river'. This was far from apparent as I leant over the bridge shared between Suffolk and Essex. Fat fish flopped up to the surface and flopped down again; wagtails snapped at flies on water-beds of crowfoot. A kingfisher sparked brief and electric blue. But on the way down to the county boundary there were farms of befitting vigour, square-built, abrupt even, some of them, yet tamed by age. A vertical sun touched their flints with gold, and trees,

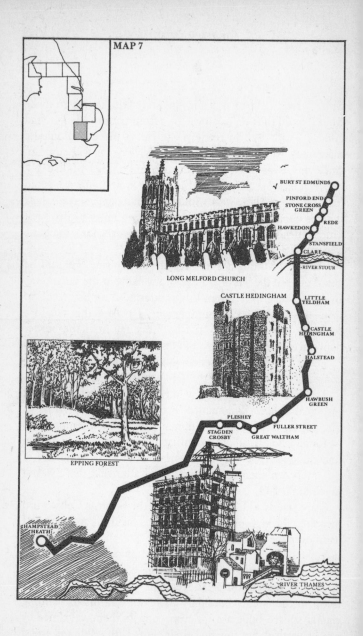

MAP 7

BURY ST EDMUNDS
PINFORD END
STONE CROSS GREEN
HAWKEDON
REDE
STANSFIELD
CLARE
RIVER STOUR

LONG MELFORD CHURCH

CASTLE HEDINGHAM

LITTLE YELDHAM
CASTLE HEDINGHAM
HALSTEAD
HAWBUSH GREEN

EPPING FOREST

PLESHEY
STAGDEN CROSBY
FULLER STREET
GREAT WALTHAM

HAMPSTEAD HEATH

RIVER THAMES

248

still set from a light shower, were freckled with points of light which in those paintings of enormous elms became known as Constable's snow.

That day I learned that old friends still called one another 'Borr', presumably from neighbour; that an affectionate diminutive is 'little', as you may hear it in 'li'l ole tempest' meaning a helluva thunderstorm. Conversely a cuckoo-loud morning is 'that fare a master fine day'. Within living memory they used to play real quoits by chucking heavy iron rings the size of sanctuary knockers along the grass verges of the roads.

Long before the police trained dogs to sniff out a few ounces of cannabis, local farmers grew the stuff by the acre for its fibre (hemp) or as seeds for caged birds. A harvest-home is a 'horkey', and not a few lonely souls are at one with Lot's daughter in feeling that incest comes closer to being a necessity than a gross misdemeanour. I heard of a young girl whose mother is her sister and whose father her grandfather. Had she a brother, there would be Biblical sanction for calling him Moab.

In Essex, I didn't pause until I took a nap in the handsomely named but otherwise unremarkable hamlet of Belchamp St Paul. I awoke to the sound of shots. Young rooks were falling out of the trees, dead.

Whereas the so-called Glorious Twelfth is known throughout the country as the start of the grouse-shooting season, some farmers who are fond of rook pie refer to the twelfth of May as 'the other Twelfth' in the sense that Thames watermen refer to the Medway as 'the other river'. It's a short season, lasting only some three or four days. Emerging uncertainly from their nests, the tender young fledgelings offer a light rifleman an easy enough target. Only the breasts are eaten, and Mrs Beeton, precise as ever, says: 'Take six young rooks and three-quarters of a pound of rump steak for some five or six persons.' I wonder what she would have made of *pie froid* which appeared on the menu of the Café Royal towards the end of the War. The *maître d'hôtel*, short of food, short of staff, but never lacking in imagination and young warriors on leave, said his chef had persuaded him that, with spice and aspic, much could be done with a few brace of magpies.

Did that surprise the elderly tenant of Tilbury Farm who was out shooting? It did not. He grinned – that's to say his walrus moustache went up under his nose to disclose almost no teeth. 'Dad told me he'd seen dressed heron several times in Halstead market,' he said. 'Big wings they've got, I know. But no body. Like a li'l ole grapefruit it is.'

Had he eaten any other unusual fowl? 'Not me,' he said, putting down his string of still-warm rooklings. 'But Dad said' (always Dad said) 'he knew no better bird than golden plover. They come down here in winter with the peewits. Taste like duck and oysters. High fliers too. Put your first shot across the bows and, as the flock comes skittling down, nobble the nearest with your second barrel. Don't see 'em much these days.' I mentioned that they were strictly protected, but he had lapsed into a private reverie about what his missus could do with them li'l rooks.

Few things are more pleasant than a village graced with a good church, a good priest, and a good pub. There is something symbiotic in their relationship. This, at least, is the impression I gained in Little Yeldham where the vicar was discussing parochial affairs over a pint of Greene King with the company around a cheerful fire in the Stone and Faggot. All jovial in-talk which, together with an inspection of his two churches and the hospitality of the rectory – for he invited me to lunch – gave a blessed touch to an afternoon in which, on my own once again, things didn't go at all well.

What drove me on was the thought that Katie would be waiting at the next township of Halstead. She had said six o'clock and I had never known her to be more than a few minutes late. It should have been an easy walk of nine or ten miles. It was nearer fifteen as, stupidly, I strayed. And all the time it rained, hard.

There is a Tibetan saying that on a long walk obstacles such as unrelenting rain, hailstorms and snow are the work of demons intent on testing the integrity of travellers and eliminating the faint-hearted among them. With that I'm solidly on the side of the Tibetans, since a succession of storms up in the mountains between the south of France and North Italy once came pretty close to putting an end to my long-distance walking. There, my sense of indestructibility came to a full stop. It seemed as if the pedestrian equivalent of the big end had gone. A wind of uncommon violence shrieked down from the Maritime Alps. It was difficult to stand up – at a time, mark you, when the airs of Provence should have been filled with the fragrance of myrtle, rosemary, oleander and the song of cicadas. It shouldn't have happened; it wouldn't have happened if I hadn't been obsessed by the notion to see the magic mountain and at the same time to continue a walk that had already taken me a thousand miles across Europe.

Before I set off for Italy my wife had died of cancer, bravely but fearfully. In an effort to come to terms with a sentence of life on my own I ventured into countries without ever really seeing them. Women friends, especially Pépé, were of solace, but rarely for long. I drank, heavily. To quote that most lucid of travellers, Peter Matthiesen, whose wife had died in similar circumstances: 'I wandered from one path to another with no real recognition that I was engaged upon a search, and scarcely a clue as to what I might be after. I only knew that at the bottom of each breath there was a hollow place that needed to be filled.'

My romantic notion on that journey was to explore a curious mountain I had seen very briefly on the final stages of a walk through the Southern Alps. In the last rays of the setting sun, Monte Bego, a contorted peak about forty miles north of Nice, had seemed to burn with cold incandescent fire. A French mountaineer affected to look horrified when I mentioned it the next day. You could scramble up that peak in a couple of hours he said, but it was inadvisable. *C'est le domaine du diable.* He had left his prints on the rocks. Even the shepherds were frightened of the place. Hokum, I thought.

Archaeologists were less sceptical. The librarian of their Institute in London introduced me to the little-known works of a Surrey clergyman, the Rev. Clarence Bicknell, who from 1840 onwards had copied many thousands of weird engravings he had found on the coloured rocks there. They were grotesque figures both of animals and human beings carrying huge weapons like halberds. There were ploughs

251

and carts of an extremely primitive kind, and cattle with immense horns. Some dated back to the Bronze Age, others had been added later by shepherds.

So Monte Bego seemed as good a place as any other to be included in a long trip. But to what end? Giovanni Caselli, a young Italian archaeologist who was living in London, suggested a walk to Rome. He had explored a track which could well be the oldest highway in the world, almost certainly palaeolithic in origin. It ran south from Bologna, clinging to the rim of the hills. Would I care to join him there so we could set off together? I wrote back saying that if a route could be worked out through the Northern Apennines which took in Monte Bego, it sounded a splendid idea. At that time of the year I reckoned I could make Bologna in a fortnight, maybe less.

Only a sort of oafish optimism stopped me from calling the whole thing off the day I stepped off the plane at Nice. Gale force nine, said the navigator, and likely to continue for days. The leaves of the huge palms that stand respectfully on both sides of the Promenade des Anglais clattered like toy windmills. That azure sea of a thousand postcards had turned bile green, and was flecked with foam. The sky looked bruised, ashamed at what had been done to that essentially feminine city.

Up in the hills it was worse. Unknown to me, Piedmonte and points south had been struck by what *La Stampa* described in huge letters on its front page as *Disastro naturale . . . Il diluvio . . . Diversi morti.* All bridges in the Val Vamasca had been carried away by torrents. The mountain railway between Nice and San Dalmazzo on the Franco-Italian frontier had been cut by landslips. I heard later that Monte Bego lies at the centre of valleys that act as wind-tunnels. Storms are common thereabouts, a fact which probably accounts for its reputation as an abode of evil spirits.

From San Dalmazzo I set off twice and fell back, bruised, knocked down by gusts of wind of astonishing violence. There was no resisting those body throws except by lying down, flat. At the third attempt I got to within three miles of the magic mountain by spending the night in a ruined chapel where the wind tried to get in at me through a hole in the roof.

During a lull the next day I saw Monte Bego as through frosted glass, a snow-covered peak, curiously skewed, with a lake below, among platforms of rocks that varied in colour from pale ochre to that streaky-red you may see in thin-skinned oranges. All hopes of seeing the monstrous engravings at close quarters were dispelled when the wind rose again. It turned the light carpet of snow into whirling dervishes. The peak disappeared and it took me a day to trudge back to square one, wondering for the umpteenth time whether to press on or go back home.

In foul weather the onward-going game is played out in the same way, no matter whether on the roof of the Apennines or the ploughed fields of Essex during a rainstorm. You either hope for respite within the hour or fortify yourself with thoughts of comfort at nightfall. I decided to strike east, towards Bologna, keeping to the crest. The first two nights were spent in Spartan fashion, attending to huge fires of ready-cut larch logs. The timber had been felled years ago and blazed like funeral pyres. On the third day I became fed up with my own company and threw away a thousand feet by scrambling down to the little hamlet of Realdo in the Verdeggia, a deep depression to the east of Mount Saccarello.

Realdo looked a bit depressed too. A rutted mountain track ended there and I must have been the first visitor they had ever seen. There was neither a shop nor a hotel. But there was a bar run by a man who hunted and netted birds, and it was in his barn that I spent the night. He hadn't a spare room. I knew that because Granny slept in the bar and when she thought it was about time the customers went home she started to take her clothes off.

The bird-catcher lit a fire by the simple expedient of putting match to an enormous bale of twigs under his arm. He waited until it blazed, furiously, before chucking them into a recess under a hole in the roof. The company watched him in silence hoping, I suspect, that he would set fire to himself.

They were kind to me. I couldn't understand most of what his four or five customers said, since they spoke a slurred variant of Mentonesi. The pasta and the chestnut pudding tasted of nothing in particular and the *vin*, which in their dialect rhymed with 'tin', was a peppery variety of Barbera. A little hospitality on my part came easily, since it worked out at about five shillings a litre. But nobody would tell me how to get on to that little high road that went on for mile after mile through the mountains. It was marked on the map, lying about two miles above the village.

They obviously knew where I wanted to go, but indicated, largely in mime, that it was difficult and downright dangerous. One dreadful-looking fellow with a blood-red eye behind his patch – which he kept taking off – stood on a chair and gave a pretty good imitation of me falling off a precipice. The rest slowly lowered their heads as I fell God knows how many feet. Orson Welles once shrewdly observed that Italy is full of actors, sixty million of them in fact. There are only a few bad ones, and they are mostly on the stage and in films. If the company that night hadn't put up such a fine performance, I might have believed them. But, they said, there were also other reasons. What were they? Was it, I asked innocently, a *via dei contrabandieri*?

Heavy coughs. Much muttering and forced laughter. Blood-eye put his head back and roared before he thought of another diversion. He came up to within two feet of my bar stool before he took off his patch again, slowly. At the sight of that awful hole in his face, I had some difficulty in not lowering my eyes. *'Ecco!'* he said. *'La guerra!'* And I knew what I was in for. We had it all that night, and when he missed out a bit about getting a shell-splinter in his bowels, the company prompted him. Fortunately Granny, who must have heard the story dozens of times, began to unbutton her blouse. They obediently downed their drinks and shuffled out, wishing me a good night.

An eerie night. In the light of a paraffin lamp, the barn looked frightful and smelt like a midden. Skins of foxes, badgers, otters, and marmots were piled high on wooden shelves. On the floor were rolls of fine netting and pots of bird lime. The Italians have an infamous reputation for slaughtering small birds. Ignoring the squeaks and the frenzied scampering of rats, I slept until seven o'clock, when I found the Val de Verdeggia swathed in mist.

After much aimless wandering about I met an old man feeding his chickens at the top of the village. I asked him point blank how much he wanted for his services as a guide. 'Where to, *signore*?' To the *sentiero*, I said, pointing up into the sky. To my surprise, he didn't seem in the least surprised. Presumably he wasn't one of the consortium of the night before. We settled for fifteen hundred lire, which was just about a £1 sterling. We shook hands on it. I was delighted. I would have given him ten times that amount.

My good friend Mario went up that track like a chamois, skipping and jumping from scree to scree, pausing only to point out where I might cut off a bend or clutch hold of a bush for support. At my request he slowed down a little, and at one point, and with some linguistic difficulties, I tried to find out why the villagers were so secretive about the track through the hills. I expected a theatrical, a voluble denial. Instead he smiled and shook his head. He didn't know, he said. I looked for signs of deceit in his dark eyes and, finding none, trudged on, more puzzled than ever.

Half an hour passed before events took a wholly unexpected turn. From far above came two reverberant hoots as from an alpine horn or a great ship, say a Cunarder, entering port. The sound echoed back from unseen peaks and died away to the north-west, perhaps from the magic mountain.

Giulio looked terrified. His whole face changed. He clutched my arm. '*Torni! Torni! subito in dietro!*' We must go back at once. He appealed to me. He tried to drag me back. I shook him off. He turned round and scampered down. I could hear his feet on the shale. After a few moments of indecision I walked up into the clouds alone.

Not difficult but arduous. The little path wound in and out of crumbling outcrops at an angle of about forty-five degrees. To my huge relief, the mist began to thin, and high above there appeared an unbroken, a pencil-thin, line – the *via militari*.

I scrambled up to a concrete blockhouse patterned with green and yellow lichen, the door heavily padlocked, a new padlock. And somebody had been there that morning. They had driven in from the west, perhaps two or three cars. To the east, beyond the blockhouse, there were no wheelmarks, no footprints in that soft damp shale. And no clues as to who the visitors might be, except a little pile of cigar-bands and cigarette-stubs, still dry. Somebody had emptied a car ashtray and thrown away a blood-stained bandage. I listened for sounds of a car but could hear nothing except the pipe of marmots and the trickle of a stream.

Among my funded capital of achievement, that highway through the clouds stands low in terms of anything approaching the heroic, but it had its moments. And some were horrendous: Stygian-black tunnels, and those *frani*, the landslips that constantly bedevil travellers in the Apennines. On that Golgotha of a track I came across skulls and kicked two or three over the edge where they disappeared into the mist. They were huge skulls. Probably draught oxen. The clouds above and the mists below were constantly at odds with each other, as uncertain as young lovers about who should order the going. And when they got together, as they did at irregular intervals, it left me wondering what in heaven or on earth lay around the next ample sweep of that track.

In places where it simply disappeared under a landslip, the going entailed arduous scrambles across a shale-grey tongue of scree. Worse by far were the tunnels which were serpentine and dark. My flashlamp gleamed feebly. In the second or third venture into the dark, I walked into a knee-deep pool of water and dropped the damned thing. Total darkness. Until a small circle of light gleamed far ahead, I shuffled along, foot by foot, with my elbow stuck out like the trolley of a streetcar, brushing the uneven walls of the tunnel.

The next day, and the day after that, the ridgeway beyond the Col di Nava and Garessio appeared grossly overgrown by young chestnut trees, all about thirty years old, the age of young Italians who had decided that life in an electronics factory, or wherever they make watches, automobiles and light artillery, was infinitely preferable to transhumation, the seasonal bucolics of the Apennines. There will be very few of those tracks left in a few years' time.

Since Ligurian place names all sound much alike to thick-tongued Nordics, it is sufficient to say that until I struck off towards Bologna I held to the ridges high above San Remo, Savona, and Genoa. In places where the ground fell sheer and was strewn with rocks, I travelled fast. But where the ancient paths had to be looked for among the riot of chestnut saplings, there were miserable delays made worse by flurries of hail. Yet some days went well and one section at least, the Route di Turkino, could be called operatic. It lies high up in the hills to the north-west of Genoa, where the top of a mountain is remarkable for a strange mixture of the sacred and the secular. After a stiff climb of about seven hours the Stations of the Cross come into view on the summit. They are truly arduous Stations, since the platforms on which they stand have been cut out of rock, one above the other. They lead up to a huge crucifix of Christ the Redeemer, aloof, austere, forlorn, against the darkening sky. Visitors are reminded that this is a *Via sacra riservata ai soli pedoni in preghiera.*

Carefully avoiding the *Proprieta privata. Lasciare libero il passagio,* I made my way to a small guest-house where, with some difficulty, I managed to book a room. The daughter of the house, a timid-looking creature, said the *padrone* had gone out and might return with some friends. But for a roll of thunder I might have settled for a meal and pitched down that night in the *Santuario Regina Pacis.* I received a key in exchange for my passport, and what lies I told about being the representative not only of English newspapers but also of the Italian Tourist Board are matters for my own conscience. The girl prepared an indifferent meal but, fortified by a bottle of superb Brunello, I watched the storm brew up and roll away, muttering. And by that time I was half-asleep.

I awoke as if at the sound of the Last Trump. From somewhere down in the valley came that noise Mario and I had heard earlier, which I have likened to an Alpine horn or the deep groan of an Atlantic liner. I heard it first as if in a dream. But it sounded again, nearer this time. And even as I looked out of my bedroom window, five cars rolled into the courtyard. A large white Mercedes first, the others equally opulent. The brethren had arrived.

They all got out: about a dozen men and three or four women, led by a stocky fellow with his arm in a sling and a beautiful-looking piece at his side. They looked as if they were dressed for a wedding or a family confirmation party.

Brunello is perhaps the finest wine in Italy. It comes from Montalcino, a Tuscan hill-town to the south of Sienna. It is kept in the dark for years before strictly controlled amounts are released. The saying is that Brunello fortifies the heart. I suspect, too, that like injudicious quantities of brandy it tends to paralyse the inhibitory cortices. I can think of no other reason why I put on a pair of clean but crumpled cotton trousers, a dark pullover and, rehearsing a small speech, went down to join the company.

All conversation promptly ceased. The stocky fellow turned to the *padrone* who looked horrified. He muttered something about the *Inglesi*. I might have been naked. Or pointing a gun. The stocky fellow turned to me and bowed, slightly. My turn for elaborate courtesy. It must have been the Brunello speaking. In English, slowly and elaborately, I wished them all a very good day. Such a surprise. My apologies, my very real apologies, for interrupting what must have been an important occasion. I bowed again. Suppressing a ridiculous idea of asking them what they were up to, I made as if to go. The stocky fellow lifted up his hand. Not at all. I must take a drink. The beautiful woman brought me a glass of wine.

With her high breasts and buttocks like mandolines, an extremely beautiful woman. By comparison her friends looked like middle-class tarts. She spoke fragments of English and had that Italian ability to lift up one eyebrow. I came from where? And where to? To Genoa tomorrow, I said. She spoke softly, almost in whispers. My bravado drained away. I thanked the company at large, and scuttled up to my room. Somebody came to the top of the stairs and stayed there.

Before I had finished my notes, I could see from my window that the company had reassembled in the Sanctuario, on chairs in a circle around a table and a crate of wine. And from their bent heads they were all listening to what the stocky fellow had to say.

To my consternation somebody tapped on my bedroom door. Quietly but peremptorily. Four taps. *Staccato.* Stuffing the little field-glasses under a cushion, I opened the door. There stood the beautiful woman.

Permesso?

Luigi Barzini has pointed out that with their excessive facility for expressing emotions facially, his fellow-country-men are often disconcerted and unhappy in the north of Europe. They find us cold. They don't know what we are thinking about. But the beautiful one can have had no doubts whatever about my emotions. They were those of a field-mouse face to face with a sleek cat, and I suspect she rather enjoyed the situation.

She held my hand just a shade longer than necessary. She looked round the room. Her eyes caught the protruding end of a strap. She pulled out my field-glasses and, in doing so, glanced towards the window. Her turn to be caught off balance. Somebody was walking back towards the house.

Hotel Excelsior, Genoa, May 28: Fulvio, the head porter thinks I was damn lucky to get out without being beaten up. Me too. Couldn't sleep. Got up at six and left at seven. Nobody about except the down-trodden daughter. Cooled me for twenty quid, nearly half of it for that wine. Apparently everyone except me knows of *Il Trombone*, the Noisy One. Big-time racketeer who specializes in busting banks and importing drugs. F. says he runs a line of whore shops in the Rue de Pre on the waterfront. Advises me not to go near them. Advice unnecessary. Am leaving early tomorrow.

At eight o'clock, lightly disguised, I trudged out of Genoa in what seemed the company of half the town in overladen, flag-decked buses, fast cars, and on noisy motorbikes. Lightly disguised, since I lowered my head each time I saw a large white car. Not the best day to storm the Passo di Giovi on foot – and on a busy road, too. It was the Festival of St Peter. But once through that ancient gateway, I regained the ridgeway and struck east towards Pontremoli.

I plunged through the first of a series of grossly overgrown tracks, hugely encouraged by a dab of blue paint on a protruding rock, the trail-mark of the local Federazione Italiania Escursionismo. It glistened in the sun. Another within a few hundred yards, and a third which not only glistened: the paint was still wet. It had been splashed on minutes earlier by Carlo Bertelli, a Genoese taxi-driver, the only pedestrian I met in the hills. An amiable, a most helpful fellow. No, he said, few people walked these days, but they were trying to encourage it. They had stowed away eight pots of paint on a twenty-kilometre stretch of the ridgeway to the Passo di Bocca. Three of his friends were following behind, slashing a patch through the chestnut saplings. In another few years the ridgeway would be completely overgrown, he reckoned. As to the path ahead, it was, he admitted, pretty rough. *Bruto. Malagevole.*

For several days I saw almost nobody between dawn and dusk, and lived on Knorr's soup, rye bread, salami and rough red wine. *Fragole,* those exquisite little mountain strawberries, were to be plucked almost everywhere. The crumbly medieval villages lay mostly in ruins, their alleyways ankle-deep in donkey shit. The remaining oldsters, the living ghosts of a way of life which is no more, peered from broken shuttered windows. They rarely spoke more than a few words, and God knows how they lived.

I asked one ancient if, to save a few miles, I could cut across the deep gorge of the Borgotara. He looked down to where the torrent foamed far below. He paused before reply and then nodded. Yes, he said. It could be done if I were a *funambolo.* He disappeared behind the shutters. It took me a few minutes to look the word up. It meant a tight-rope walker.

When two eagles circled round and round against a sunset like the end of the world, there were some compensations for dawdling in the Passo di Bocca. But not many. If I laughed it was to cheer myself up. Through glasses I saw a black-coated figure plucking cherries at the top of a tree. He surely would know the path down to Pontremoli. It was a scarecrow.

In that town with its arched fifteenth-century bridge held together, it seemed, by clumps of valerian, the news wasn't good. At the post office they turned aside, reluctantly, from their daily task of sticking lira notes together with adhesive tape to look for my letter 'to await arrival'. They found it. From Giovanni Caselli: could I join him in Florence instead? Presumably he hadn't received my apologetic telegram sent several days earlier. I should by now have been with him in Bologna to start the walk down the Tuscan Way. Bologna was about a hundred miles away and Florence at least half as far again, depending on what route I took. But what was the point of continuing the walk in any direction?

I knew the answer. It was a critical date ringed in red in my diary. A date more important even than the reassuring company of Giovanni on the Via Roma. In an effort to achieve what I had set out to do, I set off that afternoon, determined on walking fast for at least another five days.

They were difficult days. A farmer set his dogs on me. More storms around Castelnuova. More landslips. The village of Succiso had literally cracked in half and pitched over a cliff two days before I saw that huge flock of scavenging kites and crows. Within twenty miles of Bologna I slipped in a gorge of the Stura, got thoroughly wet and twisted my ankle. It became difficult to walk more than a few hundred yards. There was nothing I could do except limp into a bus station – something that had never happened before. It worried me the more since that date ringed in red in my diary was getting nearer.

Since all power corrupts I shall say nothing about how Giovanni and I made our way from Bologna over La Futa, La Calvana and Monti del Chianti to Montepulciano, mostly on foot but occasionally by car. Nothing except that in the Frignano Hills he drank to my continued health on the slopes of a mountain higher than anything which has reared up in the Alps or Africa: Mount Sexagenary. My sixtieth birthday.

That was five years ago. As the jet plane slowly circled the Mother of Cities I looked down on that long winding road I had failed to reach. No matter. *Stet.* Let it stand. Bernard Shaw makes Caesar say to Fulvio, we may grow old and die 'but the crowd upon the Appian Way is always much of the same age'.

To the north of Genoa, high above the Apennines, I looked down again and wondered how far Carlo Bertelli and his friends had managed to walk with their pots of blue paint. Not far, it was sad to think. Perhaps a fifth of the way between the Franco-Italian border and the valley of the Po. The Ligurian ridgeway is reverting to what it looked like more than three thousand years ago. As for myself, I had been determined on walking to my limits and had come very close to them on the Stura. But unless you fall by the wayside there is no dropping out of the column. On active service you cannot resign.

For most people in so-called civilized parts of the world, a walk is occasional activity. It is recreation, and what a good word that is. All fortunate holiday travel, like all good recovery after illness, is a renewal of youth. But for thousands of others a walk is part of the daily way of life. We can scarcely live without it. Even in that sombre, chastened mood in which I flew back to London, it never occurred to me for one moment that I had done with walking; but it did seem unlikely that I should ever again essay much more than a score of miles.

And now all that is over and done with, killed stone-dead, literally trodden into the ground over a distance of several hundred miles. And I have for too long turned aside from the person who brought all this about. My wife, Katie.

Journey home

We met, warmly, on the sloping High Street of Halstead; we might have been parted for weeks. We bought food for supper and breakfast and struck south, out of town, for some place to put up the wigwam. No matter how simple the food, a meal eaten in the open on a warm evening in May achieves a touch of sacramental significance. In his story of Marius, Walter Pater describes his hero's recovery of a lost interest in common things, of household customs, the daily meals, just the eating of ordinary food at appointed and recurrent times. I watched her as she moved about in the flickering light of our little lantern. Homer did not try to describe Helen's face, he said only that the sight of it moved even elderly men. We ate, we gossiped, we slept.

During the remaining four days our journey became more and more of a coherent whole. It was from nearby Coggeshall, for example, that in 1220 or thereabouts an unknown writer set down the first convincing facts about what happened to King John's 'lost' treasure. A town now much devoted to the sale of antiques, but not, unfortunately, those of local importance. Could that writer have been John Godard of Coggeshall, a Cistercian monk with great skill in mathematics and difficulty in breathing through his nose? He was injured and imprisoned in Jerusalem when Saladin's army besieged the place. Or so he affirms: 'The face of him who relates these things was wounded by an arrow which pierced through the middle of his nose, and although the shaft was extracted, the iron head remains to this day.'

To the south of that town we took to the new-made Essex Way which would bring us, we hoped, to Epping on the outskirts of London. We clung to it faithfully, crossing three handsome rivers, and found it difficult going – though not because of man-made obstructions. In Essex there are more signs proclaiming public rights of way and fewer about the prosecution of trespassers than anywhere else of comparable size. The difficulties lay underfoot, for clay is adhesive stuff and scores of paths were boot-deep in ochrous mud.

Many people regard Essex as a sort of Cinderella county with a front door in Liverpool Street and a backyard overlooking the docks at Harwich. Wrong, this. We walked through some beautiful country. In his *Dream of John Ball*, William Morris – who was born at Walthamstow – wrote that he 'came not from heaven but from Essex'. Norden said, 'This shire seemeth to me to deserve the title of the Englische Goshen, the fattest of the lande, comparable to Palestina that floweth with milke and hunnye . . .'

It is a county of the unexpected, a fit place for those alien to compromise. A Nonconformist country, and has been for centuries since the Commonwealth and the influx of Flemish weavers and Huguenot refugees. The church is expected to be there for births, marriages, deaths, and cases of need, but the number of committed church people is small.

My host of the day before, the vicar who gave me lunch, had recalled that when he lived in an adjacent village his parish was graced by a sacristan-verger-cum-everything-else by the name of Lizzie Mitchell. Lizzie was a brown, wrinkled nut of a woman aged about seventy when he knew her, but, as he puts it, she now rejoices with the saints. She had never been to London, perhaps not even much further than Ipswich. On her coat she wore a tin badge with the legend *Jesus Saves*. She would attend the parish church every Sunday morning come hail or shine, and every Sunday evening she would go to the little tin tabernacle down the road. When reciting the Creed her mouth would shut firmly over the words, 'I believe in the Holy Catholic Church', because she didn't.

Yet below the Nonconformity there are inclinations towards far older faiths. That hospitable vicar told me how, to his surprise, he was asked to bless the extension to a cottage, and duly did so with holy water and appropriate prayers. At the same time a piece of holly was stuck in the cottage chimney to keep the witches away. It seems it wasn't successful. A few months later there was a fire and the old part of the cottage was gutted. The extension was completely undamaged, in fact the fire stopped just short of the sanctified stone.

To find two churches in one churchyard – as there are in the vicinity of Willingale with Shellow Bowells – is unusual but not unique. Except in that extraordinary name. At the Maltsters Arms, conveniently close to them both, they will tell you that they were erected by two rich sisters at odds with each other. This story simply won't stand up: the architectural styles are two hundred years apart. The rector agrees, but says he has no other explanation to offer.

But earlier, in the park of Great Waltham, we had heard of a church embarrassed by a clerical duet between two vicars. This was in 1823. The first on the scene, the Rev. G. S. Clarke, was a learned but eccentric scholar who insisted upon giving his own translations of various portions of the Bible when reading the lessons in church. Being requested by the bishop to conform to the Authorized Version, he refused. He was then 'inhibited', and a substitute was despatched to conduct his services. Mr Clarke, however, persisted, and continued to read and perform his office at one end of the church while the bishop's nominee was in the act of doing so at the other. This made for confusion. The vicar was finally suspended and went to the cooler at Chelmsford.

The humour of rural Essex has distinctly dry qualities. A village grocer was rebuked by the butcher for not attending the funeral of the undertaker the previous day.

'But why should I have done?'

'Well for one thing,' said the butcher, 'he'd have gone to yours.'

That night we had experience of what was described to us as a 'very conservative and deeply entrenched land-owning squirearchy'. It may not have been typical, though we like to think it was. The place: Pleshey, the site of a truly enormous moated castle on a mound some nine hundred feet in circumference, for centuries the abode of the High Constables of England. Shakespeare made great play of it in *Richard II*:

> Sirrah, get thee to Plashy, to my sister Gloster;
> Bid her send me presently a thousand pounds: -
> Hold, take my ring!

Alongside that moat are the well-laid out grounds of a gentleman farmer. During a cautious reconnaissance for somewhere to sleep, we almost literally bumped into the fellow on a tour of inspection. We were obliged to explain what we were doing there. He heard us out and asked if we would care to accept the hospitality of his lawn running down to the moat. And he offered what he delicately referred to as 'other facilities', adjacent to the house. At dusk he and his son came down to ask if we were in need of anything and, on being reassured that we could not have found a more pleasant site, they wished us both good-night.

We were up and away at seven, and the gods of good adventure saw us kindly home. All the next day, and the day after, the country was overhung by masses of Constable skyscape. Nightingales *jug-jugged* in the thickets of Good Easter; butterflies were more profuse than I had seen in years, especially the nettle-eaters, the Comma, the Red Admiral, the Tortoiseshell and the Janus-eyed Peacock. And as for plants, the Rodings, the bed of that fine stream which rises by Stansted Mountfitchet, were so beflowered that we agreed to stop and try to identify only the most spectacular.

In Norfolk I thought we had come close to the absolute in the oddities and absurdities of place-names. By contrast with Essex, they were fairly elementary. What history, what conflict between heritors, feofees and tenants-on-sufferance gave rise to Helions Bumpstead, Bottle End, Tolleshunt D'Arcy, Fingringhoe, Ugley, and Bung Row? We neither knew nor cared. But between one diversion here and another there we speculated, wildly. What a great day that was!

The river Roding, a tributary of the Thames, brought us to the fringe of the great Forest of Epping. We walked the length of it from the north-east to the south-west where at Whipps Cross we spent the night in the Georgian home of my old friend the Alchemist, and met his friend the Verderer. A memorable night, our last in anything which could be described as rural England. A touch of symbolism here, since it was at Hackney, scarcely three miles away, that my literary companion Celia Fiennes died. Only connect . . .

For many years I have quartered that expanse of hornbeam, beech and holly for birds and beetles, wood wasps and fungi, seeing there a dismal decline of its beauty, and the Verderer told us more about *woodwards*, *agistors*, *regarders* and *reeves*

266

than we really wanted to know. But as that knowledgeable man talked, I realized that, almost imperceptibly, we had arrived back home on the London clay.

As for the Alchemist, it is difficult to make a thumb-nail sketch of a man who for half a century has been passionately concerned about pharmacy ancient and modern, Sherlock Holmes, Count Dracula, vintage wines and field sports. But no man could be more at home in a forest renowned since the days of Edward the Confessor for

> Heorte and hynde, doe and bocke,
> Hare and foxe, Catte and brocke,
> Wylde fowel with his flocke,
> Partrich, fesant hen, and fesant cocke
> With green and wylde stob and stocke . . .

For the last chaotic ten years he has acted as my Grand Inquisitor, enquiring in shrewd but kindly fashion into my precise relationship with a number of women. There was, for example, the Sorrel Nag from Cardiff, a gifted architect who treated me like a building site. She had a sad smile, a singing accent, strange mysteries in her eyes and a temperament somewhere between sulphuric acid and fulminate of iodine. Once in his presence she emptied a bucket of water over me. He sighed. 'It is,' he said, 'in the nature of corgis to bite.' He wasn't altogether in favour of the hunting woman who he referred to as Lady Debrett. 'Voice irritating,' he said, 'and moves her arms like a water beetle.' As for Madam he has on several occasions threatened to carry her off. They are extremely fond of each other.

To reach Hampstead Heath, that same heath from which Celia Fiennes set off nearly three hundred years ago on the greatest of her journeys, we braved the worst industrial squalor in East London, much of it on a thunderous freeway. Without making an elaborate detour there was no avoiding one of the city's main drains of locomotion. But there were compensations in what has been nicely called the unofficial countryside, the flowering of the wasteland.

To allow for extensions to the width of the North Circular Road, the county council has left a broad strip of grass, remarkable for its self-sown plant life, and on that refuge we walked, gratefully, sometimes arm in arm. Knotweed and willow-herb, London rocket, blackberry and trailing convolvulus partly hid the concrete posts of miles of fencing. White dead nettle which, being a relative of aromatic thyme and therefore having nothing whatever to do with its irritating namesake, made better looking the ruins of old bedsteads and bicycles. Pussy willow and the enormous leaves of dock and coltsfoot marked the ditches that dribble into the now grossly polluted Roding, Ching, and the Lea, drabbest daughters of London's river. And everywhere, from dumps of rusting car bodies to the austere brick fronts and truck parks of industrial lots, the manscape was gloriously splashed with butter-yellow bouquets of ragwort.

The domain of the commonest species, the almost ubiquitous groundsel, bane of gardeners, is being challenged by a seemingly ineradicable alien, the so-called Oxford ragwort, a native of Sicily where it frequents volcanic ash. It used to be a rarity confined to the Oxford Botanical Gardens but, feeling more at home on the cinders of railway tracks, it escaped and cautiously explored the surrounding lines until Goering's fire-bombers provided it with huge spaces for sustenance and decoration.

Above the urban commons where new factories are spreading like eczema, the sky at any time of the year is made fascinating to look at by the most aesthetically pleasing, the most useful, sculpture of the second half of the twentieth century: tower cranes, poised pencil-thin and exquisitely balanced against a backcloth of sky, sunlit or sullen. Some sculptors of metal, say Malevitch, Kandinsky and George Fullard, have lifted their enormous mobiles above the concepts of the Bauhaus. But in my opinion not one of those heirs of Constructivism can match the aerial T-junctions. They are commonplace. They are beautiful. The marvel is how they seem to defy the basic laws of leverage.

Somewhere to the west of that conurbation where Waltham Forest once stood we saw, far ahead, a ridge topped by trees and television masts: the park that houses the ruins of the Alexandra Palace. We were almost home. If we didn't stop for any threshold ceremonials beyond a drink gulped five minutes before closing-time, I reckoned we could climb up to Hamp-

268

stead Heath in a couple of hours. We made it in fifteen minutes under par.

'It is impossible to write about the vortex of north-west London, especially Hampstead and Highgate, without being conscious of its artificiality.' Impossible? Then let us try.

'Vortex' I'm prepared to go along with. It means a swirl, a rapid movement around an axis of relative calm. By comparison with the great highways that cut off Hampstead Heath from the motorists' conception of the countryside, those eight hundred acres with their relics of the ancient hunting Forest of Middlesex are almost Arcadian. The air is superb. Light flashes from a dozen ponds. Above the subdued hum of traffic from all quarters, sensitive ears can detect the reed-thin calls of nesting warblers. Hundreds of wild plants have been recorded from its woodlands, water courses, meadows and hummocky dunes. This is an oasis of life miraculously preserved.

Artificial? For over thirty years I have tramped every corner of that bed of impermeable clay overlaid with a thin stratum of porous sand. As a self-appointed census-taker, I have been on more than nodding terms with its native inhabitants, botanical, vertebrate, and invertebrate, and consider the region no less artificial than, say, limestone pavements of the fells which were brought about by neolithic over-grazing, or man-made grouse moors. Or the Norfolk Broads, which are the filled-in basins of peat-diggers. By comparison with the arboreal slums of the Forestry Commission, it offers a spectrum of habitats carved out and honed down from the days when the ancestral Thames flowed ten miles north of Tower Bridge.

The Heath has suffered a great deal, but never from the plough. Its soils are too poor, the product of glacial downwash: for the ice cliffs expired, worn out, before they reached the heights of Hampstead and Highgate. But those downward-sweeping vistas towards the City have provided countless millions of recreation-seekers with views which John Constable considered unsurpassed in Europe. For years he trudged up to the Heath to 'do his skying'. At one period, during a strained relationship with John Linnell, it is reported that the two artists sat painting back to back. Conservationists are constantly bickering about what should be done with this or that, for, as one shrewd observer put it, 'throughout its long history the Heath has always been a place where one lot of people were vehemently trying to stop another lot of people from doing whatever they wanted to do – intended to do – and, in fact, eventually did.' What all are agreed about is there is no place quite like it anywhere else in the world. Better than what we had seen on our long tramp?

Not 'better' meaning 'superior', but certainly made the better by comparison with what we'd seen, since all places when properly looked at illuminate or set off one another. And when you've got the hang of whatever you choose to call your own country by walking several hundred miles towards it, the contour lines begin to sing together like the Biblical stars.

As we hastened home, do you suppose we talked about the quiet lanes of Suffolk, the mists of Howl Moor or that occasion when, within four days of our standing together in front of a priest, Madam slipped more perilously than she knew on the flanks of Angle Tarn? We did not. Our minds were on domestic matters. Spring is the time when all creatures rearrange their nests. A respite first, and then the enormous romance of planning yet another journey. That was Celia's way of ordering her life. She was nearly eighty when she died at Hackney, probably in the house of one of her nieces. Almost a generation had elapsed since she last told us what she was up to. It may be that one day more manuscripts will be found in the library of some old country house, and what treasure that would be.

We may picture her as an old lady, sitting upright and with a complexion still fresh from those uncountable miles in the saddle. No doubt she often talked to visiting friends and relatives, for few women of her time could have had a greater store of memories to draw on. We know something about her circumstances and possessions, since she left behind a detailed will with the last codicil added some three months before her death. She still maintained six or seven servants and provided something for them all. She had already given away much to her nieces. One would eventually receive her ring, 'sett with diamonds and rubie to be worn by her unalter'd', and her nephew, her repeating clock, 'for his closet to remind him that time passes'.

270

As Celia fingers that ring and hears the clock slowly ticking, how often, one wonders, does she travel back in time to the fens and flats of Norfolk, the grey moors of the North? Can she remember that day not far over the Border from Cumberland when, tired of it all, she decided to lead her retinue home? Can she still hear the roar of the sea at Land's End, the wind on Salisbury Plain, and the explosions that freezing night when the oak trees in the park around her family home at Newton Toney were shattered by the frost? Almost certainly she can, and one feels she often thanks God for giving her so much to sustain her remaining years.

In *Lorna Doone*, that story of Celia's times, R. D. Blackmore says: 'That night such a frost ensued as we had never dreamed of . . . the kettle by the fireside froze . . . many men were killed and the cattle rigid in their head-ropes. Then I heard that fearful sound which I have never heard before, neither since have heard . . . the sharp yet solemn sound of trees burst open by the frost blow. Our great walnut lost three branches, and has been dying ever since, though growing meanwhile as the soul does in the body.'

In that last sentence there is something of the very essence of travelling.